Elena, Princesa of the Periphery

Disney's Flexible Latina Girl

DIANA LEON-BOYS

RUTGERS UNIVERSITY PRESS

NEW BRUNSWICK, CAMDEN, AND NEWARK,
NEW JERSEY, AND LONDON AND OXFORD, UK

Names: Leon-Boys, Diana, author.
Title: Elena, princesa of the periphery : Disney's flexible Latina girl / Diana Leon-Boys.
Description: New Brunswick : Rutgers University Press, 2023. |
    Series: Latinidad: transnational cultures in the United States |
    Includes bibliographical references and index.
Identifiers: LCCN 2022028197 | ISBN 9781978830172 (paperback) |
    ISBN 9781978830189 (hardback) | ISBN 9781978830196 (epub) |
    ISBN 9781978830202 (pdf)
Subjects: LCSH: Elena of Avalor (Television program) | Hispanic American
    women on television. | Disney Channel (Firm) | Disney characters. |
    Girls on television. | Branding (Marketing) | BISAC: SOCIAL SCIENCE /
    Ethnic Studies / American / Hispanic American Studies | SOCIAL SCIENCE /
    Women's Studies
Classification: LCC PN1992.77.E428 L46 2023 | DDC 791.45/72—dc23/eng/20220926
LC record available at https://lccn.loc.gov/2022028197

A British Cataloging-in-Publication record for this book is available from the British Library.

References to internet websites (URLs) were accurate at the time of writing. Neither the author nor Rutgers University Press is responsible for URLs that may have expired or changed since the manuscript was prepared.

♾ The paper used in this publication meets the requirements of the American National Standard for Information Sciences—Permanence of Paper for Printed Library Materials, ANSI Z39.48-1992.

rutgersuniversitypress.org

Manufactured in the United States of America

Elena, Princesa
of the Periphery

Latinidad
TRANSNATIONAL CULTURES IN THE UNITED STATES

This series publishes books that deepen and expand our understanding of Latina/o populations, especially in the context of their transnational relationships within the Americas. Focusing on borders and boundary-crossings, broadly conceived, the series is committed to publishing scholarship in history, film and media, literary and cultural studies, public policy, economics, sociology, and anthropology. Inspired by interdisciplinary approaches, methods, and theories developed out of the study of transborder lives, cultures, and experiences, titles enrich our understanding of transnational dynamics.

Matt Garcia, Series Editor, Professor of Latin American, Latino and Caribbean Studies, and History, Dartmouth College

For a list of titles in the series, see the last page of the book.

For my daughter, Zoila

Contents

Elena, Princesa
of the Periphery

Introduction

LATINA GIRLS' MEDIA STUDIES

As I walked through Magic Kingdom's *Fantasyland* on the morning of June 2, 2019, I spotted five young girls walking out of the Bibbidi Bobbidi Boutique after their princess makeovers. The girls were all wearing *Elena of Avalor* dresses, and it seemed that they knew one another as they laughed and talked while making their way to the *Prince Charming Regal Carrousel*. At Disney World, the Bibbidi Bobbidi Boutique sits next to Cinderella's Castle, and to have an "enchanted makeover," you must secure your spot through a reservation made well in advance. Inside the boutique, several "fairy godmothers" provide makeovers for young children between the ages of three and twelve. The makeover packages range from $74.95 to $450 (plus tax), and children can select the princess dress and accessories of their choice. On that morning, I noticed the five girls because they were all wearing *Elena of Avalor* dresses. *Elena of Avalor* (2016–2020) is a television series, but more importantly she is one of Disney's newest princesses, a princess whom the conglomerate describes as its "first Latina princess."[1] Although Jasmine and Pocahontas were the two princesses of color available to me as a young Latina growing up in the 1990s, I never quite felt as though I should dress up as either of them. Seeing those young girls that morning and knowing well that they paid a significant amount of money for their perfect buns, princess heels, tiaras, and Elena dresses reminded me of the representational significance of Disney's "first Latina princess." I then wondered what it would have been like for me to have a "Latina" princess growing up. Elena's existence not only fills a huge gap as far as Latina representation within the world of Disney but also functions as a way for non-Latinxs to make sense of Latinidad.

As many scholars before me have noted, media allow us to make sense of ourselves and others. As a young child, I may not have realized this, but I was searching for recognition on the screen. I was searching for a recognition that would allow me to feel a sense of belonging. I was also searching for a type of recognition that could transcend the television screen so I could implement it via dress up. Unfortunately, I was not able to fully find that recognition as a young child growing up in the United States in the 1990s. I did not grow up with images of young Latinas on any screen, but now my daughter sees Latina girlhood on Netflix, Disney+, Hulu, and the like. During the fall of 2020, as she watched Netflix while I worked on this book a few feet away from her, she shouted at me from the living room, "Mom, Kaylie is a Latina. I didn't know, but they are planning a *quinceañera* for her in this episode." *Team Kaylie* (2019–2020), a Netflix original series, is one of a handful of series that highlights Latina girlhood in a way that is different from what I saw on television growing up. Now my daughter and other young Latinas can watch *Diary of a Future President* (2020), *The Expanding Universe of Ashley Garcia* (2020), *Spirit Riding Free* (2017–2020), *Elena of Avalor* (2016–2020), and even reruns of *Dora the Explorer* (1999–2019), and see a version of themselves represented on the screen. If, as Nick Couldry (2000) notes, audiences see media as an authority that determines who and what is important, then young girls form a part of this conversation. Young girls, like other audiences, look to the media to understand themselves and the world they live in.

    Elena, Princesa of the Periphery analyzes a contemporary example of a location where young Latina girls can possibly find the recognition I was seeking long ago. It focuses on one narrative franchise, which purports to represent Latina girlhood, to illustrate how Latinxs remain marginalized as mainstream media continuously claim to produce Latinx representations that are actually Latin American and Iberian Peninsula peoples and narratives.[2] Elena and her kingdom reside on an island, firmly located somewhere in relation to Latin American narratives as Disney continues to invoke the eternal foreigner trope. For *Elena of Avalor* to be accepted and recognized by non-Latinx, mainstream audiences, Disney created her as a familiar and stereotypical representation of Latinidad, tied to Latin America rather than U.S. Latinidad more broadly.[3] Although Elena appears on merchandise, television, and around Disney theme parks, the three nodes (production, text, and audiences) explored in this book, demonstrate that she holds a position as a permanent outsider within the U.S. national imaginary. Even though Elena, the princess and all that her kingdom stands for, provides a new space for Latina girls to find recognition and possibilities for existence, these new possibilities are momentary, nonthreatening, and tangential. This book highlights the intersections between Latinidad, age, and girlhood as presented in the discourses in *Elena of Avalor*, a television series that forms part of Disney's privileged global patriarchy (Blue, 2017). As a company producing media content for girls, which has started to incorporate animated Latina girlhood, Disney must be theorized in relation to contemporary discourses of Latinidad and postfeminist girlhood, while acknowledging that the company's incorporation of Latina girlhood privileges white patriarchy and a global media conglomeration.

"Dream Big, Princess"

On July 22, 2016, Disney Junior released the first episode of *Elena of Avalor*, an animated series following the adventures of Disney's first (teenage) Latina princess.

Disney executives describe Elena as a Latina princess, while the creative team says she is "inspired by Latin American cultures" (McDermott, 2016). For the purposes of this book, it is essential to note that Disney goes back and forth between Latin America and Latinidad (and sometimes even "Latin" and "Hispanic"), constantly conflating the terms. Even though this Latina princess was not a full-length feature film (which upset some Latinx audiences) *Elena*, the series, was quite popular while it aired and it secured multiple awards, including the Daytime Emmy Award for Outstanding Writing for a Preschool Animated Program, and the Imagen award for Best Children's Programming (e.g., B. Cantor, 2016a; Coffey, 2020; Common Sense Media, 2016; TV News Desk, 2016; Whyte, 2018).

Elena forms part of Disney's multiple strategies to increase revenue and expand its audience base through the representation of more nuanced versions of girlhood, which include princesses of color and minimal male love interests. Advertised as a born leader responsible for saving her kingdom, she rescues her sister from elves, repeatedly saves her family from magic spells, leads the way in archaeological digs, helps coach her olaball team, and fences disguised as a man to prove she is a worthy girl ruler, among many other quests.[4] The series is action packed and frequently showcases Elena engaging in tremendous physical feats, as she attempts to prove she is worthy of soon becoming a queen. As she exerts physical agency, she also consistently puts her family first and teaches her younger sister family values as they face many challenges, occasionally incorporating Spanish words or references to go along with her supposed pan-Latinidad throughout the narratives. The series provides a restrained and palatable Latinidad (actually Latin Americanness), which is reflective of institutional visions that seek to highlight diversity in a nonthreatening way.

Elena of Avalor consists of seventy-seven episodes, which are all available on Disney+, Disney's subscription streaming service, and sometimes as reruns on Disney Junior and Disney Channel. The series came to an end with a one-hour finale that premiered on August 23, 2020. The finale culminated with Elena's coronation, transitioning her from the realm of princess to queen, thus ending her renewed presence in the world of Disney. Elena lived on the small screen as a princess for three seasons from 2016 to 2020. However, she continues to live in merchandise, including clothing, accessories, gadgets, books, household products, and the like (this synergy is common with most Disney characters). Additionally, from August 2016 (just a few weeks after her small-screen debut) until March 2020, Elena consistently held meet and greets at both U.S. theme park locations. Following the reopening of the Disney theme park in Florida after the COVID-19 closures, Elena continued to make quick appearances at the park, but via a float on a parade rather than one-on-one interactions with guests. Almost a year later, when the California park opened its doors post COVID, Elena held occasional meet and greets ten feet away from park guests.

Elena, in all her iterations, is supposed to be a representation not only of Latinidad but also of girlhood in animated form. In particular, Elena is meant to target pre-tween audiences, through her incorporation as part of Disney Channel, the television company associated with the much larger entities of Walt Disney

Television and the Walt Disney Company. Elena's televisual airtime was first and foremost through Disney Junior, which is nestled within Disney Channel and aims to attract children ages two to seven. The entire Disney Junior library content is now available via Disney+, and within this, the *Elena of Avalor* series is available either in the "princess" category or in the "Disney Junior" content. Elena is thus positioned within the realm of animated girls, but a specific type of girlhood very much aimed at attracting pre-tween girls. This specific iteration of girlhood, due to its existence as an animated princess, is less likely to attract tween and teenage girls who typically tend to favor live-action content.

As a testament of Elena's inclusion within a new wave of girlhood, the series debuted five months after Disney launched its Dream Big, Princess campaign, which seeks to "inspire girls and kids around the world to realize their full potential and dream big" (Epstein, 2016). While the campaign says its goal is to target all children, it has an obvious focus on girls. This campaign consists of commercials, posters, and initiatives that showcase girls and Disney princesses playing extreme sports, getting dirty (literally), and taking on STEM (science, technology, engineering, and math) roles. Further, the campaign often highlights both pre-tween girls and phenotypically nonwhite girls. Disney princesses, the most well-known of the mediated princess narratives, have existed for over eighty years, and since then have been used as a representation of Disney's girlhood in a variety of promotional materials, now including the Dream Big, Princess campaign. In fact, most of the commercials forming part of this campaign feature an even distribution of screen time for real girls and animated princesses, often done using a split screen. The commercials explain that real girls draw inspiration from the animated princesses. They usually conclude with the line: "For every girl who dreams big, there's a princess to show her it's possible." Through the Elena Dream Big, Princess public service announcements (PSAs), nonwhite girlhood is linked to princess discourses of possibility and leadership. The animated princesses and the live-action girls on the PSAs are supposed to demonstrate that achieving your dreams is possible.

This campaign is part of Disney's latest princess wave, which showcases princesses as brave, fearless, and often without a love interest—though their body shapes remain consistent with the slender princesses of the early Disney days, with the slight exception of Moana (I use the word slight because the most significant difference is the size of her legs). Though the Dream Big, Princess campaign is the paradigm of Disney's new initiatives, Disney princesses have actually been in the process of morphing for twenty years as Disney attempts to mark its transition from passive princesses like *Snow White* (1937—the first Disney princess) to more empowered representations of animated girlhood. Tiana (*The Princess and the Frog*, 2009), Rapunzel (*Tangled*, 2010), Merida (*Brave*, 2012), Elsa (*Frozen*, 2013 and *Frozen 2*, 2019), and Moana (*Moana*, 2016) are the most recent animated Disney princesses (in full-length feature films), along with the new versions of Mulan (2020) and Jasmine (2019) via live-action movie remakes, who showcase their agency by seemingly rescuing themselves, albeit often relying on the help of a strong man or demigod to assist them in achieving their goals.

Figure 1. Two sisters stand with their backs against each other in the closing shot of the "Dream Big, Princess—Dear Future Us (Elena)," PSA (Disney YouTube).

The Walt Disney Company debuted *Elena of Avalor*, whom it calls its first Latina princess, at the tail end of 2016, coinciding with the aforementioned animated feature films and during a moment of prominent girl presence in the media. This moment was also marked by an increased awareness of postfeminism, popular feminism, and neoliberal feminism in academia (Banet-Weiser et al., 2019). Disney has not only attempted to back away from passive princesses/heroines but has also actively tried to expand its audience market by including the Latinx demographic, often through ethnically ambiguous characters (Valdivia, 2008c, 2011, 2020). Disney's strategy to appeal to larger audiences worldwide attempts simultaneously to target a growing market of Latinx audiences domestically. This multilayered process of flexible and ambiguous Latinidad redounds to Disney's economic advantage while at the same time opening a window for some segments of the audience to identify with a character and recognize themselves, perhaps for the first time, within the Disney universe. *Elena, Princesa of the Periphery* provides an in-depth, multi-method, study of *Elena of Avalor* that examines the commodified construction of Latina girls by a transnational media giant during a very specific cultural moment, when immigration debates continue to create hostile climates toward Latinxs,[5] while simultaneously media react to population and demographic changes by creating more content that showcases nonwhite populations. This book further highlights the ways in which the policies and practices of the Disney conglomerate both shape and reflect contemporary understandings of Latina girlhood and the place of Latinidad in U.S. popular culture.

Media and Latina Girlhood

I still remember the time in first grade during recess when my classmate told me I could not pretend to be the pink Power Ranger because "Kimberly is white." From that day forward, I very consciously avoided pretending to be the white character and always selected the Black character, even though I am phenotypically white. Back then there were not many choices other than Black or white, at least not that I can recall. As I think back to my classmate's comment, it is clear to me that she was not interested in casting based on skin color (as our skin colors were practically the same) but was instead grounding her argument in something much deeper than skin. This was the same classmate who once told me I was not white because my parents did not speak English. For this classmate, whiteness was much more than the color of our skin. Her comments throughout my early years not only influenced how I continued to play throughout the rest of elementary school but also how I began to understand myself in relation to my peers. On rare occasions there would be an opportunity to play an Asian or Asian American character and I often found myself gravitating toward that one. I selected anyone but the white characters. The same could be said for Disney princesses, and though I did not see myself represented in either Pocahontas or Jasmine, they were always my go-tos for Halloween or pretend time with friends.

This was my way of searching for cultural recognition and belonging through fictional characters. This is a process, which now as a parent, I witness as I watch my daughter and her peers play. Searching for this recognition is something children do from an early age, often subconsciously.

Media texts have the ability to showcase or erase the nuances of gender, race, class, nationality, age, ability, sexual orientation, and the like. As a child, I saw few Latinas on the television screen and none at all in animated form. Further, most of the representations I saw of animated girlhood, or girlhood at large, depended on a heroic male to solve the central conflict. For the most part, they were thin, white girls belonging to middle- or upper-middle-class settings. As media scholars have long argued: representation matters, whether it be animated or live-action. Media representations influence the world beyond the screen, from politics to how people understand their very own identities and those of their peers (Hall, 1997). They transcend images and script writing and become tools for understanding the world, especially for young children. In their canonical work on how media cultivate audiences' understandings of reality, Gerbner et al. (1986) explain that television "serves primarily to extend and maintain rather than to alter, threaten, or weaken conventional conceptions, beliefs, or behaviors" (p. 18). Audience studies find that audiences are neither fully passive nor fully active, but usually fall somewhere in between, and this book understands that the representations of Latina girls are meaning laden and therefore most likely read by audiences in multiple ways.

Latinas, especially Latina girls, in the media bear the burden of representation, where far too much is expected of these representations in the absence of a wide array of options. Images of Latina girls say a lot to society and the world at large about the value ascribed to this group of people. As Báez (2018) illustrates in her research on Latina audiences, "Latina/os' place within the nation is often thought to be not only imagined by media, but also secured by media" (p. 3). Latina girls and children in general come to understand themselves and young Latinidad through and by the images they see on the movie screen, television screen, and mobile screen.

Young girls consume media at an incredibly fast rate. For example, as part of a national survey of over 1,600 eight- to eighteen-year-olds in the United States, Rideout and Robb (2019) found that children in general, ages eight to twelve, consume about five hours of entertainment media each day. Girls, in particular, outnumbered boys by over 5 percent when it came to television consumption. As Báez (2018) explains, "Age is an undertheorized category of analysis within media and related fields like Latina/o studies, Women's and Gender Studies, and American Studies. In addition, media industries largely focus on young adults, ages eighteen through thirty-four, as the ideal (read: most lucrative) market" (p. 113). While Báez's work challenges teenage and young adult-centered research by including older women, my research extends this scholarship in the opposite direction by focusing on pre-teen and pre-tween populations, which are mostly understood under the umbrella of "children." As Latinxs continue to be the youngest and fastest growing group in the United States, media companies, including Disney, continue to demonstrate their response to these newly acknowledged yet long-standing demographic changes by altering the media landscape.

However, with increased presence and what could appear to be a recent hypervisibility, media scholars and audiences must continue to interrogate these representations. Why the sudden boom in the representation of young Latina girls? How are these young girls represented? How much longer will this representational boom last? When Noble (2013) writes about the recent hypervisibility of Black women celebrities, she notes that this type of visibility actually works to make Black girls less visible. She defines the "invisibility" as the lack of acknowledgment for the discriminations these women and girls face. This is invisibility redefined. I extend her findings to the representation of young Latinas and the dismissal of intersectionality and systemic oppression. While it is exciting to see young Latinas on the screen who received their PhDs before they turned fifteen,[6] it is striking to note that the narratives rarely consider any struggles or issues the young girls had to overcome due to their race, nationality, immigration status, gender, sexual orientation, or age. This is the type of invisibility that Noble refers to when she connects hypervisibility to invisibility. This book engages a tripartite media studies approach to examine Latina girlhood post 2015 through a Disney property. Using the tripartite approach, I engage in a deep ethnographic analysis combined with substantive consideration of production and representation.

METHODS: ANALYZING CORPORATE REPORTS, EPISODES, MOBILE APPLICATIONS, THEME PARKS, AND MORE

One of the topics that students bring up themselves every time I teach a course on Disney is the types of effects the company's animated content has on children. Some students share very personal experiences about how Disney films have shaped their

understandings about certain concepts, while others speculate on the type of influence certain films could have on people in other countries. Research on children
and the media often resides within media effects literature—children's identity for-
mations, their eating habits, relationships to education, cognitive development,
sexuality, views about violence, and even their safety (ontological and physical).
Instead, *Elena, Princesa of the Periphery* draws on and extends research on children's
mediated representations as they are tied to issues of commodification of childhood and markets catering to children as consumers. Cook (2004) illustrates the
influence of children on industries: "Estimates of the monetary value of the overall children's market (including the 'influence' that children exert on household
purchases) run into hundreds of billions of dollars annually for the United
States alone" (p. 2). These numbers continue to rise year after year. Although Cook
looks specifically at the clothing industry, he explains how the market culture of
childhood is a symbol of the status of capitalism today. Whether we are looking at
clothing, the commodification of childhood, or media representations, childhood
studies only distinguish between girls and boys on rare occasions. Additionally,
studies within this sector have a long way to go in terms of the commodification
of ethnicity. My work takes all of this into consideration and analyzes childhood and mediated content aimed at attracting children from a perspective that
takes seriously issues of race, ethnicity, nationality, and gender.

Through three case studies, *Elena, Princesa of the Periphery* addresses the above-
mentioned gaps in scholarship by examining Disney's creation and deployment
of animated Latinidad through the commodification of the ethnic category in relation to Latina girl bodies. *Elena, Princesa of the Periphery* merges critical theory,
political economy, digital studies, industry record analysis, discourse analysis,
and ethnography. I conduct discursive analyses of Disney's online, social media, and
television promotion of the series, as well as extensive reviews of corporate social
responsibility reports through a political economy lens to uncover prominent
themes related to the production of the series. My analysis of the series includes
discursive analyses of the three seasons, focusing on purposefully selected episodes
and analyzing Latinidad through a continuum of flexibility, which is a tool I developed for my analysis of televisual Latinidad. Finally, I created a "modified situated
ethnography" methodology to study on-site performance of Latinidad by princesses at both U.S. Disney theme park locations. Using this innovative process I
combine photo-documentation, participant observation, and critical technocultural discourse analysis to study frequency and patterns at the theme parks, both
digitally and on the ground. This nimble multi-method approach included pre- and
post-digital analyses as well as on-site ethnography.

This book takes a circuit of culture approach (du Gay et al., 1997), which emphasizes the interrelated nature of culture and power permeating key moments of a
cultural text. *Elena, Princesa of the Periphery* provides three case studies contributing to the emerging subfield of Latina girls' media studies. Using the three case
studies, I examine how Latina girl subjectivities are produced and disseminated

to young girls through Disney's *Elena of Avalor*, while also investigating how the discourses come to life through the character's presence in other synergized locations, such as corporate social responsibility reports, celebrity social media platforms, YouTube videos, and the U.S. Disney theme parks. I capture as much of the "circuit" as possible, and focus on the production, text, and audiences (my three nodes) to achieve triangulation. *Elena, Princesa of the Periphery* addresses gaps in the disciplines of children and media, girls' media studies, and Latina/o/x studies by asking: How does Disney's construction of *Elena of Avalor* fit with its history of ambivalent inclusion of Latinidad? And is Elena a consistent figure of girl power in the various nodes analyzed?

THEORETICAL LENS

As an intersectional media studies project, this book draws on a combination of feminist theoretical perspectives against the backdrop of contemporary postfeminism, situated within cultural studies. As my project focuses on a Disney text aimed at young girls in a postfeminist moment, I theorize the company's mediated productions in relation to postfeminist discourses and discourses of girlhood, keeping in mind that the company is driven by the profit motive and may not prioritize the best interest of the girls. I take a discursive and ideological approach rooted in Michel Foucault's (1980) conceptualizations of discourse and power and Antonio Gramsci's (1971) hegemony. Through these lenses, I intersectionally analyze discourses of Latina girlhoods and theorize Disney in relation to postfeminism, race, and girlhood.

Elena, Princesa of the Periphery follows both Stuart Hall and Foucault in situating discourse and representation within structures of power at specific sociohistorical moments and locations. I take a constructivist approach, and I understand representation to mean the representation of the world to others through spoken language and visual discourses that are interpreted in a variety of ways by active audience members (Hall, 1997). As an active audience member myself, I bring in my own positionality to interpret my texts and therefore keep in mind the different readings that can take place when consuming a text. As a white cisgender Latina, who migrated to Texas from Mexico and became a U.S. citizen at the age of nineteen, my different identities influence how I understand my objects of study. Additionally, I am a native Spanish speaker who grew up in Texas in the 1990s and this frames how I understand the sites I analyze. All these identities and experiences are interwoven and inextricable from one another in numerous ways. It is from this perspective that I very uniquely approach my study of *Elena of Avalor*, Disney, Latinidad, and girlhood. By considering the multiple and sometimes contested meanings in the various texts, this book is guided by cultural approaches to issues of representation. Drawing from cultural studies, I focus on the interactions between textual productions, the text itself, reception of the text, and the social context under which the text operates.

Feminist Discourses through Girls' Media Culture

Feminist media theory provides an "unconditional focus on analyzing gender as a mechanism that structures material and symbolic worlds and our experiences of them" (Van Zoonen, 1994, p. 33). In this way, feminist media studies analyze how this structuring takes place through and with the help of media, while carefully focusing on issues of power. I do not seek to provide a clear-cut definition for feminist media studies in this work, but rather to "promote recognition that feminist studies of the media represent an open, dynamic and contested field of inquiry" (p. 6), one in which pre-tween girls play a key role, although this role is not always highlighted. Further, it should be noted that feminist media studies emerged in the 1970s due in large part to the increased availability of feminist discourses and second-wave feminism, though it was not an intersectional endeavor at the moment of inception (Cepeda, 2015).

By analyzing my texts through a feminist theoretical perspective, I prioritize media content that privileges women (girls), analyzing social constructions of gender, and focusing on the relationships between feminist discourses and representations of gender, namely, at the pre-tween level. More specifically, by drawing on feminist girls' media scholarship, I am focusing on media content featuring girls and directed toward girls. Throughout my chapters, I call attention to various identity markers, such as class, race, age, nationality, and gender as these are all interwoven and inextricable from one another in numerous ways. Further, in relation to age, this book's focus on a pre-tween generational category positions the research within the purview of childhood studies.

As I situate this book against the backdrop of contemporary postfeminism, I draw on Tasker and Negra (2007) to operationalize the term. This book understands postfeminism as constructed through popular culture as a surface-level praising of feminism and simultaneous rejection of it (McRobbie, 2009). The "post" in postfeminism does not simply mean "after feminism," but rather a moment that ironically declares the struggles of the feminist movement as no longer necessary because feminist goals have already been achieved. Postfeminism often highlights themes of self-discipline, individualism, and empowerment, while constructing it as other to ease the rejection of feminism as an antiquated concept (Tasker & Negra, 2007). Gill and Scharff (2011) outline the many ways in which postfeminism is related to neoliberalism and contend that they both highlight women's and girls' individualism, while asking them to "work on and transform the self . . . and to present all their actions as freely chosen" (p. 7). Indeed, postfeminist "culture's centralization of an affluent elite certainly entails an emphatic individualism, but this formulation tends to confuse self-interest with individuality and elevates consumption as a strategy" (Tasker & Negra, 2007), which seeks to fulfill voids caused by dissatisfactions by creating the figure of a woman/girl who relies on consumption to achieve success.

Harris (2004) argues that girls are constructed as a "vanguard of new subjectivity" (p. 8) and as the modern subjects who exert self-regulation and discipline to model the future of the Western world. Within these discourses, girls are hailed as powerful/agential consumers, who must maintain a strict level of self-surveillance and self-discipline to operate as "model" citizens. One of the most prominent neoliberal tensions in general is that we must control and discipline our bodies to prove that we are good citizens, but we must let go of that control in relation to consumption. This applies to discourses surrounding women and girls. As Valdivia (2020) reminds us, "combining girlhood studies with postfeminism reveals that can-do authenticity in the tween universe can only be achieved through postfeminist practices of individualism, working on the self, and self-surveillance" (p. 80). *Elena, Princesa of the Periphery* explores postfeminism as a mainstream strategy used to displace and postpone feminist goals. I also draw on post-racial approaches to the body, which like postfeminism, serve to once more halt social justice demands in favor of market-driven profit through commodification of bodies.

Additionally, a central postfeminist theme is the value placed on youth, and as such, it appears that the young (often teenage) girl becomes the central figure or symbol for postfeminism (e.g., young, white, middle class, straight, often blonde, physically fit, able-bodied, and powerful). A brief explanation of postfeminism's origins helps explain its purchase for the study of girls and the media. Gill (2007) discusses three ways in which postfeminism has been conceptualized since its inception and her third definition contends that postfeminism is a reaction to feminist movements, specifically those related to second-wave feminism. What she labels as more than a backlash becomes "a sensibility," one that must take seriously the role of "post-feminist media culture [as] . . . our *critical object*" (p. 151). Gill invites us to analyze mediated representations of gender by exploring common tropes and interrogating their meanings in our culture. Gill's postfeminist sensibility informs my readings of *Elena of Avalor*. More recently, Banet-Weiser et al. (2019) conceptualize the "sensibility" as a way to understand the contradictions inherent in the representations of women in the media after the 1990s. Banet-Weiser et al. explain that this sensibility is to be used empirically to analyze popular culture.

As tween and pre-tween popular cultures continue to expand drastically, feminist media scholars continue to raise concerns about popular culture's relations to neoliberal and postfeminist frameworks,[7] most notably through narratives and characters that foreground beauty, consumerism, individuality, and authenticity (Rottenberg, 2014). Media, after all, provide spaces for feminist discourses to emerge and thrive. Following Kennedy's (2018) lead, I wish to highlight the significance of both neoliberalism and postfeminism as terms that help outline the increasing expansion of tween (and pre-tween) popular culture. In a response to what some would explain as a "growing sense of exhaustion" (p. 425) with the two terms, Kennedy encourages us not to take these terms for granted as they "allow us to make sense of the ideological work of tween culture's fairy tale narratives in the retelling of feminism's history and the construction of feminist identities" (p. 425). Moreover, postfeminism and neoliberalism are deeply embedded in the texts of both tween and pre-tween popular culture, particularly through their focus on an ideal, postfeminist girl subject who embodies an "authentic" can-do spirit.

The postfeminist discourses surrounding girlhood can be further grounded by drawing on the work of scholars like Harris (2004) and her concept of the "can-do" girl. Harris extends the work of both McRobbie and Gill by exploring the representations of the "can-do" girl as a model of success, a girl who is empowered and who serves as the new face of girlhood. She distinguishes between the "can-do" girl and the "at-risk" girl by noting that the "can-do" subject becomes a beacon of hope for the neoliberal future, while the "at-risk" subject acts as a symbol for oppressive social systems. The "can-do" girl exerts responsibility and looks after her economic development all on her own. Harris's scholarship strengthens the previous claims about postfeminism and its relationship to girlhood: postfeminism positions girls as powerful agents, while exploiting their consumption through these same discourses of power. Harris ties postfeminism to our neoliberal moment by explaining that it is not systemic constraints but "good choices, effort, and ambition alone that are responsible for success that has come to separate the can-dos from the at-risks" (p. 16). There are, however, instances where the "at-risk" morphs into the "can-do" and vice versa, or instances that are more complex than Harris's dichotomy. To move beyond the "can-do" and "at-risk" binary, Projansky (2007) asks girls' studies scholars to "focus attention on the inextricable combination of disruption and containment, and of at-risk and can-do, in the contemporary popular discursive construction of girlhood" (p. 69). Additionally, she urges feminist media girls' studies scholars to think outside of the binary of "feminist" or "anti-feminist" when it comes to exploring media representations. Postfeminist discourses mostly focus on women, particularly successful women who perform paid labor. Some scholars, like Blue (2017), McRobbie (1982, 1991, 2009), Projansky (2014), Kennedy (2014, 2018), and Valdivia (2011, 2018, 2020), outline the ways in which girlhood fits into postfeminist and neoliberal discourses. Projansky (2014) conceptualizes "spectacular" girlhoods as Molina-Guzmán (2010) theorizes spectacular Latinas, both of which inform my analysis of a spectacular Latina girlhood.

Elena, Princesa of the Periphery focuses on a narrative franchise targeting a younger subset of girls before they become tweens, and situates these discourses within feminist media studies. In her work on feminist theory and childhood studies, Lemish (2013) posits that feminist theory can offer the field of children and media nuanced perspectives in four areas: "First, a mapping of gender segregation of children's leisure culture and an explanation of the mechanism driving this segregation; second, a theoretical understanding of gender as a form of social construction rather than a biological fact; third, a particular view on the form and role of methodology in the study of children and media; and fourth, a model of engaged scholarship that is attempting to advance progressive social change" (Lemish, 2013, p. 68). The scholarship on younger populations within feminist media studies is indebted to the work started by the feminist sociologist Angela McRobbie, "who in the late 1970s launched the field of Girls' Studies by insisting on attention to sex and gender in analyses of adolescence and youth culture" (Kearney, 2006, p. 4). McRobbie's intervention directed the attention of cultural studies scholars to the study of girls and feminist issues.

Through girls' media studies, media are often explored from a cultural studies lens, and media texts are understood as "complex [and contested] artifacts of ideologies that operate to shape their symbolic form and content" (Lindlof & Taylor, 2011, p. 66). Drawing on Hall's work on hegemony and ideology, much of the literature on girls and the media analyzes not only texts but also how girl viewers have responded to different texts, whether these texts are meant to represent them or not. As an extension of this already rich subfield, Latina girls' media studies creates avenues for the exploration of Latina girlhoods, their mediation, and mediatization.

INSERTING THE LATINA INTO GIRLS' MEDIA STUDIES

Research within Latina/o media studies seldom focuses on young girls or girls in general, so the intersections between girls' media studies and Latina/o media studies are few, which is why this book substantially contributes to the expansion of Latina girls' media studies. The existing scholarly work about girls and the media tends to focus on a white, Western, middle-class, normatively gendered, heterosexual girl as the subject of study. Except for my own research and that of a few other scholars (e.g., Valdivia, 2008b, 2008c, 2011, 2020; Vargas, 2009), Latina girls have not been central to the research agendas at the intersection of girlhood studies and media studies.

Latinx children face numerous challenges coming of age in the United States. Research shows that a significant number of these children/youth face deportation, food insecurity, high obesity and diabetes rates, and high dropout rates (e.g., Fry & Passel, 2009; Krogstad, 2016; Livingston, 2009; Office of Adolescent Health, 2016; Wiltz, 2015). Girls, in particular, deal with additional challenges facing Latinx teenage parenthood. Even though the numbers have been in flux and the percentages sometimes decline, in 2018, "the birth rate for Hispanic and Black teens ages 15 to 19 was almost double the rate among white teens and more than five times as high as the rate among Asians and Pacific Islanders" (Livington & Thomas, 2019).[8] Given these numbers, the current social climate toward race, and the fluctuating role that girls play in our nation, research focusing on Latina girls has never been more necessary.

The past twenty years have witnessed the rapid blossoming of girls' media studies within media studies. Most of the girlhood studies literature focuses on adolescent girls, with a recent (late 1990s) interest in the tween girl market as well within feminist media studies. The research begins with adult women, then extends to teenage girls, with a 1990s burgeoning focus on the tween demographic. However, scholars have focused very minimally on pre-tween girlhoods and their relationship to the media. Scholars and marketing experts alike recognize that girls generate a significant amount of revenue (Durham, 2008), and the same can be said about the Latinx demographic, in particular Latinx pre-tween children, and their increasing purchasing power (Nielsen Company, 2019). For example, in 2019, Latinxs at large "overrepresented in the share of movie tickets purchased (25%)

relative to their proportion of overall population (18%)" (Motion Picture Association, 2020). Marketing firms are aware of these numbers as they continue to adapt and reimagine their products.

Much of the research on children tends to focus on issues concerning health, education, and violence, but there are media-specific studies that focus on the relationship between children and television. Although there are studies that examine gender representations on television (e.g. Aubrey & Harrison, 2004; Baker & Raney, 2007; Banet-Weiser, 2004; Bell, 1995; Blue, 2013; Lemish, 2010), when research focuses on the younger demographic of children and on children's relationships to animated content, this category is usually treated as a whole, without differentiating between young girls and boys. Moreover, most of the research in children and the media falls under the umbrella of effects scholarship wherein gender is treated as a variable. My analysis of Elena is different because my audience approach does not treat gender as a variable, but rather firmly understands that this text will be read in specific ways according to children's gendered Latinidad. Work does exist on representations of children in the media (e.g., Ariès, 1962; Avery & Reynolds, 2000; Higonnet, 1998; Zelizer, 1985), but these studies vary drastically from my work in methodology and sites of analyses. A few studies do delve into issues of race in mediated texts aimed at children and featuring children (e.g., Aladé et al., 2020; Lemish & Russo Johnson, 2019; Valdivia, 2008a, 2008b, 2011), but we certainly need more of such scholarship, particularly with a focus on young girls. As the terrain of children's television continues to change, media studies scholars must pay careful attention to how children, in particular children of color (and even more in depth, girls of color) are portrayed. In a study focusing on U.S. and Canadian children's television content, Lemish and Russo Johnson (2019) note that whereas "the majority of human characters on children's TV are Caucasian," female characters are twice "as likely to be portrayed as persons of color or as racially ambiguous" (p. 14). Given this finding, my book analyzes one such instance within children's animated content.

Elena, Princesa of the Periphery firmly inserts Latinidad into girls' media studies. As previously mentioned, the increased presence of Latina girls in the media is noticeable. Also noticeable is the increased media visibility of Latinas in general and the robust body of scholarship on Latinidad and media representations documents this growth. Negrón-Muntaner (2014) draws on findings from *The Latino Media Gap* report to highlight the "status of US Latinos in movies, television, radio, and the Internet" (p. 2). She argues that although the numbers of Latinxs on the screen have increased within the past few decades, "numbers, of course, do not tell the whole story" (p. 2). Her analysis highlights the types of roles Latinxs play on the screen, and she concludes that the same stereotypes continue to be prevalent. Research on Latinas in popular culture abounds (e.g., Aparicio, 2003; Báez, 2007a, 2007b, 2008, 2018; Beltrán, 2002, 2004, 2009; Cepeda, 2015, 2017; Mendible, 2007; Molina-Guzmán, 2005, 2007, 2010, 2018; Valdivia, 2000, 2007, 2008a, 2010, 2020). The literature often focuses on spectacular bodies, particularly the "hypervisibility of Latinidad as central to the future growth of global cultural industries" (Molina-Guzmán, 2010) and general narratives of Latinidad, which include prominent mediated representational practices (Aparicio, 1997; Valdivia, 2000, 2007, 2008a, 2010, 2020).

In a capitalist economy, purchasing power should make a difference, but it has not generated equality or equity in media representation, suggesting that the inclusion of ethnic representations is ruled by an ideology stronger than capitalism. As Cepeda (2015) explains, "The increase in Latino numbers and buying power rendered the Latina/o market more legible to mainstream media outlets and therefore ripe for increased media attention across all formats" (p. 348). Some could even assume that "liberal racial thinking would tell us that racially based stereotypes would lessen, as racial 'minorities' are everywhere present" (Dávila, 2014, p. 12). However, race-based stereotypes remain prominent and often lurk under ambiguous representations that seem to indicate a step in a different direction. Valdivia (2005) argues that Latinxs are "a metaphor for or a window to the ravages of globalization and the erosion of democratic rights and citizenship status" (p. 307). This book extends the research surrounding Latinas in the media to focus on girls and explore the possibilities, continuities, continuums, and ruptures present through the animated Latina girl.

Theorizing Flexible Latinidad

Media studies has explored the relationship between Latinxs and the media through hybridity (Molina-Guzmán, 2005, 2010; Molina-Gumán & Valdivia, 2004; Rinderle, 2005), issues of representation (e.g., Aparicio, 2003; Báez, 2007a, 2007b, 2008; Beltrán, 2002; Cepeda, 2015; Dávila, 2001, 2014; Molina-Guzmán, 2006, 2010, 2013; Valdivia, 2000, 2007, 2008a, 2008b, 2010), identity formation through the media (e.g., Mastro, 2003; Moran & Chung, 2008), and prevalent stereotypes and their consequences among Latinxs (e.g., Casas Peréz, 2005; Mastro, 2003). Within these studies, some have specifically focused on issues of gender and ethnicity in mainstream media (e.g., Aparicio, 2003; Báez, 2018; Beltrán, 2002; Cepeda, 2015; Mendible, 2007; Molina-Guzmán, 2006, 2010, 2013; Negrón-Muntaner, 2016; Valdivia, 2000, 2007, 2008a, 2008b, 2008c, 2010, 2020), calling attention to the Latina body as site of analysis. *Elena, Princesa of the Periphery* builds upon these media analyses and interrogates Disney's incorporation of ambiguously brown characters (mostly via animation), and its back-and-forth process of conflating Latin America and U.S. Latinidad as a mixture of discourses come to life via Elena, in all her iterations. It further explores Valdivia's (2005) assertion above that Latinxs serve as a metaphor to the effects of globalization, and interrogates what Elena, in all her iterations, reveals about local and global understandings of gendered Latinidad.

To explain how flexibility exists through this Disney animated character who then comes to life in a theme park space, *Elena, Princesa of the Periphery* extends the work of Ong (1999) and Amaya Schaeffer (2013) to conceptualize a "flexible Latinidad." Ong argues that "flexible citizenship" allows disenfranchised individuals in the era of globalization to thrive and adapt amid uncertain conditions and take advantage of different privileges afforded by their respective nations. Amaya Schaeffer builds on the notion of "flexible citizenship" to introduce "pliable citizenship" (p. 7) for contemporary Latinas. Amaya Schaeffer's focus shifts to neoliberalism, gender, postfeminism, and Latinidad to argue that newly minted Latina U.S. citizens enact a malleability to ensure that "they will not be a threat to the U.S. family or nation" (p. 7). I build upon both concepts to account for Disney's incorporation of what I call "flexible Latinidad." The Latinidad I trace allows for a nonwhite character to be molded in various ways to appeal to diverse audiences in the United States and beyond. Just as Amaya Schaeffer traces the malleability enacted by U.S. Latinas, I trace a malleability that is created by a global media giant as it provides a representation that will not be a threat to the nation, a representation that is supposed to reach out to all children while simultaneously representing Latinidad. The flexible Latinidad, in my analyses, is made even more flexible through Elena's existence as a girl in a fantastical animated land and her grounding in Latin America rather than in the United States. The flexibility I highlight varies from chapter to chapter. It is dependent on the site of analysis and is multilayered. *Elena, Princesa of the Periphery* teases out moments of flexibility carried out in complex negotiations by Disney, producers, and audiences as they navigate cultural flows.

Studying the Production, Text, and Audiences of a Princesa: Chapter Overview

Chapter 1, "From Black-and-White Mouse to 'Latina' Girl," lays the groundwork for the case studies to follow by providing a brief overview of Disney from multiple perspectives. It traces the history of Disney (from Walt's early days to its current existence as a conglomerate monopoly), examines the corporation's history with animation, and breaks down the history of its engagements with Latin America.[9] The chapter also considers the significance and incorporation of the theme parks within these components. The chapter concludes with a lead-in to the debut of *Elena of Avalor* a year before *Coco*'s U.S. release date. Here, I argue that through the creation of an animated Latinx universe, Disney presents a rhythmic, vacillating pattern between Latin America and U.S. Latinidad. This pattern is consistent within the production, series, and theme park experiences related to *Elena of Avalor*, and is indicative of Disney's tenuous attempts to reach out to the Latinx market through Latin American specific narratives.

Chapter 2, "The Flexible Production of a 'Latina' Princess, builds on chapter 1, and analyzes the company's inclusion of Latinidad through its explanations of the series' production and creation. Understanding production as the link between industry and audience studies, and focusing on political economy and ownership, the chapter explores the production of *Elena of Avalor* (in corporate reports, Disney Instagram pages, Girl Scouts and Disney YouTube channels, popular press coverage, and celebrity social media accounts) and highlights three salient themes of the production practices behind *Elena of Avalor*. The chapter analyzes Disney's corporate, social media, and television promotion of *Elena of Avalor* (before and after its debut). The chapter is grounded in political economy, calling attention to the interplay between symbolic and economic dimensions of production and meaning. It further highlights the genre of corporate communications, which is designed to facilitate the sharing of information with stakeholders (including investors, potential clients, and media analysts) to whom an organization is beholden. However, it also weaves analyses of social media accounts and various social network platforms, almost all of which are controlled and regulated by Disney.

Chapter 3, "Animated Latina Girlhood and the Continuum of Flexibility," situates the *Elena of Avalor* television series against the backdrop of the 2012 *Sofia the First* controversy. In 2012, after rumors came out that *Sofia the First* was Latina, Disney executives were quick to explain that *Sofia the First* was inspired by a mixture of cultures but was not specific to any location or region. This strategy positioned her as a hybrid, ambiguous animated subject. The disavowal of Sofia's Latinidad in 2012 became the undeniable backdrop to the creation of *Elena of Avalor*. Chapter 3, the "text" chapter, analyzes the three seasons of the Disney Channel series, focusing on ten purposefully selected episodes. It focuses on the series in relation to contemporary discourses of Latinidad and postfeminism in mainstream popular culture and explores how Disney attempts to represent and reach out to Latinx audiences, in particular Latina girls. To carry out the analysis, I developed an architecture for studying flexible Latinidad within a continuum of flexibility. This continuum of flexibility expands postfeminist scholarship to analyze how the flexibility of an animated Latina girl expands her visibilization. Elena and the series are analyzed according to different categories and levels of flexibility. Among the episodes analyzed are episodes about Christmas (Navidad), Day of the Dead (Día de los Muertos), *quinceañera*, and Hanukkah. All these celebrations, except for Hanukkah, have come to signify stereotypical Latinidad in mainstream U.S. popular culture and are overused in live-action and animated content.

The final case study, chapter 4, "On-Site Performance of Latinidad from East Coast to West Coast," extends the previous case studies to the live-theme-park setting. The Disney theme parks allow their guests the opportunity to encounter embodied representations of animated characters in live form. When *Elena of Avalor* occupies a live setting, audiences can interact with this character and vice versa. Chapter 4, the "audiences" chapter, provides an analysis of Disney's control of the identity and lived transactional space of the production of the princess in the zone where the company allows real-time audience interaction. Guided by a "modified situated ethnography" methodology that I developed, this chapter analyzes on-site performance of Latinidad by princesses at both Disneyland and Disney World, alongside audience reactions to and interactions with the princess. Comparing the embodied location of the princess at the parks in relation to her digital park presence, this method engages a three-stage process conducted at both Disneyland in California and Disney World in Florida, including a physical visit to the theme parks and two stages of digital data collection. Elena's physical presence at the park, in conjunction with her digital representation through the

Disney Parks mobile application, illustrates how a major media conglomerate commodifies and tames complex hybridity in real time, and in accordance with the *Elena* paratexts (these paratexts include posters, corporate reports, toys, Disney parks' mobile application, and other discourses existing outside the series, which supplement the main text). Disney selects, positions, and backtracks, but nonetheless unambiguously commodifies ethnicity through different tropes of "authenticity" invoked at different times, in different locations. The analysis here demonstrates that the existence of this princess varies drastically from coast to coast. Such a conclusion allows us to understand that the inclusion of the princess at the parks is malleable, situated within the geographic setting (i.e., theme park location), and dependent on distinct factors, which the conglomerate does not disclose.

The conclusion, "A Princess for All Is a Princess Without a Home," summarizes the book's main arguments and implications, but most importantly it encourages readers to interrogate media representations such as the one in this book, through various lenses. It further asks readers to take Latina girls' media seriously as a site of scholarly research as well as through avenues outside of the academy. If Elena no longer has a future, or a home, within the Disney universe, what does that mean for Latina girls? What's next? In August 2020, the *Elena of Avalor* series came to an end with the culminating episode of her coronation. Now that Elena is no longer a princess, but a queen, her remaining time within the Disney princess universe seems unclear.

This concluding chapter highlights the overarching argument that *Elena of Avalor*, as analyzed through the production, text, and audience components, remains marginalized from the U.S. mainstream. Her existence within the Disney universe is therefore indicative of the overall presence of Latinxs in popular culture and at large. Not only do Latinxs continue to be portrayed as foreigners or outsiders, but the representations actually fall much more in line with Latin American and Iberian Peninsula peoples. *Elena of Avalor* is a perfect example of this. Although Disney worked hard to promote this princess as its "first Latina princess," Elena and her kingdom reside within Latin American narratives and implicit geographic locations. Thus, not only is Elena marginalized from the U.S. mainstream, but the research in this book indicates that she is not a Latina princess. U.S. Latinxs and Latin Americans are not the same, yet the media conflate us at large to create an easily digestible and recognizable image for non-Latinx viewers. Whether at the theme parks, on the mobile applications, or in the corporate reports, Elena does not call Disney her home. She is an outsider, an eternal foreigner, a princess of the periphery. This book provides a key example of how Disney carefully produces a version of animated Latina girlhood that is intended to court domestic Latinxs as well as global brown audiences, while actively appealing to normative white audiences via exoticization. The book's multilayered analysis of Disney's approach to mediated Latina girlhood interrogates the complex relationship between the largest ethnic minority in the United States and a global conglomerate that stands in for the United States of America on the global stage.

❋

CHAPTER 1

From Black-and-White Mouse to "Latina" Girl

I begin the first session of my undergraduate Disney course by asking the students a simple question. What is Disney? Following this question, I ask them to think through their experiences with Disney and their personal histories with the company. Most students talk about characters, films, experiences, products, and fond memories. Students are also often eager to share personal stories about their trips to the parks. One semester, though, I was struck by a student who asked, "Isn't Disney practically everything?" We wrapped up that portion of the class discussion as she explained that it would be easier to count what Disney does *not* own than what it does. This student answered my question by thinking about Disney ownership. She did not describe memories, experiences, or visits, but rather came up with a long list of what Disney owns. And while the Disney Company *is* composed of all that it owns, it is also much more than that. Before delving into the Elena circuit of culture case studies, it is important to think through the question I pose to my students. What is Disney? Given that the name is iconic around the world, what is it that defines "Disney" beyond the conglomerate? And how does the answer to this play a part in the inception, deployment, and consumption of *Elena of Avalor*?

This chapter provides a brief overview of the Disney Company from multiple perspectives. It traces the history of Disney (from Walt's early days to its current existence as a conglomerate monopoly and brand), examines the corporation's history with animation, breaks down its engagements with Latin America and later U.S. Latinidad to trace Disney's long use of flexible Latin Americanness in conjunction with a more recent flexible Latinidad, and outlines the history of its (gendered) princess discourses. The chapter also considers the significance and incorporation of the theme parks within the components. This information helps contextualize the debut of *Elena of Avalor* a year before *Coco*'s U.S. release and four years after the *Sofia the First* Latinidad controversy (which I carefully analyze in chapter 2). This chapter also sets the backdrop for understanding Elena's flexible Latinidad. I trace Elena's flexible Latinidad back to the various objects presented in this chapter: summaries of Walt Disney biographies, compilations of Disney's vast ownership, reports of Disney's internal leadership, analyses of Disney scholarship (including animation history), explorations of Disney princess culture discourses (including some newer discourses), a breakdown of the history behind the "Good Neighbor" films, and an in-depth analysis of the history of the theme parks.

Throughout the book, I argue that in its creation of Disney's animated "Latinx" universe, the company presents a rhythmic, vacillating, pattern between Latin America and U.S. Latinidad. This flexible pattern is consistent within the production, series, and theme park experiences related to *Elena of Avalor*. Further, the pattern is indicative of Disney's flexible and tenuous attempts to reach out to the Latinx market through its animated content. These representational decisions should not be surprising given Disney's history.

From *Alice in Wonderland* and *Oswald* to the Disney Multiverse

The Walt Disney Company has come to mean happiness, magic, and love for audiences around the world, but where did it all begin? Walt Disney's story (or at least pieces of it) is known by people all over the United States and beyond. Both his story and his journey to success are often presented through a lens of praise. I have quickly discovered this in my Disney classes as well. Students are eager to excitedly share information concerning what they know about this infamous man: where he was born, how he came up with the idea for Disneyland, details about his childhood, or whether his body remains frozen under the theme park. Some of the details are a bit off, while others are spot on. One can find many biographies of Walt, so rather than delve into the depths of his story (or that of the company), I will instead provide a few key details in this chapter that will set the backdrop for the chapters to come.

Walter Elias Disney was born in Chicago in 1901 and spent most of his childhood moving throughout the Midwest due to his father's job instability. Reports indicate that his fondest memories growing up stemmed from his two-year period in Marceline, Missouri (Croce, 1991; Wasko, 2020; Wills, 2017). His stay would later inspire Main Street Disneyland, though a much more sanitized version of Marceline (Francaviglia, 1995). Even though Walt did not live in a rural setting for too long, he idealized small-town life and grew alarmed by the disarray of urban settings, a feeling that later inspired him to create EPCOT as a prototype for the future (Croce, 1991).

Walt left his parents' home when he was sixteen years old to serve in World War I. After his time abroad, he returned to the United States and worked at his father's jelly factory for a short time. He then started working as a commercial artist in Kansas City, not long after leaving his father's jelly factory, to pursue a more creative outlet. It was in Kansas City that Walt formed his own company at the age of twenty and started producing the *Alice* series (1923).[1] After the company failed, he joined his brother Roy in Los Angeles and picked back up with his *Alice* series. It was in Los Angeles that the Walt Disney Company was formed in 1923. Following his production of *Alice*, Walt created yet another short-animated series starring "Oswald the Lucky Rabbit." Oswald's story is known by many: Universal owned the rights to the character and Walt was left with nothing. However, Oswald is said to have inspired Mickey, the mouse that started it all. Walt was often quoted saying, "I hope that we never lose sight of one thing, that it was all started by a mouse" (Colt, 2015a). In fact, this quote can be found throughout many of the Disney parks.

Although the creation of the mouse did start it all, the company's history (and now its present) are much larger than the mouse, though the mouse has come to signify the brand internationally. Society's fascination with Walt's history and the story of his struggles and successes often obscures the corporate nature of the Walt Disney enterprise and Walt's existence as a businessman above all else. Back in the 1920s the Walt Disney Company was actually much smaller compared to other corporate giants in the film industry. According to Wasko (2020), the Walt Disney Company was able to survive amid intense competition due to three strategies: (1) distribution deals with large film companies, (2) product differentiation, and (3) the money earned from merchandising contracts. Walt Disney's commitment to mass culture allowed the company to expand rapidly and become larger than he ever imagined.

Currently, the Walt Disney Company not only continues to produce Disney films at a rapid rate but also owns companies, television channels, film studios, and the rights to characters, ideas, and other types of intellectual property. Some brands and companies owned by Disney are: Vice, Pixar, Lucasfilm, Marvel, the Muppets Studio, Maker Studios, A&E, Touchstone Pictures, ABC, Hollywood Records, ESPN, Lifetime Channel, History Channel, and Twenty-First Century Fox. With its recent purchases of 21st Century Fox (2019), Lucasfilm (2012), and Marvel Entertainment (2009), Disney's massive ownership allows it to remain at the forefront of Hollywood narratives and retain its place as a major player among rapidly expanding media giants. More recently, its streaming service, Disney+, which launched in November 2019, has been quite successful both nationally and internationally (e.g., Bean, 2020; Goodfellow, 2020; Mendelson, 2020; Zacks Equity Research, 2020). Additionally, the streaming service significantly helped the company with revenues during the early months of the COVID-19 crisis when theme parks, live sports, and movie productions came to a halt. The launch of Disney+ coincided with the outbreak of COVID-19 on a global level and by the spring of 2021, Disney+ subscriptions had more than doubled (Faughnder, 2020; Jarvey, 2021).

Disney's global presence and influence are undeniable, and the company continues investing in attempts to grow its global presence every day. In describing Disney's global ownership, Wasko (2020) notes that the Walt Disney Company has moved beyond consideration as a "Disney universe"—a term coined by Real (1977) to refer to Disney's ownership—to a "Disney multiverse." Wasko explains that given the company's vast expansion within the past twenty years, we cannot understand it as one universe, but rather as a collection of universes. She uses the concept as a metaphor, which refers to the company's "corporate management, directors, share-holders, and employees; its corporate ethos, policies, strategies; its divisions, products, services, and properties; its content, values, and meanings; and its audiences, consumers, and fans; as well as the other universes that it owns (Pixar, Marvel, Lucasfilm, and 21st Century Fox)" (p. 3). The Disney multiverse continues to hold one of the most dominant roles in the entertainment industry with no end to its expansion in sight.

But who are the major players, who are the people making the major decisions about the multiverse? The Walt Disney Company has transitioned from family ownership to a publicly traded enterprise, where the largest stocks are owned by a few wealthy individuals. The company's board of directors is composed of people who oversee decision making for and about the company. This group of people typically represents key shareholders, legal firms, or financial organizations. They are also often "key managers of other corporations and thus provide corporate inter-locks between the companies" (Wasko, 2017, p. 21). During one of the class sessions for my Introduction to Media Studies course, my students and I briefly discussed political economy and ownership. Part of the activity for that day consisted of their visiting the Walt Disney Company website and analyzing the "Executive Leader-ship" tab. On that day, in the spring of 2019, my students were shocked to find that the top two rows consisted solely of Roberts/Bobs and Alans. The top six people were named either Robert/Bob or Alan, were all men, appeared (phenotypically) to be white, and were all over the age of fifty. It took a bit of scrolling for them to finally come across any women or people of color. Although there have been a few changes within Disney's executive leadership since we completed that activity in April 2019, most notably the inclusion of a chief diversity officer, almost all the major players on the executive team continue to be white males. The Roberts/Bobs and Alans are still there, though they have shifted locations within the leadership tab. As Valdivia (2020) explains when juxtaposing Disney's animated break-throughs with its leadership team, "Little bunnies might be breaking through the glass ceiling in *Zootopia*, but not at Disney Studios" (p. 133). The multiverse continues to be run by normative, older, white male bodies. This level of ownership has not broken the glass ceilings quite yet.

Disney's Cultural Universe Reshaped by Expansion and Ownership

Even before the conglomerate was a universe of universes, numerous Disney products and the histories behind their creation secured their fair share of controversies and analyses. Dating back to the 1930s, Disney products were celebrated as art, while at the same time being analyzed by others for their potential influence on society. Members of the Frankfurt School interrogated the role of Disney products and characters within the scope of the culture industry, warning of their dangers (Adorno & Horkheimer, 1944). Internationally, the Walt Disney Company stands for U.S. mainstream media, and because of this, Disney has a strong influence in shaping understandings of what "America" means, both domestically and abroad. In fact, a former student of mine who was studying abroad in the United States, once told me that for him and his family, Disney means the United States of America and vice versa. He and his family understood Disney as the quintessential U.S. American icon. This student always had a lot to say about the role that Disney played in his life as he was growing up in the early 2000s in Spain.

Through the years, Disney has sought to "communicate an unambiguous ideology" (Wasko, 2001b, p. 26) via its products, whether these are films or the experiences provided by their resorts or multiple parks around the globe. Regardless of how many countries Disney films and television shows are exported to, the making of the mediated products occurs in the United States. As noted by Wasko and Meehan (2001), most of the participants in a study they conducted around the world agreed that Disney promotes a vision of American culture that is different from that of other cultures. The vision positions U.S. American ideals and norms as central and normative, with all others falling outside the scope of normativity. This is similar to what my exchange student noted. Disney has achieved this massive reach through many platforms (e.g., ABC, ESPN, Lifetime, and even 21st Century Fox), and via its synergy across those platforms. As Meehan (2005) explains, "Transindustrial conglomeration presents a unique opportunity to use each project to feed every operation. Called synergy, this practice has been championed by Michael Eisner, the current CEO of the Disney Company" (p. 123). Even though Eisner is no longer the CEO (he served in that position from 1984 to 2005), it was not until the 1980s that Disney's synergistic practices began to unfold at an unprecedented rate, both vertically and horizontally (Meehan, 2005).

Eisner came in with an aggressive growth plan, and one of his goals was to develop and deploy the animated characters broadly across platforms. Through horizontal integration, a company competes in multiple product markets to achieve synergy across businesses. Through vertical integration, a company competes in one product market, along different points of the supply chain. Disney was and continues to be a worldwide leader in both arenas. It might have all started with the mouse, but it was Michael Eisner who began promoting the idea to share the Disney characters across different businesses to enhance the value of their theme parks, television shows, stores, ice shows, and so on (Wasko, 2020).

Robert Iger, the Disney CEO from 2005 to 2020, implemented a slightly different expansion strategy. He began leveraging characters as he bought Pixar, Marvel, and Lucasfilm, and deployed them across multiple businesses. In other words, Iger expanded Disney through intellectual property purchases that, in turn, increased synergistic possibilities. Even though the Lucasfilm production company was famous and quite powerful before Disney purchased it, when we take into consideration corporate strategies, the decision to sell Lucasfilm seems wise. Synergistic corporate strategies aim to have the whole of the company be worth more than the sum of its parts. For example, the Walt Disney Company should expect its theme parks to be worth more as a part of the Disney family, and not independent of that family. Further, as Disney continues to acquire more companies and channels, its hope is that they become stronger because they are working together now, under the name and brand of Disney (Great Courses, 2015). Another great example here would be a franchise like *Toy Story*. Through its acquisition of Pixar, the hope was that *Toy Story* would become stronger and generate more revenue for the Walt Disney Company. Evidence of the franchise's worth is the inclusion of *Toy Story Land* at both U.S. theme park locations. The same can be said for Lucasfilm, all the *Star Wars* films, and the opening of *Galaxy's Edge* at both U.S. theme parks. Disney is unique when it comes to synergy, in that it has key characters, who are known worldwide and bring the brand together (characters ranging from Mickey to Chewbacca).

By implementing strategies like these, the power of Disney can be seen around the world as it continues to extend its global reach. Central to its attempts to extend the conglomerate's global influence lie attempts to invest in audiences of color within the United States and globally. As previously noted, Disney's indistinguishable ideology is recognized worldwide as distinctly situated within the United States, which is, however, made up of a plethora of nationalities, so what does this mean for the conglomerate as it attempts to cater to nonwhite audiences domestically and abroad? It is important to interrogate what falls under this well-known vision of "American" culture, especially as the demographic composition of this country continues to shift and Disney continues with its attempts to diversify its products and audiences for the sake of profit. Is the diversification of Disney a direct result of the changing demographics of the country in an attempt to promote a newer vision of U.S. American culture? Or is it more about attracting new, multigenerational, multiethnic, multiracial markets? It appears that Disney is still in the process of figuring out how to cater to youth (and families) of color, particularly Latinxs in the United States, through transmedia franchising while remaining consumable for white audiences. Part of that strategy hinges on producing flexible nonwhiteness, which is often animated. Flexible nonwhiteness refers to groups of characters who will appeal to most nonwhite people, instead of just one race or ethnicity. Notably, almost all of Disney's new releases featuring nonwhite characters are animated. Some of these films include *Encanto* (2021), *Raya and the Last Dragon* (2021), *Luca* (2021), and *Soul* (2020). This could be indicative of a trend where Disney first tests out its diversity moves via fantastical, animated content. This process also involves less risk for Disney. Not only is animation generally more affordable to produce and easier to translate and alter for international markets, but because it does not involve real humans on the screen (such as live-action characters), it is easier for Disney to avoid critiques or backlash for the content present in these fantastical cartoon lands.

Given that the Walt Disney Company is a global purveyor of content and constantly vying for the position of largest media conglomerate in the world (e.g., Le, 2015; O'Reilly, 2016; Seth, 2020), the significance of Disney's programming, and the shifts therein, continue to attract scholarly attention worldwide. The scholarship on Disney is vast (e.g., Blue, 2017, 2018; Bryman, 2004; Dorfman & Mattelart, 1971; Giroux & Pollock, 1999; Project on Disney, 1995; Sammond, 2005; Smoodin, 1994;

Wasko & Meehan, 2001; Wasko, 2017, 2020) and tackles issues from political economy to audience effects and theme park attractions. Wasko (e.g., 2001a, 2001b, 2017, 2020) not only traces the depth and scope of the Disney corporation but also the universality of the brand and company name across the years. In 2001, Wasko, Phillips, and Meehan edited one of the most popular projects within Disney studies, a global analysis of Disney audiences (referenced above) that traced different aspects of the Disney corporation as they were perceived by groups of audiences around the world. Again, one of the main findings was that Disney is recognized internationally as a symbol for U.S. society.

Publicly examining Disney, however, is no simple feat. The scholars Dorfman and Mattelart (1971) conducted an in-depth analysis of the Disney corporation, in particular the character of Donald Duck, in their text *Para leer al pato Donald* (How to Read Donald Duck). This analysis of Disney Donald Duck comic books concluded that Disney promotes ideals of consumerism, capitalism, and imperialism. Like Theodor Adorno, they warned about the dangers of Disney in reproducing harmful ideologies, especially as these posed a threat to Latin America. Their study concluded that Disney imposes U.S.-centered ideologies on the world, and when it comes to Latin American peoples, these ideologies are particularly dangerous because, as the authors state, "It forces us Latin Americans to see ourselves *as they see us*" (p. 95). The Disney Company was not only quick to react to this text, but even locals and military officials in Chile, where the book was published, took to the streets, where they publicly burned the text. To this day, the text is difficult to access in many U.S. libraries. The text is foundational not only to Disney studies but also to media studies.

To further echo the statement of the dangers of publicly exposing Disney, it is worth mentioning Giroux and Pollock's work (1999). In *The Mouse that Roared*, Giroux and Pollock warned about the dangers of Disney and how these dangers were more harmful particularly for children, who were more often the direct consumers of Disney's content. Giroux and Pollock (1999) argued that while Disney purports to disseminate positive messages about race, gender, and democracy, the company's main goal is to convert children and their families "from a democracy of citizens to a democracy of consumers" (p. 162). As was the case with Dorfman and Mattelart in Chile, Giroux and Pollock received numerous complaints from people expressing their frustration about the criticisms aimed at what they understood to be such an innocent and pure company. However, the criticisms are not all that outlandish, particularly when you look at them alongside a statement Michael Eisner made in 1981 in an internal company memo. When asked about the accuracy and specificity of Disney's films, Eisner replied, "We have no obligation to make history. We have no obligation to make art. We have no obligation to make a statement. To make money is our only objective" (Cox, 2000). "We" refers to Disney, and his point does not get any clearer than that.

As previously mentioned, when Bob Iger took over as chairman and chief executive officer of Disney in 2005, the company started a more aggressive push to expand globally even farther than Eisner had as CEO before him. With his team's global expansion came the release of more nonwhite characters to appeal to different demographics around the world through Disney fantasy tales. Although Disney claims that its tales are purely fantastical (they are supposed to be magical and not ideologically or politically motivated), throughout the years the conglomerate has adapted, updated, and modified its representations in attempts to meet economic, cultural, and demographic changes around the world (hence the release of more nonwhite characters and different storylines). Wasko (2017) reminds us that "Disney fantasies are offered as commodities, produced and manufactured in accordance with definite commercial parameters" (p. 23). These "fantasies," driven by commercial needs, help shape realities for certain groups of people, especially young children. Given that Disney is associated with ideas of purity, magic, childhood, happiness, and innocence, these ideas often tend to go unquestioned (Giroux & Pollock, 1999).

We must not forget that Disney's appeal hinges on an idea that the brand and what it stands for are universal, even though the company is based in the United States. Even with the newer, darker-skinned characters, the company represents the United States. In this sense, the company is promoting U.S. values and ideas as universal, although they use transnational talent, transnational locations, and borrow from stories and legends outside of the United States. Wasko (2020) warns, "We also need to remember that this 'universality' is not necessarily automatic or natural. It has been and continues to be deliberately manufactured and carefully controlled" (p. 24), something that viewers often fail to remember or even recognize. Wasko further notes that "Disney's power is related to the ability to define childhood and family life, as well as its control over widely popular and successful media and entertainment franchises. It is an active player in the concentrated media business and thus is active in shaping our cultural universe" (p. 24). It shapes our cultural universes through its storylines, characters, and many decisions, which we are rarely aware of.

On February 25, 2020, the Walt Disney Company transitioned into the hands of a new CEO, Robert Chapek. Chapek stepped in at a critical point for the company, weeks before COVID-19 changed people's lives around the globe. Since then, Chapek has been making decisions that he hopes will stabilize the company given the ways in which consumer trends have shifted (Swineburn & Chapek, 2021). Chapek is not only changing film distribution strategies through Disney+ early releases, but he has also explained that he is committed to continuing the company's changes in relation to diversity and inclusion (Hough, 2021). In the closing lines of the *2020 Corporate Social Responsibility Report*'s "letter from our Chief Executive Officer," Chapek explains that "one of the things I'm most proud of is the progress we've made in the area of Diversity & Inclusion. Last June, I outlined a multi-faceted plan to bring about important changes across our company, comprised of six pillars: Transparency, Representation, Accountability, Community, Content, and Culture" (Walt Disney Company, 2021). Thus far, Chapek has demonstrated that he is incredibly mindful of consumer trends. His approach and direct reference to his commitment to diversity are situated at the tail end of the narrative franchise I analyze, but they continue to form a part of Disney's vision for its future.

Culture through Animation: Girls, Princesses, and Nonwhite Characters

Well before the inception of media studies, Disney's animated representational strategies had already gained scholarly attention from distinct fields (Giroux & Pollock, 1999; Jackson, 1993; Real, 1977; Watts, 1997). Researchers focused on issues including gender and racial representations in Disney animated films and shorts. Within the realm of girlhood in particular, the literature on teenage and tween girls' relationship(s) to Disney is much more extensive than the research pertaining to younger groups of girls. Researchers like Blue (2013, 2017), McGladrey (2014), and Kennedy (2018), among others, have explored the way that Disney Channel and Disney products deploy girlhood, but their focus is on tween and teenage girls, and most of this research focuses on white girls as well. It must be noted that animated cartoons are a large part of the Disney empire and, as indicated by many scholars, animated series and films greatly influence and shape young children's understandings of the world (Aladé et al., 2020; Aubrey & Harrison, 2004; Greenberg, 1982; Roberts, 2004; Swan et al., 1998). For young girls, in particular, animated representations of princesses and heroines inform not only how they play, but how they understand themselves and others around them. For example, for children who have never met or been around a Pacific Islander, watching a film such as *Moana* (2016) could prove to be the only type of information they receive early on about this group of people and about Pacific Islander girls in general.

Since the inception of its animated films and television series in the 1930s, Disney has had a long history of portraying its animated heroines and princesses as passive and mostly white. The animated representational practices employed by Disney, however, do not begin or end with the princess culture. As briefly outlined above, Disney as a cultural phenomenon has gained attention from fanatics, film critics, and scholars alike. Starting in the late 1990s, Disney studies has exploded even more and has taken on the form of rhetorical, feminist, Marxist, psychoanalytic, critical, and other such analytical methods that allow for the exploration of social issues (Jackson, 1993; Wasko, 2001a, 2020; Watts, 1997). Much of the existing literature that focuses on racial issues within Disney animation explores the problems surrounding the fact that most of the Disney animated characters throughout the history of the company's existence are white, with nonwhite representations being relegated to archaic stereotypes or animals (Wasko, 2001b). In recent years, and since the beginning of the inception of the literature cited above, there has been an increase in animated heroines and princesses who are more active and diverse. In 2009, *The Princess and the Frog* became the first Disney full-length animated feature film to feature a Black princess, although audiences were only able to see the Black princess for one-fourth of the film because Tiana (the princess) turns into a frog and spends the majority of the film attempting to turn back into a human. It is possible to count on our two hands the few Disney princesses or heroines of color, or supposedly nonwhite, although many of them claim (through executive producers and the like) to be ethnically ambiguous or belong to make-believe kingdoms with no claims or ties to any real regions (Sieczkowski, 2012). Ambiguous make-believe kingdoms will be further expanded on in chapter 2.

When it comes to nonwhite princesses or lead female heroines, films like *The Princess and the Frog* and *The Hunchback of Notre Dame* gained much scholarly attention after their release (Breaux, 2010; Gehlawat, 2010; Lacroix, 2004) as researchers attempted to explain that these representations were still highly racist and problematic. For example, Breaux (2010) explains that even though *The Princess and the Frog* takes place in New Orleans during the Jim Crow era, the film contains no references to any of the obstacles that would have been present for the characters, as issues of race and segregation are whitewashed in typical Disney fashion. Although *The Princess and the Frog* is an animated Disney film from 2009, the same type of whitewashing still exists in more recent cases. For example, some audiences have been very vocal in expressing their resistance and opposition to *Moana* (2016), even going as far as to create a Moana syllabus to be used in critical studies classrooms nationwide (Miyashiro, n.d.).

Princesses in general form a vast portion of Disney animation. The princess culture plays a large part in Disney's influence on young girls. Princess discourses abound in U.S. mainstream popular culture, and the Disney Princess line, without a doubt, is the most successful and popular. Disney's princess franchise earns billions for the corporation, not just from the films but through a vast range of products including dolls and toys (Giroux & Pollock, 1999; Hains, 2014; Meehan, 2005). Many reports on toy sales indicate that the Disney Princess franchise consistently ranks in the top categories for worldwide sales (Burns, 2015; Suddath, 2015; Whitten, 2016). Disney is well aware of this, and the conglomerate continues to generate animated princess stories year after year. The stories turn into films or television series, which then turn into countless types of merchandise including books, toys, Halloween costumes, ice shows, dance party shows, tiaras, gowns, and the like, all of which convey discourses about girlhood. Disney secures the largest claim on the princess narrative, due in large part to the fact that Disney brought the narrative to life in animated form and continues to produce these animated stories year after year.

Disney princesses, however, are not all created equal. Princess scholars have traced the many iterations of princesses throughout the years and even developed different waves and labels for the distinct phases of Disney princesshood. Whelan (2012), among others, traces the first Disney princess narratives and distinguishes between the first wave of princess films (*Snow White*, *Cinderella*, and *Sleeping Beauty*) and the second wave (*The Little Mermaid*, *Aladdin*, *Mulan*, *Beauty and the Beast*). In this work, Whelan traces the representational shifts present within animated princess discourses, situates them within the corresponding time periods, and concludes her piece with provocative questions about whether a feminist

progressive princess representation is fully possible. Similar to findings surrounding postfeminist representations in live-action form, most Disney princesses still remain glued to traditional heteronormative narratives of romance,
despite their engagement in more seemingly progressive journeys throughout the
past fifteen years. Whether or not progressive feminist princesses are fully possible is a question that many scholars, teachers, parents, and children have sought
to answer. It continues to be a prominent question as heroines and princesses like
Sofia from *Sofia the First*, Lilo from *Lilo and Stitch*, Moana, and Mirabel from
Encanto (all seemingly powerful representations of teenagers and young girls)
appear on screens and on merchandise across the nation.

Even though recent animated princess films like *Tangled* (2010), *Frozen* (2013),
and *Frozen 2* (2019) appear to be indicative of superficial changes, the archetype of
the submissive princess still exists and has a long history. Overall, when it comes
to a consensus about the "princess culture," there is no clear-cut answer. While
some scholars acknowledge that we can clearly see progress within the princess
narrative, others believe that this "progress" merely veils a continuity of traditional
narratives, even within the realm of racial or ethnic representations. In this conversation of progress, or lack thereof, the live-action *Aladdin* (2019), *Mulan* (2020),
and *The Little Mermaid* have garnered quite a bit of attention. Regardless of the
many different viewpoints herein, we must acknowledge that these conversations
point to the layered nature of Disney princess representations.

Disney's more recent animated full-length feature film representational shifts
are not just racial and ethnic but are also exemplified in the topics the narratives
address. Additionally, these are not limited to princess representations. Since 2010,
some examples of Disney films with animated representational shifts include:
Arjun: The Warrior Prince (2012), *Wreck-It Ralph* (2012), *Zootopia* (2016), *Moana*
(2016), *Cars 3* (2017), *Coco* (2017), *Ralph Breaks the Internet* (2018), *Soul* (2020), *Raya
and the Last Dragon* (2021), *Encanto* (2021), and *Turning Red* (2022). These films
not only feature nonwhite characters, but some also address topics ignored by Disney in previous years. *Zootopia*, for instance, addresses issues of prejudice and
racism through the animal characters. The film also highlights a lead female character, a rabbit by the name of Judy Hopps, who is not a princess or looking for
love. *Wreck-It Ralph* and *Ralph Breaks the Internet* focus on the story of Ralph and
Vanellope von Schweetz, both video-game characters. Vanellope, although not an
official Disney princess in the princess pantheon, is a princess in the narrative of
the story. However, she is practically the antithesis of a Disney princess, and in a
scene in *Ralph Breaks the Internet*, she meets all the Disney princesses (in modern
and updated form). This scene mocks common tropes of princess narratives, such
as the traditional princess's dependence on a male hero, her constant singing, and
her magical ability to commune with animals. The scene also points out and ridi-
cules the frequent narrative of the princess being kidnapped or enslaved. Here,
Vanellope illustrates some of the many critiques surrounding princess culture.

Even though it is only in one scene, *Ralph Breaks the Internet* challenges frequently used princess tropes. The film not only does so in this specific scene but it

also deploys a unique representation of girlhood and princesshood, albeit in a video-game character format. As previously mentioned, these narrative shifts are not just limited to girlhood, they also include elements of race and ethnicity, some of which focus on Latinidad and Latin Americanness.

Cars 3, for example, features a lead Latina anthropomorphic race-car character, voiced by Cristela Alonzo, who showcases her Latinidad through her slight accent and in her family story of success (and meritocracy) in this country. The Latinidad in *Cars 3*, however, can very easily go unnoticed. *Coco* (2017) provides a specific Mexican representation of nonwhite characters in a full-length animated feature film, although the focus is not on girlhood and the story does not address U.S. Latinidad, instead showcasing the story of a family living in rural Mexico and the Land of the Dead, in the overused celebration of Día de Los Muertos (Day of the Dead).

Since 2010 (and even a bit earlier), Disney and Disney Junior animated television series have also expanded the breadth and depth of their characters. *Handy Manny* (2006–2013), *Doc McStuffins* (2012–2020), *Sofia the First* (2012–2018), *Elena of Avalor* (2016–2020), and *Mira, Royal Detective* (2020–2021) are five examples of this expansion using animated series. *Handy Manny* was originally pitched by Disney as "edutainment," and according to Brayton (2013), the series "portrays Latina/os as valuable and congenial to the multicultural community" (p. 336). Manny represents a hardworking model minority invested in helping his community by repairing of local infrastructures. *Doc McStuffins* also perfectly exemplifies Disney's efforts to shift its narratives toward a more all-encompassing path. Created and produced by Chris Nee, an openly gay screenwriter, producer, and activist, the series tackles issues of childhood cancer, adoption, and same-sex parents (topics not often addressed in animated series). Doc is a young Black girl who "fixes" her stuffed animals, emulating the ways in which her mother, a medical doctor, treats her patients. Her father is a stay-at-home dad who is always one step ahead of the game when it comes to making dinner and planning extracurricular events, thus the show rejects normative gender roles through the portrayal of her parents. Doc does not necessarily complicate Disney's pervasive princess tropes, but rather is constructed outside of these. Not only is this an animated television series (instead of a film), but the narrative falls outside of traditional princess scripting that is central to the Walt Disney Company.

Although different versions of animated princess representations exist (even princesses who are not interested in finding a romantic partner), many critics believe that Disney's new line of princesses, and female characters at large, still need much more improvement. One area in need of improvement that is often highlighted is the limited construction of princess bodies (Bell, 1995; McGladrey, 2014). In her piece on the construction of the female body in Disney's animated works, Bell (1995) found that some of the key aesthetic features used when portraying princesses or heroines were small waists, slender legs and arms, and an ability to move gracefully. Eighteen years later, McGladrey (2014) similarly noted that the tween participants in her study found that the "just-right ideal" body was represented in Disney girls (not limited to animated girls) and the participants associated this type of body with a "normal girl" body. While Disney's representations of girls, heroines, and princesses is limited when it comes to race, the depictions are also limited when it comes to a variety of physical attributes, different body types, and different abilities, much of which can be traced to the privileging of white, normative bodies. These representational strategies continue to gain attention from scholars in different disciplines, especially as issues dealing with body image disorders continue to plague girls around the world. Although animation has provided new opportunities for Disney to re-create and revise its previous images, plenty of modifications have yet to be made.

DISNEY'S ENGAGEMENTS WITH LATIN AMERICA AND U.S. LATINIDAD

Long before the company's attempts to reach out to global audiences and more diverse audiences nationally, Walt Disney himself had been a part of a push to reach out to Latin Americans, and people of Latin American descent in the United States. In 1941, Walt headed to South America for a U.S. government-commissioned research trip. This venture was a strategy formed as part of the Good Neighbor Policy, which sought to strengthen ties between North America and Latin America. Initially, the government asked Walt to take part in a goodwill tour of Latin America, but the idea of a simple tour did not sit well with him. A second offer consisted of a proposal to create two films showcasing Latin American people and ways of life. The U.S. government specifically asked that Walt focus on the ABC countries: Argentina, Brazil, and Chile (though these are all countries in South America). Again, this trip was fully underwritten by the U.S. government (at half a million dollars) in an attempt to strengthen ties between Latin America and the United States during World War II and secure Latin American countries as allies.

Walt was tasked with creating media texts that would appeal to Latin American populations and express sentiments of friendship. The government hoped he would represent Latin American people and culture as friendly and nonthreatening, in order to win their favor. At the same time, the government also felt that Walt would be the perfect representative of the United States abroad. Walt and eighteen artists participated in the research trip and tour. It started in August 1941 and lasted ten weeks. Scheduled by the governments in each of the countries were research tours and outings for Walt and "El Grupo." "El Grupo" was the name given to the crew shortly after their arrival in Rio de Janeiro. The research trips consisted of visiting farms, attending gaucho dance performances and musical performances, and sampling local cuisine to gain inspiration for the film. The end results were the two films: *Saludos Amigos* (1942) and *The Three Caballeros* (1944), known as the "Good Neighbor" films from the 1940s. Because the governments of these countries were responsible for offering the perspectives that would inspire the films, the Good Neighbor films must be understood as state-sponsored representations.

Traveling to South America for the research offered Walt a welcome distraction. In South America he was welcomed and revered by many. The situation back in Los Angeles was strikingly (literally) different. At home, Walt was dealing with tense situations among his employees, who had begun to unionize. In May 1941 half of his art department walked out and went on strike due to unfair wages and working conditions. Walt blamed the unionizing and strike on communism and even after the situation was resolved (though not necessarily in a way that favored the studio), many people said he continued to hold grudges against those who had stood on the picket line.

After the chaos with the studio ended and they wrapped up the research trip, Walt and the creative team immediately began working on the films, which came out a year and a half apart. In 1943, at the U.S. premiere of *Saludos Amigos* (the film opened in Rio de Janeiro in 1942) at the Hollywood bowl, audiences were surrounded by mariachis, sombreros, and vibrant colors (Cerejido, 2017). *The Three Caballeros* (1944), premiered shortly after, similarly relying mostly on Mexican artifacts as markers of Latinidad. Moreover, both films conflated distinct regions in Latin America to create a single unified consumable version of the entire region. For example, in both films, when Disney showcased Mexico, audiences saw mariachis, sarapes, piñatas, and heard heavy accents. This was the case even though the films did not specifically focus on Mexico. But the whole of Latin America is more than just mariachis and piñatas. The thirty-three countries that make up this huge land mass have a variety of climate zones, geographical attributes, languages, histories, and traditions.

It should also be noted that Disney did not travel to Mexico during this research trip; "El Grupo" traveled only to South America, which does not represent all of Latin America. Yet, "El Grupo" relied mostly on Mexican markers in both of their films. As Valdivia (2020) observes, both films "represented Latin American cultures and characters through the recurring, continuous, and still familiar tropes of the bandido, señorita/spitfire, the Latin lover, the dark lady, with heavy doses of dancing, colorful tropical settings, happy natives, and talking animals" (p. 83). If we take a close look, many of these images continue to circulate through Disney representations of Latin Americans and U.S. Latinxs. We can see this more recently in *The Legend of the Three Caballeros* (2018) and *Stuck in the Middle* (2016–2018).

Both films were commissioned to dispel negative stereotypes about Latin American people in the media. They were created for the U.S. population to see a friendlier representation of Latin American people as well as for Latin American people and Latinxs in the United States to see themselves in a different light. However, as Goldman (2014) finds, "Close analysis reveals that the films actually promote other, no less inaccurate stereotypes, and, in particular, underscore the long-standing unequal relationship between the U.S. and Latin America. They continue to depict the flow of cultural texts from north to south as natural and unequivo-cal" (p. 25). Unfortunately, we continue to see extensions of these tropes in the new *Legend of the Three Caballeros* (2018), an animated series based on the original film, which is available on Disney+. Although there is only one season, it suffices to illustrate that there truly have not been many revisions when it comes to the Good Neighbor films. We continue to see vibrant colors, dancing natives, strong accents, and the same overused tropes via animals.

As already noted, part of Disney's formula for representing all of Latin America and to aid in the U.S. government's quest to forge solid ties with this region included reproducing frequently used tropes that flattened the many differences among Latin American countries. This flattening is often accompanied by the "outsider/insider" dichotomy, whereby the person or region outside of the United States functions as the eternal outsider, often closer to nature and more primitive than the modern United States (these topics will be expanded on in chapter 3). Disney has a long history of othering (Valdivia, 2017) nonwhite animated characters through strategic representational choices in television and films (Breaux, 2010; Gehlawat, 2010; Lacroix, 2004; Wasko, 2001a; Whelan, 2012), and these early films are only two examples of many in which Disney represents Latin America and Latinxs by relying on archaic tropes that position this group as outside the norm. The strategies used in "othering" make it easier for white audiences to consume these texts, especially if they fall in line with representations (or tropes) that they are already familiar with. Two examples of othering include language and accents. By its inclusion of characters who do not speak English or characters with a strong accent, Disney "reinforces the mainstream by differentiating individuals and groups and relegating them to the margins" (Valdivia, 2017, p. 133). Moreover, these strategies are likely symptomatic of having been produced in a white, male-dominated industry. I will continue to call attention to these strategies throughout this book as I highlight Disney's approaches within the *Elena of Avalor* narrative franchise.

Even though the Good Neighbor films were created in an attempt to win the favor of Latin America during a time of strife in the world, the stereotypical representations offered by the texts were not readily accepted by everyone. During the early 1940s, the U.S. government was hopeful that Disney, the visionary and creator of dreams, would help strengthen relationships between the United States and Latin America through animated representations, but the success of the films is still hard to gauge. Regardless of whether the films successfully achieved what the government hoped they would, this marked one of the first attempts by Disney to represent the United States' neighbors to the south. Valdivia (2020) reminds us that when exploring the relationships between Disney and Latin America we should understand that "there is a long history, that this history flattens difference, and that this history is more influenced by geopolitics and economic issues rather than by ground level issues and narratives occurring within Latin America and US Latinidad" (p. 20).

Disney continues to respond to demographic findings and changes, both nationally and abroad. Disney's acknowledgment of an ever-growing nonwhite population is heterogeneous in that it continues to produce supposedly ethnically specific characters and narratives while simultaneously courting a broad range of global audiences through tenuous ethnic ambiguity. The analyses of Disney's nonwhite live-action characters is growing, especially as Disney's ownership goes on expanding (Bucciferro, 2021; Griffin & Rossing, 2020; Leon-Boys & Chávez, 2021). Within these critical cultural analyses, those focusing on Disney's representation of live-action Latinidad, however, are minimal, especially in relation to girlhood (Leon-Boys, 2021a; Leon-Boys & Valdivia, 2021; Valdivia, 2011, 2020). As noted earlier, Brayton (2013) explores the inclusion of *Handy Manny* within the animated Disney Junior lineup, and Chávez and Kiley (2016) provide an insightful approach to Disney, Latino children, and television labor through an analysis of corporate reports. These are two of only a few studies currently available.

In her previous work on Disney Channel, Valdivia (2008c) finds that the channel is unique in many ways, including its previous status as a "noncommercial" channel and its strong push to appeal to the tween demographic through series like *Lizzie McGuire* and films like *The Cheetah Girls* (2003, 2006, 2008). After *Lizzie McGuire* (2001–2004) ceased to be in production, other series such as *Wizards of Waverly Place* (2007–2012) quickly took its place in bolstering Disney's efforts to appeal to tweens/teens of color, specifically Latinx youth. In her analysis, Valdivia finds that Disney ultimately uses difference very carefully so as to avoid alienating white viewers and still appeal to a G-rated audience seeking a happy ending. Part of the strategy involves ambiguous racial representations. These findings still apply to current Disney Channel live-action series. *Stuck in the Middle* (2016–2018), which showcases a Latinx family navigating life with seven children, provides a perfect example of the conglomerate's more recent attempts at ambiguity and flexibility. Disney Channel's Latinx universe, as exemplified by the series, incorporates overused Latinx tropes, such as hyperfertility, *quinceañeras*, and spitfires, but also presents yet another example of what is becoming a secondary trope, the overly successful STEM-savvy tween (Leon-Boys & Valdivia, 2021). Through the narrative, the series presents a flexible and nonthreatening Latinidad that is barely perceptible.

By providing images that are ambiguously brown, Disney takes a flexible approach to representation that is not limited to Latinidad. Currently, many speculate that the Walt Disney Company is transitioning into a new stage of representations with the inception of its new darker-skinned characters and their ties to more specific cultures. The examples of *Elena of Avalor, Moana, Coco*, and *Encanto* suggest that this could be the case, although of course, these shifts are driven by profit. These films indicate that Disney continues to implement various strategies to extend its representational possibilities, but this potential is currently only available in animated form. It is important to note here that the animated characters and storylines are recirculated at the Disney theme park locations. One of the most prominent possibilities afforded to animated characters, which does not necessarily translate to all the live-action characters, is that they are also able to exist in a live setting at the theme parks around the world. Disney keeps this in mind during the development of the films' narratives.

Theme Parks

An area of Disney in which diverse representational tactics continue to be tested is the theme parks. The Disney parks have a long and complex but often romanticized history, much like the story of Walt and the company's inception. However, one cannot gain a well-rounded understanding of Disney as a media giant without tackling the significance and history of the theme parks. Walt Disney did not initially set out to create theme parks, but they form a central part of his synergistic legacy and the Disney multiverse, responsible for generating a significant amount of the conglomerate's revenue. Shortly after Walt's research trips to South America, and amid the ongoing tensions at the studio in relation to the strike and Walt's open accusations of communists within the company, he embarked on a train tour in Illinois. After wrapping up this tour, he put together his own large-scale model train back at home. In 1951, Salvador Dalí visited Walt in California, where he was mesmerized by Walt's train village and realized that Walt's fascination with and dedication to the train could be channeled into something else, something much larger. Dalí took note of the carefully created village, from the tunnels to the curves on the tracks, and pointed out the model's creativity and precision to its maker (Colt, 2015b). It is unclear whether Walt's initial idea to build Disneyland came about after Dalí's visit or was already in place and only strengthened by Dalí, but what is evident is that Walt began the planning and plotting shortly after Dalí's 1951 visit.

As the story goes, one day Walt was at an amusement park with his daughter when he noticed that the park was not necessarily clean or wholesome. As he sat on a bench with her, he realized that he yearned for a park that was fun-oriented, could provide a nice environment for the entire family, and was clean. Croce (1991) notes that "in planning his park, Walt Disney created a relentlessly clean entertainment through an almost compulsive passion for order and control" (p. 95). Order, cleanliness, and control were central to Walt's vision of his theme parks. His vision also hinged on the idea that the park would be divided into separate themes, which would revolve around Disney's cartoons and films. The park would not only provide the opportunity for a wholesome and clean park experience, but it would also allow the company the opportunity to recycle Disney characters and stories in live form.

Early in 1952, Walt began quickly liquidating his assets and even sold the rights to his own name. He was determined to make his park dream a reality. Shortly after selling the rights to his name, he started a new company for a new enterprise, an enterprise that he remained relatively quiet about in the beginning. Later that year, Walt's plans had outgrown his initial vision so much that he outgrew his studio. Initially called "Mickey Mouse Village," Walt hoped that his theme park would appeal to every family member, not just children. This vision remains central to the corporation to this day. He sought to distance his park from the carnival concept, particularly by allowing the park guests to enter a live, three-dimensional adventure.

The timing of the park opening could not have been more perfect given the state of the economy in the United States. Middle- to upper-middle-class U.S. Americans during the mid-1950s found themselves with extra amounts of disposable income, and families began to plan more leisure activities revolving around travel and entertainment. By creating the Disneyland park in California, Walt was able to provide families with both of these pleasures. To draw in as many crowds as possible before the grand opening, he sought out different forms of advertising through synergistic practices and even created a television series called *Disneyland* (1954). The objective of this show was to provide in-depth information about the park to attract audiences. On July 17, 1955, Disneyland opened its doors, and the line to enter the park was backed up for seven miles. The first few days after the grand opening consisted of quite a few hiccups, such as issues with rides, theme park guest concerns, hot temperatures, lack of sufficient food, and so on. However, despite reports of melted asphalt on Main Street and a flooded deck on Mark Twain's Riverboat, guests continued to pour in, and even political leaders and celebrities from around the world made sure to visit the park within the first few months of its opening.

Since 1955, the Disney parks have gained popularity domestically and abroad. Some of the most popular locations are the two parks in the United States (California and Florida), Disneyland Paris (1992), Hong Kong Disneyland (2005), and Tokyo Disneyland (1983), with Disneyland Paris (otherwise known as EuroDisney) constantly ranking as the top attraction in Paris (Muir Packman & Casmir, 1999), although it is not actually located *in* Paris. Disney parks are carefully crafted to showcase the town squares, Main Street, and quaint shops that line the entrance, in order to allow guests to partake in a unique vision of the U.S. collective memory. While this vision is not shared by all U.S. Americans, it is the vision showcased at the parks. Even though parks outside of the United States have made slight modifications through glocalization, Main Street and most of the landmark constructions at the parks remain the same throughout. Baudrillard (1994) and Eco (1986), among others, argue that Disney crafts a particular kind of reality through its parks, the layout, and the experiences it provides park guests. Disney employs different signifiers that attempt to represent moments, memories, and things that do not exist, referred to by Baudrillard as "hyperreality." Albeit fully embedded within this hyperreality, Disney theme parks are first and foremost commercial spaces, where tourists and park guests are encouraged to pay admission and patronize shops, restaurants, and hotels. In the process, however, Disney's theme parks perform significant ideological work. Most theme park scholarship suggests that the parks promote Walt's normative U.S. American values, which "reify existing social relations and the status quo, or, in other words, the present" (Wasko, 2020, p. 192).

Theme parks are complex, dynamic spaces. The ideological work that takes place within all the Disney park locations has become a prominent topic of interest within Disney studies (e.g., Bryman, 2004; Fjellman, 1992; Leon-Boys & Chávez, 2021; Mills, 1990; Mittermeier, 2021; Smoodin, 1994; Williams, 2020). The research, however, is not limited to the ideological significance of Disney parks. Another area of research within this sector concerns the actual labor performed at the parks. This type of scholarship goes beyond issues of labor disputes at the Disney parks and encompasses issues of affective labor performed by the employees. As previously mentioned, Disney is known by many as a magical entity, a producer and creator of dreams. The work of the Disney employees is therefore often invisibilized and disguised as magic (Bryman, 2004). The Project on Disney (1995), notes that through its parks, Disney "marshals the creative and emotional energies of its workers and creates a situation in which they are always performing for the company" (p. 113). Disney parks, forming an integral part of the corporation's image, strategically position their employees as extensions of the company as a whole, continuously laboring to secure the conglomerate's ideological fantasies. As Blue (2017) expands on her operationalization of "corporate imagination," she contends that "conglomerates such as the Walt Disney Company clearly foster particular working cultures and discourses that can constrain how and what meanings are made within and beyond the organization" (p. 12). In this book (particularly in chapter 4), I draw on her work as well as the above-referenced literature concerning theme parks and Disney parks to interrogate how Elena of Avalor's positioning at the park and her interaction with the park guests foster discourses about Latinidad and girlhood.

Disney theme parks rely on the performative and emotional labor that their characters engage in. One of the most significant appeals of the parks, particularly for younger demographics, is the ability for park guests to interact with characters from movies and television series, along with the classic Disney characters such as Minnie Mouse, Mickey Mouse, Pluto, and the crew. The costumed employees are not the only ones partaking in the process of performative labor, however. Every single employee at the Disney theme parks performs specific roles to cultivate the aura of magic that the parks are so well known for. Even the employees at Starbucks, for example, employ certain terms and references to solidify the performances. In fact, Disney employees are not referred to as employees, but as "cast members" (O'Connell, 2014), and they operate under strict rules and guidelines (including but not limited to how to smile, point, and wave). I draw on Bryman's (2004) work to operationalize performative labor in relation to Disney. He explains that when employing this term, he means "the rendering of work by managements and employees alike as akin to a theatrical performance in which the workplace is construed as similar to a stage" (p. 103). For the Disney "cast members," their work is theater. This book concludes with a case study of the performative labor (along with the positioning) of Elena and interrogates how this labor works to challenge or reproduce certain ideologies within the larger cultural context in which my theme park trips were taken.

This project draws on the history of the corporation and traces the revisions, continuities, and ruptures present via the *Elena of Avalor* narrative franchise. I ground the following case studies within the historical significance of the Walt Disney Company, which, alongside its standing as a top transnational media conglomerate, had previously engaged in attempts to represent Latin American cultures. Disney has always thought in global terms, and continued global expansion remains at the core of its mission. *Elena of Avalor* released its first episode in the summer of 2016, *Coco* premiered on November 22, 2017, and *Encanto* opened in theaters almost exactly four years later, on November 24, 2021. *Encanto*, set in Colombia against the backdrop of magical realism, yet again takes Disney animation to Latin America. Currently, there are no rumors of a U.S.-specific Latinx representation on the horizon for Disney full-length features, but perhaps the data gathered on the inception of their Latin American (though labeled Latina) princess will shift that conversation moving forward. Chapter 2 introduces the first case study of this narrative franchise, an in-depth analysis of the production of *Elena of Avalor*.

CHAPTER 2

❦

The Flexible Production of a "Latina" Princess

I grew up going to Disney. Disney's been in my family for a very long time . . . and just to see my own images represented, my own culture represented is really special and I hope it will be for everybody watching.
> —Aimee Carrero, 2016 *interview on* Good Morning America

Our creative team has delivered a universal story with themes that authentically reflect the hopes and dreams of our diverse audience.
> —Nancy Kanter, *former general manager of Disney Junior Worldwide*

What Disney really does well is create fairytale kingdoms. It makes it very inclusive—you don't have to pick just one nationality. No one really asked if Arendelle was Norway or Sweden, it's just inspired by a Scandinavian country. The idea for us was that we wanted Avalor to be more broadly accessible.
> —Craig Gerber, *executive producer and creator of* Elena of Avalor

As was previously discussed, Disney claims Elena as its first Latina princess. Even well before the debut of *Elena of Avalor* in the summer of 2016, the Walt Disney Company went to great lengths to promote Elena as its "first Latina princess" (Amatangelo, 2016; Del Barco, 2016). In the above quotes, Aimee Carrero (the voice of Elena) explains the significance of the princess's role within the Latinx community; Nancy Kanter creates a bridge between the story's authenticity and universality; and Craig Gerber rounds it out with his corporate framing explaining that the series is to be broadly accessible. In many similar interviews and social media posts, Disney carefully situated *Elena of Avalor*, the series and the princess, within the realm of Latinidad, while making sure the narrative franchise remained universal. After many blunders in the terrain of ethnic representations, Disney continues to employ a variety of industrial and representational strategies meant to seek out ethnic audiences, while continuing to center the normative and universal white audiences (Real, 1977; Shuggart, 2007; Valdivia, 2020; Wasko, 2020). Whereas the story behind the creation of *Elena* could be understood as unique and genuine, given that it is Disney, it is also a strategy to secure a large Latinx audience and to represent diversity sensitivity. Although audiences and scholars cannot be privy to Disney's internal marketing strategies, we know narratively that *Elena of Avalor* owes her existence to Sofia, from Disney Junior's *Sofia the First* and we suspect that, economically, Elena makes sound profit and economic risk-averse sense in that it will appeal across a broad demographic swath.

Shortly after *Sofia the First* debuted on Disney Junior in 2012, Latinx audiences were thrilled to hear from the show's executive producer that the princess was Latina, as many suspected. Days after the executive producer spoke out, however, other Disney executives stepped in and gave the official statement that Sofia was not Latina. The former general manager of Disney Junior Worldwide, Nancy Kanter, explained that Disney characters are not intended to reflect or represent any specific culture or ethnicity because they all belong to fantasy locations (C. Rodriguez, 2013). In a halfhearted apology, she laid to rest claims that Sofia was Latina. Of course, Disney films and television series locations are often inspired by real places, and frequently even take place in actual locations. Kanter, however, made it a point to explain that the creation of Sofia was inspired by and based on a mixture of many nations, positioning Sofia within the realm of Disney hybrid and ambiguously ethnic representations (Valdivia 2008b, 2008c, 2011). This situation and the responses to Sofia's ethnicity suggest that Disney narrates the creation of its animated characters as a post-racial and post-nation production process, very much in line with Gerber's quote about not picking one nationality at the beginning of this chapter. The disavowal of Sofia's Latinidad took place in 2012 and undeniably composed the backdrop to *Elena of Avalor*'s creation and royal debut. Indeed, given Disney's approach to developing franchises long ahead of their release, it is possible that the controversy was planned to increase attention and coverage of the true Latina princess release.

Unlike the situation with Sofia's Latinidad, with *Elena of Avalor* Disney proudly hailed this princess (in all outlets) as a Latina. With a long history of commodifying ethnicity (Halter, 2000), Disney brings to life what it claims to be its "first Latina princess." The princess, her kingdom, and the storyline showcase elements of both the specific and the ambiguous ethnic, while highlighting broad "can-do" (Harris, 2004) girl power discourses in another iteration of the "can-do Disney princess utopia" (Valdivia, 2020). Against this backdrop, this chapter provides the first case study in my circuit of culture approach, where I analyze the node of production. The chapter examines Disney's strategies in promoting and producing *Elena of Avalor* following the *Sofia the First* Latinidad fiasco of 2012. I analyze production in a unique way, blending an analysis of corporate communication with other promotional materials. Corporate communication is rarely analyzed via a cultural studies approach, except for a few studies (Brulle et al., 2020; Ciafone, 2019) in which the objects of analysis are vastly different (oil corporations and Coca-Cola). By analyzing corporate communication as a cultural artifact, indicative of the time period when it emerged, I contribute to the literature on production studies and create a bridge between industries and culture. Following the circuit of culture approach, a focus on production and labor provides one-third of a project that explores production, representation, and audiences.

Between 2010 and 2019, Latinxs' share of the total U.S. population increased from 16 percent to 18 percent, accounting for almost half of U.S. population growth during that period (Noe-Bustamante et al., 2020), and the numbers continue to rise. Additionally, Latinxs are the youngest and fastest-growing group in the country, which also factors into projected growth. Awareness of this population growth coincides with awareness of Latinx purchasing power and media consumption. Disney's acknowledgment of these findings is multiplicitous. The conglomerate's latest attempts to showcase its inclusivity through Latinidad came in animated form with the full-length feature film release of *Coco* in 2017, *Elena of Avalor*'s three seasons on Disney Junior from 2016 to 2020, and the latest full-length feature film *Encanto* (2021). These representations, however, continue to be situated within Latin America rather than the United States. The images we see are supposed to represent experiences outside of the U.S. national imaginary.

PRODUCTION IN MEDIA INDUSTRY STUDIES

When one hears the word "production," behind-the-scenes footage found on DVDs as well as promotional materials might come to mind. Production, as a set of practices, is multidimensional, vibrant, and composed of many people performing various roles. In this chapter, I conceive of cultural media production as broadly defined and inclusive of audiences' production of meaning(s) through media, especially in light of the fact that young audiences and nonwhite audiences are so often only discussed in terms of market value. Within media studies, production studies engages ethnographic, critical, material, sociological, feminist, and political-economy methods that span a variety of disciplines (Mayer et al., 2009). Media producers in all their different ranks are culture makers. Mayer et al. (2009) note that production studies scholars "draw their intellectual impetus from cultural studies to look at the ways that culture both constitutes and reflects the relationship of power" (p. 2). Production studies are vast, and some prominently highlight the role of audiences as producers. As Johnson (2017) notes, "Rather than trying to impose a new unifying name on an intellectual endeavor well under way by this point, it may be better to simply embrace the theoretical potential of production study to explain how each link in the industrial chain participates in a production process more broadly and radically conceived" (p. 150). Here, I draw on this approach in providing an account of the production of *Elena of Avalor* by highlighting some of the salient "link(s) in the industrial chain." I look at various links, though not all, that constitute the production elements behind *Elena of Avalor*. The links I analyze (including YouTube videos, Instagram pages and hashtags, corporate reports, and other digital spaces) are often overlooked in this type of research.

My analysis focuses on the ways in which Disney articulates the series' connection to Latinidad through corporate materials, online promotional materials, Disney employees, and Latinx actors. I purposefully analyze mediated instances that highlight the company's production strategies (i.e., where Disney explains how the creative team conceived the mythical land of Avalor and its inhabitants), specifically the strategies tied to Latinidad. My analysis is also the result of many incidental readings of social media posts referencing the series' ties to Latinidad. Part of my methodological process consisted of closely following all the Instagram accounts belonging to *Elena of Avalor*'s voice actors, along with the official *Elena of Avalor* Instagram page and the *Elena of Avalor* hashtag. Additionally, multiple Google Alerts for "*Elena of Avalor*" yielded useful information about Disney corporate reports.

Grounded in political economy by calling attention to the interplay between the symbolic and economic dimensions of production and meaning, I focus heavily on the genre of corporate communications, which is intended to facilitate the sharing of information to stakeholders (including investors, potential clients, and media analysts) to whom an organization is beholden, while also paying close attention to social media and the television promotion of *Elena of Avalor*. I critique these materials as rich discursive and ideological objects that demand analysis. As previously noted, very few studies offer a cultural studies approach to the analysis of corporate communication materials. I approach the corporate materials as my texts, which I read alongside many other texts. Textual analysis qualitatively focuses "on the underlying ideological and cultural assumptions of the text" (Fürsich, 2009, p. 240) and aids the researcher in unlocking embedded meanings by allowing us to understand "which gender, class, and ethnic identities in the current cultural sensibilities are encouraged and which ones are excluded" (p. 241). Following Fürsich's steps for textual analysis, I conducted detailed readings of each of the selected texts, followed by contextualized interpretations. Drawing on Foucault's theory of discourse and Stuart Hall's representational analysis pedagogy, I examine the ways in which a young, animated Latina is packaged and created for dissemination through many efforts on behalf of the Walt Disney Company.

Additionally, ownership of media factors prominently into this study. A political economy approach is central for understanding how a massive media giant like Disney operates and produces mediated content. The fact that Disney functions as a global entertainment oligopoly, with vertical and horizontal integration, as well as highly developed synergistic and convergent strategies, can only be analyzed using a political economy approach. Critical political economy calls for an interplay between the symbolic and economic dimensions of the production of meaning (Hardy, 2014). As an added layer, this approach examines how audiences are interpolated into broader corporate interests (Meehan, 2005; Wasko, 2001, 2020). With solid data indicating that the Latinx population will continue to grow, the Disney Company has found multiple ways to incorporate this in its corporate interests. This means also looking at how the company is organized, funded, and regulated (Wasko, 2020). Thus, this chapter operationalizes production as a process, which "enables us to understand not just distinct media institutions and industry sectors, but also how those forces figure into larger processes of communication, culture, and meaning creation" (Johnson, 2017, p. 151). I heed Johnson's call to action detailing how "we need to recognize the potential that an emphasis on production offers for seeing the intersections between industry and other cultural fields" (p. 150). By focusing on *Elena of Avalor*, I highlight how the production process of this narrative franchise creates intersections between industry and culture through Disney's mainstream and digital content about the production of the series.

Focusing on the production of *Elena of Avalor* in corporate reports, Disney Instagram pages, Girl Scouts and Disney YouTube channels, popular press coverage, and celebrity social media accounts, I posit that Disney uses three prominent production practices to construct ethnicity in relation to Latina bodies in *Elena of Avalor*. First, the company produces a flexible Latinidad through the corporate narrative and via its social media platforms. Second, Disney produces a specific kind of Latinx talent and utilizes the labor of the Latinx actors to promote the series' Latinidad. Finally, Disney produces Elena as a way to showcase its corporate social responsibility through Elena's partnership with Girl Scouts of the USA (hereafter, Girl Scouts USA) and through the new cultural and ethnic component highlighted in the yearly *Corporate Social Responsibility Reports*. My engagement with production focuses on the visibilization of the production process to highlight diversity through culture and "authenticity." Girls' media studies scholarship engages production studies prominently, but such studies to date have focused primarily on technical production aspects (i.e., YouTube video production practices and explorations of girl filmmakers). In contrast, Latinx media studies scholarship typically focuses more on media activism, digital storytelling, independent (rather than mainstream) media production, and struggles for Latinx access to media channels. My analysis provides insight into how Disney produces discourses of Latinidad through girl culture.

DISNEY AND THE PRODUCTION OF MAGIC

As one of the largest media conglomerates in the world, Disney offers audiences symbols for fantasy, happiness, magic, and love, which have contributed to long-lasting success and popularity domestically and abroad. When it comes to the conglomerate's production process, Disney is often viewed as a magical entity. Such an understanding suggests that its production decisions and methods are not to be understood in a rational way, and therefore ought not to be subjected to rational critique. What is "magical" implicitly cannot be comprehended by others, and therefore cannot be challenged. This "magic," however, is deeply rooted in hegemonic ideals, and invisibilizes material, ideological, and affective labor (Bryman, 2004; Smoodin, 1994; Wasko, 2020; Wills, 2017). Disney's historically and culturally specific notion of U.S. American normativity is linked to the aura of magic that comes with the conglomerate's name. Its original brand of American exceptionalism seeps into every aspect of production.

Performative production processes are often publicized. By actively framing its production practices for promotional purposes, the Walt Disney Company attempts to create an aura of transparency, though like everything else Disney, this is a carefully orchestrated and staged mediatized product and process. According to Sammond (2005), when Disney began television production, its public relations efforts enabled the company to appear to "celebrate the productive process behind its commodities rather than masking them. By placing an emphasis on the creative process behind its shorts and features while downplaying the repetitive labor of animation (as well as its extensive operations involving licensed products and the mundane administrative and support services that are part of the industrial operation), the company reinforced an idea of Disney as a sort of magical entertainment factory" (p. 319). Disney's role as a "magical entertainment factory" aims to reproduce a version of the hopes and dreams of the company's normative American audiences, invisibilizing both labor and conflict throughout the process. Even though Disney's production practices have changed drastically over the years (and will continue to do so as new technologies emerge), it still invests in showcasing mediatized production strategies. For example, three decades ago, Disney might not have promoted the cultural "research" employed in the making of its animated films. As the company incorporates more ethnically and culturally diverse representations to address changing demographics, the showcasing of these production strategies becomes more layered, and staged visibilization joins the many other strategies of self-representation so expertly and successfully deployed by Disney. Indeed, as leading practitioners of synergy, Disney has series on Disney+, such as the multi-episode *The Imagineering Story*, which detail the company's production strategies from numerous angles.

Disney's history representing Latin America and Latinxs is not unique in the context of U.S. commercial television. Historically, Disney has represented Latinidad through the use of archaic tropes like the Latin lover or the spitfire (Ramirez-Berg, 2002). During the Eisner era, Disney began to incorporate more characters of color in various roles. The company did this in productions such as *Johnny Tsunami* (1999), *The Cheetah Girls* (2003), and *Wizards of Waverly Place* (2007–2012). Although these representations provided more color for the Disney screen, Valdivia (2008a, 2010, 2011) argues that the characters either serve as bridges between the white and the Black characters, or they appear as ambiguous ethnic characters with no specific mention or link to a place of origin or culture, to allow multiple types of audiences to identify with the characters. This same type of representation still functions today in series like *Stuck in the Middle* (2016–2018) (Leon-Boys & Valdivia, 2021). Recent animated films like *Coco* (2017) and *Encanto* (2021) appear to provide a rupture in representational practices because they do not rely on ambiguity, but rather highlight the specificity of the supposed Latinidad they represent (through Mexico and Colombia), though this is Latin Americanness and not

Latinidad. This supposed specificity, however, is strongly highlighted via promoting the production of these films. For example, before the feature film *Coco*, audiences were shown a "making of *Coco*" touting all the expert knowledge brought to bear on the production of the film. As a conglomerate that strives to represent itself as ever-changing and up to date on trends and societal issues, catering to Latinxs along with visibilizing a mediatized version of this process becomes a central aspect of Disney's production efforts.

FLEXIBLE LATINIDAD VIA ELENA'S PRODUCTION

Research on Disney and Latina girls is limited, but it suggests that ambiguous or subtle Latinidad in U.S. media applies to Disney's representations of Latina girlhood. Disney's strategies for representing Latinidad often hinge on the talent it employs. For example, in live-action media, Disney often casts actors who appear ambiguously ethnic or ethnically flexible enough to play multiple nonwhite roles. This strategy allows for multiple types of audience identification (Blue, 2017; Valdivia, 2008a, 2008b, 2010, 2011, 2020), resonating with media representations of Latinidad outside of Disney as well (e.g., Báez 2018, Beltrán, 2004; Molina-Guzmán, 2010). *Elena of Avalor* appears to be a specific representation of Latinidad, and Disney finally avows one of its princesses as Latina, but this princess and her kingdom still fall within the scope of pan-Latinidad/Latin American identity and ambiguous, bridge representations of Latina girlhood, similar to Selena Gomez from *Wizards of Waverly Place* (2007–2012), Miranda from *Lizzie McGuire* (2001–2004), and Harley from *Stuck in the Middle* (2016–2018). To remain a competitive media giant, Disney implements strategies to maximize its profit by simultaneously reaching out to mass and niche markets, remaining vigilant about not alienating the normative white audiences (Valdivia, 2020). One of the most prominent components of Disney's promotion of production for *Elena of Avalor* is the fluctuation and flexible navigation between specific and ambiguous representations of Latinidad. Uniquely, here it occurs within the same narrative franchise.

Some of these ambiguating strategies consist of the flattening and dehistoricization of the locations onto which Disney casts its white gaze, a broad pattern in U.S. media texts, in older Disney films and non-Disney productions, both animated and live action. For example, *Aladdin* (1992, 2019) has been criticized for taking place in a vague location that draws from a multiplicity of far-east cultures, such as India, China, and Russia, a classic example of Orientalism. *Dora the Explorer* (2000–2014), although not a Disney production, has also been analyzed for the vagueness of its Latinidad, though it is apparently set in some tropical location in Mexico. These ambiguating strategies flatten diverse geographies and cultures to appeal to white cultural fantasies. The flexible use of locations is present in the production (and the promotion of the production) of *Elena of Avalor*, which is supposedly "inspired by Latin America." The creative team frequently uses the term "inspired by Latin America" to explain its creative process. As Valdivia (2020) notes, using "inspired by" allows Disney greater license to draw on and invent tales of origin. Disney claims that the characters and storylines are Latinx, but they are often "represented as generic Latin Americans, not only without national or regional specificity, but also with the commonality of being eternally foreign in the United States" (Valdivia, 2020, p. 84). This flexible navigation between Latin America and U.S. Latinidad consistently places Elena and Avalor on the periphery of U.S. normative culture.

Through *Elena of Avalor*, Disney claims to use a vast range of Latin American markers by drawing its inspiration for the images, storylines, and ideas from Chile, Mexico, Argentina, Bolivia, Brazil, and Peru. The creative team draws its inspiration solely from Latin America, but the company (through the promotion of the production) conflates Latin America and U.S. Latinidad quite broadly. Moreover, Elena's dress also evokes Spanish flamenco style, although Disney does not include this "inspiration" in its promotion of authenticity. Here, the company is once again creating a flexible Elena, an image that now (via the dress) also extends to Spain. Disney thus equates Spanish culture with Latin American culture and U.S. Latinidad more broadly, exploding the flexibility beyond the Americas. This strategy is not uncommon in mainstream media representations of Latinidad, but the conflation of all of these reduces various groups of people into one tight category and entirely flattens differences. In this way, at a surface level, the series and the storylines appear to specifically represent Latin America, U.S. Latinidad (the two conflated by Disney), along with Spain. Yet the stories and the series at large can appeal to anyone not familiar with the origins of the stories. For example, in season 1, episode 4, in a quest to remain young, Chancellor Esteban drinks too much water from the fountain of youth and turns into a baby. Esteban's story potentially appeals to most people because aging is a universal concept (everyone ages), regardless of whether one fears or embraces the process. The specificity of the fountain of youth, however, refers to a myth surrounding Ponce de León, the Spanish conquistador who is said to have discovered the fountain of youth in Florida. These images and storylines simultaneously draw in a Latinx audience, while remaining familiar and universal enough to the non-Latinx audiences that they do not feel alienated.

As noted in the introduction to this book, these flexible back-and-forth strategies employed by Disney make economic risk-averse sense. Drawing on Ong's (1999) "flexible citizenship" and Amaya Schaeffer's (2013) "pliable citizenship," this chapter traces how Elena's flexibility is created through the promotional materials about the production of the series, which then leads to various degrees of flexibility in the series itself, and finally find its way to the U.S. theme parks. Disney's employment of flexibility, however, is not new. Lustyik (2013), for example, outlines a similar strategy in Disney's globalization efforts surrounding the High School Musical franchise. She argues that High School Musical "conquered the world" (p. 240) from the United States to China, to Latin America, to India by creating a "flexible new model in the creation and exploitation of brands targeting young people" (p. 240). The flexibility she finds exists within Disney's customization and glocalization efforts in numerous countries. The flexibility I highlight is a bit different (especially at the production level), but it remains consistent with Disney's economic risk-averse strategies.

The kind of flexible authenticity that Disney presents through Elena is a response to globalization and rapidly changing demographics in the United States. As Banet-Weiser (2012) argues, consumers' authenticity is grounded in a desire to seek out genuine emotions and experiences that exist outside of the global marketplace. However, although Disney claims that it is authentic, Avalor is an entirely fictitious space, which means that positioning it as a real place can be a challenge. In doing so, Disney draws from a different kind of authenticity, termed by Gilmore and Pine (2007) "referential authenticity," in which an offering refers to some other context, drawing inspiration from human history and our collective memory. Disney's attempts to highlight the series' authenticity avoid any type of rationalization or critique because of the company's insistence on its "magical" production process and an inspirational approach rather than data driven research. Discourses of "magic" that claim authenticity cannot be challenged due to the aura of magic within which Disney products are encased. Claiming "inspiration" also gives the company great creative leeway. This resembles the situation where Nancy Kanter used *Sofia the First*'s fantasy element and "inspired by" Europe claims to avoid any ties to a culture, region, or group of people. While Disney engages these flexible strategies through the description of the creation and production of *Elena of Avalor*, the company further continues to reinforce the discourse of the Latina as eternal foreigner (e.g., Aparicio, 2003; Flores-González, 2017; Jimenez, 2009; Valdivia, 2010, 2020) by drawing on inspiration from Latin America rather than U.S. Latinidad. This type of flexible Latinidad allows for greater creative license to construct ambiguity and foreignness through the series and its many iterations.

"BEHIND THE SCENES" AND "THE MAKING OF . . ." CREATE A FLEXIBLE LATINIDAD

If you type "Disney's the making of . . ." in the YouTube search bar you encounter dozens upon dozens of short (and sometimes not so short) clips detailing the arduous creative practices behind the conception of numerous films, series, theme park rides, and even shops. These productions date back to the "Making of *Snow White and the Seven Dwarves* (1937)." These seemingly transparent clips or segments of Disney's creative processes have long been part of the company's promotional efforts. They are not found only on YouTube, however. Audiences can access "behind the scenes" or similar explanations of how Disney produces certain media in corporate reports, Instagram pages, press coverage, and now even in a specific section on Disney+. As part of the "Behind the Magic" section on Disney+, audiences can access a wealth of documentaries or docuseries that explore the "behind the scenes" of Disney-produced weddings, the *Star Wars* empire, theme park decoration processes for the holiday season, specific series and films, and even themed areas within the parks (*Star Wars Galaxy's Edge: Adventure Awaits*). These slick, produced, staged, edited, and performed "documentaries" must be understood as promotional material and paratexts.

Elena of Avalor's flexible Latinidad comes to the forefront in the "making of" content produced by the company. A quick Google search for "Making of *Elena of Avalor*" yields dozens of YouTube and Disney Channel clips dedicated to explaining the inspiration behind the creation of the series, the storyboarding process, and details about some episodes that celebrate "traditional" holidays. In most of these clips, there is some mention of or reference to Latinidad, Latinx culture and heritage, and Hispanic influence (with all these terms used interchangeably). For instance, on October 15, 2017, the *Elena of Avalor* Instagram page dedicated a video post to its celebration of Hispanic heritage month. The post was captioned "Celebrating #HispanicHeritageMonth with the team that creates #ElenaofAvalor! We're going behind-the-scenes to see how tradition and culture inspire the show" (Elena of Avalor, 2017). The video post on Instagram includes a voice-over that mentions: "Our show has delved into Hispanic heritage from Mexico all the way down to the South of Chile. One of the great things about this show has been the research and really taking myths from all over Central and South America and incorporating those myths, legends, and folk tales into the show. From the very first day we were thinking about, you know, how we could make this fairy tale universe feel authentic to Hispanic culture" (Elena of Avalor, 2017). The "authenticity" that this creative team claims to implement relies on a type of fantastic pan-Latinidad, where Disney flattens difference and essentializes Latinidad under the umbrella of "Hispanic culture" without claiming ties to any specific or actual Latinidad, but instead creating a flexible representation that can go back and forth between U.S. Latinidad and Latin Americanness.

Given that Disney claims an "authentic" universe, the conglomerate's selective sampling provides viewers with a world that is in many ways foreign to everyone, as few people can be familiar with cultural "myths, legends, and folk tales" from over thirty countries. In sum, as Disney hopes concerning all its products, it hopes that audiences will accept this flexible Latinidad, regardless of their ethnicity. The creators of the series seek to reach as many segments of the audiences as possible through the creation of this pseudo-authentic implausible universe, where Latinidad is flexible enough to be from every corner of Latin America, but not necessarily based in the United States. The flexibility that I analyze includes not only the character of Elena but also the series and all the paratexts associated with it. It is a flexibility that allows the narrative franchise to appeal to all audiences. In this sense, the series is much more *fantastically universal*—as in the production of a universe—than specific.

While Disney claims (in the promotion of its production) to engage in this culturally and ethnically specific storytelling process through Elena, another similar video from a year prior, *Behind the Scenes of "Elena of Avalor"* describes the animation and storyboarding process, and presents a short interview with Aimee Carrero, who voices Elena. In the video interview Aimee, an actress whose family is from the Dominican Republic, explains that she was excited to lend her voice to the animated princess "because I think the story is so universal. Even though she is so unsure of herself sometimes, there is a natural confidence to her" (*Animation Magazine*, 2016). Although the short video begins with an explanation of the cultural significance of the series, the animators (and Carrero) soon explain that this is a universal story with a classic "Disney feel" that can inspire anyone (*Animation Magazine*, 2016). As Carrero notes, this is supposed to be a universal storyline that should appeal to many demographics, although it also claims specific ties to one culture in particular (or to many Latin American cultures). As previously noted, Nancy Kanter, the former general manager of Disney Junior Worldwide, shared a similar statement before the debut of the series. She explained that the series was meant to be a "universal story with themes that authentically reflect the hopes and dreams of our diverse audience" (Llona, 2015). The flexible Latinidad showcased in these interviews, positions Elena as both culturally specific *and* universal, a twofold strategy that Disney implements to appeal to a niche market without alienating those outside the niche.

Similar "making of" clips for *Coco* (2017) engage in this flexible twofold strategy to sell the story as both culturally specific *and* universal. In the documentary *A Thousand Pictures a Day*, Lee Unkrich (a director of the film) explains that *Coco* is supposed to be "a love letter to Mexico." The documentary, like other "making of" *Coco* segments, outlines the research trips to Mexico embarked on by the directors for the laborious creation of this "authentic" film. A significant portion of this documentary, and other similar "making of" content, consists of highlighting the broader universal components of the film that could attract larger audiences. These themes include but are not limited to perseverance, family, optimism, grieving, and good triumphing over evil. Like Carrero's testament above, many of the voice actors in this film explain that the story of *Coco* is "universal" and appeals to a wide range of audiences, especially those with memories of having lost a loved one. Although they highlight how they draw on the expertise of several "culture consultants," who are not permanent Disney employees, the "making of" segments usually conclude with some mention of how the storyline is for everyone. Thus, the promotional efforts for both *Elena of Avalor* and *Coco* put forth a Latinidad that is flexible enough to be culturally specific enough as well as universal.

"ELENA OF AVALOR" INFOGRAPHIC AND MEXICO UNNAMED

Elena of Avalor is constructed as a *fantastical universalism* as she is, according to Disney, an embodiment of over thirty countries. While searching for "making of *Elena of Avalor*" videos and reports, an "*Elena of Avalor* infographic" appeared in various marketing efforts as well as in Disney corporate reports. In examining corporate reports, I kept in mind the central goal of sharing information with the company's stakeholders, for whom this infographic was produced. By studying how power relations and ownership constitute production, media scholars can better understand the impact of cultural products (Mosco, 1996). These reports function with corporate interests in mind, and I have examined how *Elena of Avalor*'s Latinidad was showcased for the shareholders before and after the series' debut.

In the "*Elena of Avalor* infographic," for example, Disney purports to represent an all-encompassing Latinidad (though there is no mention of the United States), while borrowing from Mexican culture, but not calling attention to the Mexicanidad inherent in the production of the series. The maroon infographic features nine images (each with a caption next to it) and a large image of Elena on the right side the graphic. Each one of the images is a real-life marker that inspired the series. The infographic references a variety of places that Disney claims inspired Elena's creation for the stakeholders to see. Even though it only minimally references Mexico directly, the infographic highlights "the Mesoamerican pyramids of Teotihuacan" two times and "a Mayan tribe" once (out of eight categories), along with three other direct references to Mexico.

The infographic is supposed to explain where the different elements in the series come from (i.e., which Latin American regions inspired the creative team). For instance, it includes a real image of the pyramids of Teotihuacan alongside two images from the series that were inspired by these pyramids. This is similar to some of the content in the "making of" *Coco* clips. The colorful Elena infographic highlights the flower that she wears in her hair as an "Apricot Mallow, which grows in Sonora Baja California in Northwest Mexico," while it says that Mateo's drum is inspired by a Chilean drum used by the "Machi (shaman) in Chile." Machis, however, are women healers in the Mapuche culture, and a male would not use that kind of drum. Further, the drum pictured on the infographic has small Mayan symbols, specifically originating from Mexico. The infographic then explains one of the most prominent landmarks in the series, the palace. It highlights the "use of wrought iron and tile" and links it to "Caribbean, Spanish colonial, and Mexican architecture." Overall, the visual proves quite messy (and far too flexible) in its attempts to draw on much of Latin America, and it borrows its inspiration mostly from Mexico, though it does not always fully reference Mexico. Additionally, this flexibility even reaches out to Spain.

For viewers who are not familiar with the region, the name "Teotihuacan," for example, can serve to mark the series as "authentic." This is only one of the many examples of similar references via the promotion of the series. In another instance, as Craig Gerber promoted the series, he noted on his Twitter account that the character of Orizaba, an evil fairy, "was inspired by the Aztec goddess Itzpapalotl" (Gerber, 2016). First, Orizaba is a city in Veracruz, Mexico. Second, the Aztecs existed in present-day central Mexico. Both drawing on "Teotihuacan" and the reference to "Itzpapalotl" have ties to specific Mexicanidad, but the Mexicanidad is not called out. Rather, it is constructed as *fantastical universalism* rooted in myth and mystery. Not naming Mexico directly is reminiscent of Silverman's (2002) findings from her analysis of *The Emperor's New Groove* (2000), where she notes that in its full-length animated film, Disney does its utmost to "not name the archaeological society in which its action is situated [Inca Peru], although this is readily recognizable to archaeologists" (p. 298). Sixteen years later, Disney continues to employ similar pre-Columbian tactics in *Elena of Avalor*. This Disney series, and the promotion of its creation, strives for a flexible type of authenticity, not directly associated with any one nation, though very clearly drawing most of its inspiration from Mexico. For those of us familiar with Mexican landmarks, we know that Teotihuacan is in Mexico and that the Aztecs inhabited what is now Central Mexico, but this may not be obvious to all the people viewing the infographic produced by Disney and disseminated to its shareholders or to all those reading Gerber's tweet. It is also possible that this is not obvious to those viewing the television series.

As Disney showcases its inspirations for the series' creation, it mentions names, locations, and regions that reinforce the claims to authenticity and specificity, albeit this authenticity is more specific to Mexico than any other Spanish-speaking location. In fact, in an interview with Ritsuko Notani, the character designer for the series, audiences learn that one of the main inspirations for the look of the series was "the Mexico pavilion at EPCOT. . . . The pavilion mixes Mesoamerican, Mayan, Aztec areas, and then you come out to this village, and there's a volcano and these Mayan things" (*Exclusive: Inside the Magic of Elena of Avalor*, 2016). In this way, Disney creates a flexible Latinidad where the referent is not always accurately situated or foregrounded (this falls in line with the hybrid flexibility I will outline in chapter 3). For example, Disney incorporates locations and names that are often inaccurate (the Chilean Machi drum), and are difficult for non-Spanish speakers to pronounce (Teotihuacan and Itzpapalotl). This is consistent with Valdivia's (2020) argument that language plays an important role in the creation of mediated authenticity, even if the language and the references may prove to be inaccurate. Further, as previously noted, Disney prominently employs pre-Columbian representations (*The Emperor's New Groove*, *Elena of Avalor*, *Coco*, and *Encanto*) when attempting to showcase Latinxs and Latin American people. In doing so, the company appears to draw on tropes of the past in Mexico and other parts of Latin America. *Coco*'s director, Lee Unkrich, for example, noted in a tweet that the film takes place in 2017 (Unkrich, 2017), though Pixar notes that it is marketed as a contemporary story with vast ties to the past (Pixar, n.d.). Elena operates in a similar way. The series heavily draws on pre-Columbian elements to create a story with myths and mysteries that situate it in a context far from modern-day experiences (i.e., Gerber's tweet about Orizaba).

As outlined above in Carrero's soundbite and the *Coco* documentary, Disney fluctuates between highlighting the specific and ambiguous elements of its Latinx/ Latin American animated productions. The company's attempts to maintain ambiguity call upon "universal" storylines that will appeal to as many groups of people as possible. After all, Disney is known for its discourses of magic and universality (Wasko, 2017, 2020), so it would make sense for it to include these elements in its representations of racial and ethnic specificity at large. Aimee Carrero's short sound bite in the YouTube clip mentioned above highlights how some of Disney's greatest ambassadors when it comes to promoting the specific, ambiguous, and flexible Elena are the actors and their talent, as they contribute to the promotion of the series on both fronts (the promotion of the racial specificity and the ambiguity/universality), particularly in their social media pages.

Latinx Actor Labor

Aimee Carrero is not the only actress to promote *Elena of Avalor*, its specific ties to Latinidad, and its appeal to universal audiences. Although it is sometimes difficult to tell whether Disney requires its talent to engage in this type of labor or not, Disney's Latinx talent engages in a specific kind of labor that is not often as visible when it comes to non-Latinx series or films. Their labor extends to promote *Elena of Avalor* and its significance for Latinx people.

Following Johnson's (2017) call to expand production studies to encompass different elements, or nodes, in the process, I heed his request "to consider the productivity of fan and amateur hobbyist cultures, to be sure, but also the everyday participation with which we use—and contribute to—Facebook and other media interfaces" (p. 152). I extend his call by including the role of actors performing as fans, a role seldom interrogated in production studies or media studies at large. I argue that actors who perform both talent and fan labor engage in what I call *managed prosumerism*. Via this managed prosumerism they enact both mediated celebrity and fandom, thereby expanding their labor capacity. Often, fandom is produced for actors as part of their public persona, and thus they accomplish a threefold goal by promoting the series for their own personal interests (ratings), for the promotion of Latinidad, and for the promotion of a specific Disney Latinidad. The labor of the Latinx actors (their managed prosumerism), in the following examples, expands to perform a type of cultural ambassador labor on behalf of the Disney corporation, a type of labor in which non-Latinx Disney actors do not engage, at least not for the purposes of promoting *Elena of Avalor*.

Actor Labor as Managed Prosumerism

Before *Elena of Avalor*'s debut, the series was promoted via numerous outlets. Not only was the future princess referenced in commercials and interstitials, but the series was also hailed on various Instagram platforms, most notably the Instagram pages of Latinx celebrities. Before the summer of 2016, a significant number of Instagram posts about *Elena of Avalor* came from the cast of *Jane the Virgin*, a CW original series featuring an almost all Latinx cast. At a glance, it appears that a Disney series is being promoted from outside of the Disney universe (as CW is not currently owned by Disney). Soon enough, however, it becomes clear that most of the *Jane the Virgin* cast members also voice characters on *Elena of Avalor* (although not all of these are recurring characters). Even Gina Rodriguez, whom many fans initially thought was the voice of Elena, joined the cast in the made-for-television Disney channel movie, *Song of the Sirenas*, which debuted in September 2018 as part of the second season of the series.

An examination of a few of the Instagram posts generated by *Jane the Virgin* cast members reveals that the Latinx talent engages in this managed prosumerism and promotes their work (for those who voice characters on *Elena*). Simultaneously, they also claim to be invested for the sake of diversifying Latinx representation, particularly in Disney animation. However, none of the non-Latinx *Jane the Virgin* cast members promoted the *Elena of Avalor* series on their personal Instagram pages. This speaks to broad patterns of unequal distribution of labor, in which those from other racial and ethnic backgrounds are expected to individually shoulder the work of advancing their ethnic group interests. It is telling that the only actors posting about *Elena*'s Latinidad are the Latinx actors.

Gina Rodriguez, who plays the lead character in *Jane the Virgin*, began advertising and praising *Elena of Avalor* well before its debut. Her initial Instagram post contained a picture of the *Elena of Avalor* poster and featured the following statement: "Very excited for this project! And feeling really blessed the Latino community has a princess for our little ladies all over the globe (A fierce, strong and intelligent princess)" (G. Rodriguez, 2016). Her post concludes with an explanation that she is *not* the voice of Elena, although some fans had speculated that she was. This speculation is not surprising given that it is common to cast the same handful of Latinx actors across series featuring Latinx characters or storylines.

Following in Rodriguez's footsteps, Jenna Ortega posted about *Elena of Avalor* the following day on her personal Instagram page. Ortega is a teenage celebrity (then tween), who starred in Disney Channel's *Stuck in the Middle*, a live-action series about a large (ethnically ambiguous) Latinx family. She is also the voice of Isabel (Elena's younger sister) in *Elena of Avalor* and plays young Jane on *Jane the Virgin*. Ortega is quite outspoken about her Puerto Rican/Mexican heritage via her social network pages. Ortega's post concluded with the following remark: "This is such huge news for all the little Princesas out there" (Ortega, 2016). Both actresses engaged in managed prosumerism as they posted about the potential and significance of the series, even before its debut. Moreover, they stress the importance of this animated princess for Latina girls/princesas.

It is not only U.S. Latinas, however, who praise and advertise *Elena of Avalor* via their social media platforms. Jaime Camil, a famous telenovela actor in Mexico who has achieved crossover success in the United States, also partakes in this managed prosumerism as he speaks about the animated series and its impact (mostly via his social media platforms). Camil previously played the lead character Rogelio de la Vega in *Jane the Virgin* and starred in *Chicago* on Broadway as Billy Fynn. He also voiced characters in both *Elena of Avalor* and *Coco*, so his ties to Disney are extensive. Additionally, on his personal Instagram page, Camil often promotes Disney products and experiences, such as the film *Bambi*, and his many Disney theme park visits, particularly by using images of his two children engaging with Disney films, series, and events. As with the other celebrities, it is safe to assume that these posts are produced, and perhaps sometimes even managed. In the 2019 annual report, for instance, the leadership team explains that the Walt Disney Company connects with millions of people around the world through their social media platforms. They further note that "a variety of TV personalities and talent at Disney, ABC, ESPN, and Marvel engage with fans through social media" (Wasko, 2020, p. 65). Disney flaunts these connections, advertising them to its shareholders. Additionally, as with most aspects of the company, they more than likely exert some amount of control over these promotional posts.

For example, as a way to promote the "A Day to Remember" Día de los Muertos–themed episode of *Elena of Avalor*, Camil took to Instagram on October 13, 2016, publishing the following text under a picture from the episode: "Don't miss a very special episode of #ElenaofAvalor THIS SUNDAY night on @DisneyJunior AND @Disneychannel simultaneously. #DiaDeLosMuertos feat; the cast of #Janethe Virgin http://www.ew.com/article/2016/10/12/elena-avalor-jane-virgin-episode" (Camil, 2016). Camil's Instagram post included the entire link to an article titled "Elena of Avalor Jane the Virgin Episode," where the first line of the piece states, "Just call her Jane of Avalor." The opening line of the article points to a larger theme previously referenced: the reusing, overusing, and recycling of the same pool of Latinx talent for the purposes of representing mainstream Latinidad. This sometimes happens within media conglomerates and often throughout the media as a whole. This labor is also often utilized to promote Latinidad across company lines. In this way, media rely on actors who are already well-known for their Latinidad and thus continue to enact risk-averse strategies. Here we see an overlap between *Jane the Virgin* and *Elena of Avalor*. Below I will extend this example to include a similar example with the cast of *Stuck in the Middle* and Disney's Hispanic Heritage month commercials and interstitials.

Although it is not uncommon for actors to promote their different projects through their social media pages, Camil's Instagram example (along with others like Gina Rodriguez's) exemplifies a type of cross-promotion synergy based on shared ethnicity rather than supporting a single media conglomerate. By using hashtags, Camil draws on #DiaDeLosMuertos and connects this episode, along with the series, to a specific Latinx holiday, notably a Mexican holiday. He also connects *Jane the Virgin* to *Elena of Avalor* (elena-of-avalor-jane-virgin-episode), and thus reinforces the finding that Latinx talent is often recycled in the media and used to represent and promote Latinidad at large. This recycling is a clear example of how Disney and media in general continue to propagate inequalities and limit access to only a handful of Latinx actors. With all the barriers already in place, recycling and reusing these actors makes it challenging for other Latinxs folks to obtain a seat at the table.

LABOR OF REPROMOTION

Disney excels in synergistic production strategies. Like many other mainstream media companies, Disney employs Latinx talent, who have already made a name for themselves in other series, within and outside of Disney. Disney often nurtures talent to recycle in its own properties, one of its many synergistic strategies, providing the conglomerate with the economic risk-aversion tools necessary to remain successful. Disney engages in these strategies on different levels, often within the Disney universe via distinct platforms. Take, for instance, the previously mentioned example of *Stuck in the Middle* and Hispanic Heritage Month. In 2017, Disney released commercials and interstitials focusing on Hispanic Heritage Month. Every one of the promotions that aired during the month of September 2017 featured a cast member from *Stuck in the Middle*. *Stuck in the Middle* (2016–2018) is a Disney Channel series that focused on the chaotic life of an ethnically ambiguous family of nine. The series is supposed to be about a Latinx family, but the Latinidad is almost imperceptible throughout all three seasons (Leon-Boys & Valdivia, 2021). In this way, Disney very strategically uses its own Latinx labor and talent to perform not only multiple Latinx roles on series and films but also roles as promoters and ambassadors for Disney's Latinidad.

Disney's engagement with Latinx labor exploits multiple opportunities for synergy. Meehan (2005) outlines five synergy behaviors: recirculation, repackaging, reversioning, recycling, and redeployment. I extend Meehan's work by proposing a sixth behavior under the Disney synergy universe: *repromotion*, the inclusion of Latinx actors' labor performances via their social media platforms. This sixth behavior is specific to the promotion of an artifact and is distinct from the others because it does not solely involve the movement of a product to another outlet. Additionally, the behavior outlines how the conglomerate exploits the ethnic actors' labor within ethnic content synergy. Different from Meehan's "recycling," repromotion does not include high costs, even if the actors are being paid by Disney to generate these posts (which we cannot be certain of). Latinx actors engage in a unique type of labor in the production and promotion of *Elena of Avalor*, and this labor is most often found on their "personal" social media pages. If we look at the example of Gina Rodriguez, who was posting about the significance of the series two years prior to becoming part of the *Elena of Avalor* cast, one can argue that this was part of Disney's long-term strategy, a strategy that the conglomerate continues to work on as it attempts to find new ways to reach its Latinx audiences. An extension of this strategy is the articulation of Elena as part of the company's corporate social responsibility. In the following section, I outline the third salient theme in my analysis of the production of *Elena of Avalor*: Disney's efforts to tie this series to corporate social responsibility.

DISNEY'S CORPORATE SOCIAL RESPONSIBILITY THROUGH *ELENA OF AVALOR*: "DO GOOD" DISNEY

Corporate social responsibility (CSR) strategies not only form a core component of neoliberal discourse at large, but they have played a central role in maintaining the Walt Disney Company's public reputation for at least the past decade. Although it does not fully address the cultural elements inherent in these strategies, CSR literature exists mostly as popular business press literature. Critical media scholars must engage with CSR components to highlight the key influences shaping cultural content and institutional practices. Philanthropy forms a central component of CSR reports, and as Valdivia (2018) notes, "Girls figure prominently as a symbol in global discourses of philanthropy" (p. 84). In this section, I outline Disney's CSR efforts in general and in relation to *Elena of Avalor* and Latinidad in particular.

Here, I round out how the company produces and promotes the production of its new girl version of an animated and flexible Latinidad.

Disney's promotional work upholds the image and name of the company around the world. Critics point out that the Disney Company's interest in making profit far exceeds its interest in philanthropy. The corporation's ultimate concern is not about cultural or civic responsibility, its first responsibility is to its shareholders (Wasko, 2017). This is hardly surprising given that Disney is a capitalist enterprise. However, within the past two decades Disney, like many other corporations, has increasingly articulated its image and brand to CSR in an attempt to align with seemingly more responsible practices. This alignment is part of a neoliberal shift, and its intent is to yield greater long-term profit by contributing to the common good through "private voluntary solutions to public problems, thus managing social risks to brands and forestalling governmental regulation" (Ciafone, 2019, p. 16). Through an exploration of "citizenship," Ouellette (2017) traces "the surge of media devoted to transforming individuals into more enterprising, responsible, self-reliant, and marketable versions of themselves" (p. 38). As many corporations pursue "good citizenship," Ouellette (2017) notes that this "does not contradict the aims of the consumer economy but is folded into them" (p. 38). As the practice of citizenship becomes more consumer oriented, we must examine how Disney narrates its citizenship efforts and aligns these with recent attempts at representing diversity. In her chapter on Disney TV and girls' citizenship, Blue (2018) contends that "international media companies, charitable organizations, and advocacy groups increasingly use images of girls as cultural and political symbols. . . . The Walt Disney Company requires a certain level of civic engagement of its talent" (p. 139). By focusing on Disney's CSR in relation to the animated representation of *Elena of Avalor*, I extend what Chávez and Kiley (2016) and Blue (2017, 2018) have identified as Disney's efforts to strengthen its CSR. I do this by bringing animated culture and the production and promotion of Latinx representations to the Disney CSR equation.

In the case of Disney's "Lead Like Elena" YouTube video, discussed below, producers expect consumers to be inspired by young girls' leadership skills and to implement these tactics in their everyday lives. Moreover, through a partnership with Girl Scouts USA, Disney is making it easy for its audiences to "support causes," in line with what Ouellette (2012) calls the "do good" turn. The "cause" here is Girl Scouts USA. Drawing on Ouellette's work, Blue (2017) argues that "Disney Channel and its affiliated websites and partner organizations thus employ images of girls and discourses of girlhood in pursuit of a 'do-good' reputation" (p. 116), which is exactly what is occurring through Disney's partnership with Girls Scouts and its use of Elena as a marker for this partnership. Drawing on both Blue and Ouellette, I argue that Disney also includes animated representations within its CSR to further drive its "do-good" reputation to increase profit and revenues, while simultaneously reaching out to viewers of color, particularly Latinxs.

The motives and driving forces behind corporations' CSR engagements are, first and foremost, financial and profit driven. Blue (2017) summarizes this notion, specifically when it comes to Disney: "Evading critical awareness and political action that might otherwise contradict the capitalist motives of the conglomerate has become the norm within the context of neoliberalism" (p. 122). Blue adds that Disney's CSR efforts "draw attention away from the environmental damage and depletion of resources endemic to material production by such global conglomerates. They also ignore the possible consequences of perpetuating inhumane, normative, hegemonic, institutionalized ideologies, discourses, and inequalities in the pursuit of capital" (p. 118). To this last statement I would add that Disney's CSR illusion of progressive ideologies as part of its reports, exemplified in its multicultural animated characters, attempts to contradict the "possible consequences" posed by its practices.

While Disney's many CSR efforts have tangible social and philanthropic effects, they certainly also help bolster the promotion of Disney's image as a wholesome, family-oriented, benevolent media giant. This public relations outcome redounds positively to the company, which implicitly, although difficult to document, leads to increases in the company's revenues. Not only do the CSR efforts help Disney continue to sell its products; they sell the ideology that society's problems can be solved through the market, that there are no solutions without capitalism. In 2012, for example, Disney took the first steps toward its CSR project to prevent childhood obesity by removing "unhealthy" commercials from its television advertising. In response to the question of whether the company would initially lose a significant amount of revenue by letting go of advertisers like Capri Sun and Kraft Lunchables, Robert Iger, then Disney CEO, admitted that "this is not altruistic. This is about smart business" (Coscarelli, 2012). Again, this is not surprising given that Disney is a capitalist enterprise. What is unusual is the naked admission that CSRs are about increasing the profit line (perhaps this was a line directed toward shareholders). Indeed, Iger followed the statement with an explanation that the initial revenue loss would turn into much more profit for Disney in the long run and healthier outcomes for children overall, a neoliberal win-win.

Iger's explanation solidifies the fact that beyond Disney's goodwill practices of corporate social responsibility lie profit-based motives. As Micheletti and Stolle (2012) explain, the term "citizenship is expanded beyond obeying laws, serving one's country, voting in elections, and keeping an eye on government" (p. 91). The authors contend that corporations have taken on new understandings of "citizenship" and incorporated them into their daily practices, often as a means of cultivating a revenue-generating image. In 2011, the Walt Disney Company explained that its success hinged upon an embedded citizenship "in our everyday actions and decisions. It's good for our planet and our people, and it makes sound business sense" (Walt Disney Company, 2011). In other words, Disney's CSR strategies are a win-win for the company. Media giants like Disney own a wealth of research about audience behavior, most of which they are not eager to make public. This research allows the company to roll out CSR efforts that serve as branding messages that appeal to children and parents alike.

In Disney's 2017 *Corporate Social Responsibility Update*, for example, there is a section titled "Inspiring Futures." This section contains an image of ten girls covered in mud, wearing Disney princess dresses. The section details how Disney inspires kids around the world to create better futures for themselves. The first example highlighted is the "Dream Big, Princess" campaign, which Disney claims encourages "kids everywhere to dream big by highlighting inspiring moments from Disney princess stories" (Walt Disney Company, 2018). The #DreamBigPrincess photography contest, for example, urged girls to share photos of themselves engaging in empowering moments, and most of the examples that Disney showcased are photos of girls dressed as Disney princesses, thus allowing Disney to recirculate its stories and brands.

Since 2008, Disney has published yearly corporate social responsibility updates, sometimes titled "Citizenship Report," "Citizenship Performance Summary," "Corporate Citizenship Report," or "Corporate Social Responsibility Update." As Blue (2018) notes, the conglomerate uses "corporate responsibility" and "corporate citizenship" interchangeably even though these concepts are not interchangeable. Therefore, analyzing the role of *Elena* within these reports as a type of cultural responsibility creates yet another layer in this somewhat messy relationship between responsibility and citizenship. The yearly reports aim to provide information for stakeholders, customers, or anyone interested in Disney's "citizenship" and "responsibility" efforts. Primarily, the reports inform the stakeholders and board of directors. In 2018, more than half of the Walt Disney Company's board of directors were linked to companies that could influence Disney's business models, thus showcasing a perfect example of interlocking directorates (Dreier, 1982). These companies include but are not limited to: Twitter, McDonald's, Facebook, Starbucks, and Apple (Wasko, 2017).

The CSR documents range from ten to one hundred pages in length, feature vibrant colors, beautiful graphics, and the newest Disney animated characters, and they always commence with a message from a Disney executive. In the 2017 Disney CSR report, Christine M. McCarthy, the senior executive vice president and chief financial officer, begins her message by recalling the Walt Disney legacy and the company's commitment to being an ethical corporation. A few lines later she notes that "consumers look at several other factors when making purchasing decisions, including things like how companies treat their employees, what efforts they make to conserve energy and water and reduce waste, and their commitment to continued improvement when it comes to good corporate citizenship and effective social responsibility" (Walt Disney Company, 2018, p. 2). Throughout the thirteen Disney CSR reports currently available online, the company is not shy in acknowledging that the reports help generate revenue and, as McCarthy puts it, "consumers look at several factors when making purchasing decisions." Profit is always at the forefront of Disney initiatives. In their piece on Disney, Latino children, and television labor, Chávez and Kiley (2016) remind readers that we must consider "CSR efforts first and foremost as rhetorical tools that are designed to advance the goals of the corporation. CSR portfolios are based on the premise that shareholders benefit and bottom-line incentives grow when corporations engage in prosocial efforts" (p. 2624). An overwhelming majority of the reports before 2016 even start with the line, "Dear Stakeholders," though the 2017–2020 reports do not address anyone in particular.

Disney and Diversity

The *2017 Corporate Social Responsibility Update* is twenty-four pages in length, and includes Disney's performance targets (environment, volunteer, and healthy living), international labor standards practices, workplace practices, philanthropy projects, and a very small portion on "engaging our talent" to bolster diversity. Traditionally, citizenship and corporate social responsibility reports highlight environmental concerns, ethical consumption practices, and volunteer hours. It is not uncommon to see pictures of executives or volunteers building wells in countries other than the United States or reading to someone who is implicitly a young cancer patient.

Disney, however, recently started incorporating a small portion describing its commitment to "diversity." This usually consists of the "diversity" heading, and a paragraph or two detailing some of the most recent forays in making the Disney universe a more diverse place, both on- and off screen. The 2008 report, for example, examines how the company uses "diversity" in its programming to "reflect the world in which today's children are growing up" (The Walt Disney Company, 2009, p. 18). The report highlights the series and movies that feature "diverse" characters, and concludes by providing links to access additional Disney diversity reports, but these links are now defunct. It is difficult to tell, however, whether this "diversity" section will become a permanent addition. The section was not included in the 2018 report (and a few others before 2015), and in the 2019 report consisted of five paragraphs solely focused on media content (most of which was released before 2016). However, the *2020 Corporate Social Responsibility Report* highlights diversity more than any other document of its kind before. In fact, the word "diversity" appears over fifty times in the seventy-nine-page document and Robert Chapek even brings up diversity in the "letter from our Chief Executive Officer," which opens the document. As previously noted, Chapek is making bold moves in the diversity sector, but this has to be put in the context of his aggressive attention to demographics and audience shifts.

In its *2017 Corporate Social Responsibility Update*, however, diversity figured less prominently. In this report, Disney devotes one-third of a page (out of a twenty-four-page document) to outline its (then) current engagements with diversity. The diversity efforts outlined consisted of engaging "diverse communities" and "diverse talent." Additionally, the "diversity" section contains a small part where Elena serves as a visual for the diversity efforts. The visual showcases Elena dancing flamenco in her traditional red dress. Her arms are shown in a customary flamenco pose as she appears to be turning while on tiptoe, lightly holding up her dress. The Elena graphic in this report contains a small blurb, stressing that Disney's diversity exists in front of and behind the camera. Further, the graphic highlights the role of Silvia Olivas as "Head Writer and Co-Executive Producer," whom audiences are supposed to understand is a nonwhite person by merely reading her name. Silvia Olivas is typically highlighted during the "making of" videos where they highlight the series' authenticity. The "diversity" section concludes by briefly highlighting the "authentic" storylines in *Moana* and *Coco*. This page in the report may appear to be short in length, but previous reports include smaller "diversity" summaries or none at all (the 2018 report, for example, does not include this section).

In 2017, Disney expanded what has traditionally been understood as corporate social responsibility or corporate citizenship by including elements that focus on ethnic and cultural acknowledgment and inclusion, though the conglomerate strategically includes these efforts very lightly, commodifying a slight engagement with diversity as do corporations when reporting to the public on how they are contributing as responsible global citizens. In 2017, for example, Disney relied on animated productions like *Coco* and *Elena of Avalor* (during the height of their popularity) to illustrate its engagement with mindful citizenship through a type of cultural responsibility. Before the 2020 report, however, at no point did the company include live-action characters, the actors who play them, or even actors who voice the animated characters to outline its citizenship efforts.

#LeadLikeElena

Disney uses *Elena of Avalor* in a variety of ways for its CSR efforts. Not only does the conglomerate use the series and the image of a dancing Elena (dancing flamenco, no less) in its yearly citizenship and corporate social responsibility reports, but it also uses her as a role model through its partnership with Girl Scouts USA, a way for it to position Elena not only as a symbol of Latinidad but also as a symbol of girl power and responsible girlhood. Disney rolled out #LeadLikeElena in 2016 as part of its partnership with Girl Scouts USA. Disney is known for forging connections with organizations and companies, but it is always careful about what these connections symbolize. I consider the Girl Scouts USA partnership broadly within Disney's corporate social responsibility efforts, particularly the new branch that focuses on gender, cultural, and ethnic diversity. Through this partnership, Disney is fulfilling its commitment to increase diversity, while showcasing its ties to an organization that is highly infused with philanthropy, altruism, and liberal gender practices. It is no coincidence that Disney uses its first and only Latina princess to serve as the image bridging the corporation with Girl Scouts USA. Elena is advertised as a fearless leader, an example of a model neoliberal citizen, and thus the branding of Elena fits perfectly with contemporary can-do discourses of Girl Scouts USA.

The collaboration with Girl Scouts has provided mutually beneficial opportunities for profit and increased audience for Disney and membership for Girls Scouts. For example, in October 2016, Disney introduced the #LeadLikeElena contest urging viewers to upload a photo of themselves, showcasing how they "lead like Elena," to Twitter, Instagram, or Facebook for a chance to be featured "on-air" (Walt Disney Company, 2017). Disney created this hashtag and the contest in

Figure 2. Girl Scouts Alexa and Maria in Disney Junior's "Lead Like Elena: Girl Scouts Maria & Alexa—Be Inspired," commercial (Disney Junior YouTube).

partnership with Girl Scouts USA to provide a space for young girls to associate themselves with Elena's leadership, and therefore align themselves with the television program and character, by tagging moments in which they were fearless leaders, thus connecting to other girls through moments of bravery and girl power. However, most of the contest rules are vague and the winners are not easy to find online. The contest rules explain that an "entry should show how the child is a leader like Elena" and one of the criteria used for judging is "personality," though this category is not defined. Moreover, most current attempts to find contest details have yielded explanations that "this contest has ended" and they provide no further information detailing who the winners were, what their airtime entailed, or what their photographs showcased. Disney does, however, readily provide a ten-page document with the contest rules, titled "#LeadLikeElena Contest: Official Rules." This lack of contest clarity is indicative of how this narrative franchise proves to be a testing ground for Disney as it continues trying to figure out how to cater to Latinxs and nonwhite audiences at large. The rules were vague and perhaps there were no winners in the end. This information highlights the behind-the-scenes messiness in creating this fantastical land of flexible Latinidad.

The #LeadLikeElena movement was also advertised through Disney/Girl Scouts USA commercials and interstitials, in which girl scouts engaged in activities that they claimed were inspired by Elena. One of the videos, "Lead Like Elena: Girl Scouts Maria and Alexa—Be Inspired | Disney Junior" features two young girls who are cousins. These two girls explain how they lead like Elena by "inspiring other girls" and putting their ideas into action by connecting with other young children. Alexa notes, "We were inspired by Elena a lot because she helps her town kind of like us, just like leading other people to do something that they have never done to make the world a better place" (DisneyJunior, 2017).

Through these commercials, interstitials, advertisements, and the #LeadLikeElena movement, Disney incorporates Elena and young girls of color to promote how they are making "the world a better place." The girls embody Harris's (2004) conceptualization of the "can-do" girl who relies on her skills to create a better world. Although Girl Scouts is a collective, these actions are primarily individualized in that Disney singles out either individual action or actions carried out by two or three girls. Disney's partnership with Girl Scouts thus promotes a neoliberal, individualist ideology suggesting that systemic issues can be altered through single actions, like planting a tree or having a bake sale (both examples used by Maria and Alexa). Disney's "can-do" Latina authenticity is achieved (mostly) through individualism and individual acts.

As part of its ongoing effort to continue expanding as a global enterprise, the Walt Disney Company must create content that accommodates pressing commercial ideologies. Increasing profit and expanding globally means reaching out to previously ignored audience segments, acknowledging previously ignored demographic trends. Disney therefore continues to aggressively seek out the Latinx market, as this population continues to boom. The company does this by including Latinidad in its production and promotion practices as well as in its fictional representations. Since the spring of 2016, the Disney team has been working hard to make sure there is no question about the fact that Elena, Avalor, and everything else within the narrative franchise is Latinx. Explaining that this was a moment for which many Latinxs had long hoped, press releases, Disney websites, and Latinx actors vigorously promoted the animated television series as the first to showcase animated Latinx royalty.

Along with the managed prosumerism coming from the Latinx actors and the company's attempts to tie its CSR to Latinidad, is the visibilization of labor and production in promotional content, which lends an aura of authenticity to totally produced and managed material. The Disney citizenship and CSR reports are created with consumers and shareholders in mind. The social media posts are as well. Although production is often thought of as taking place in studios separate from consumers and audiences, the many processes occurring under the name of production cannot function without awareness or understanding of audiences and their consumption practices. As the examples in this chapter have demonstrated, production and consumption are anything *but* isolated. Chapter 3 addresses a middle ground within production and consumption—the actual components of the television series, where Elena's flexible Latinidad comes to life on the small screen. Guided by the previously outlined concepts of Disney's flexible Latinidad, managed prosumerism, and repromotion, an analysis of *Elena of Avalor*'s three-season run provides another layer from which to understand Disney's mediated Latina girlhood.

CHAPTER 3

Animated Latina Girlhood and the Continuum of Flexibility

We created the character of Elena with the hope that she would be a role model, not just for young Latina girls watching, but for all children to be able to see what a true leader looks like. From the beginning, Elena's story arc has been that she would one day become queen. With the series finale, the creative team has been able to bring Elena's story to the thrilling conclusion that we always envisioned.
—*Craig Gerber, creator and executive producer,* Elena of Avalor, *July 2020*

After exploring the layers composing the production of *Elena of Avalor*, we move to a textual analysis of the television series. Craig Gerber reiterates two significant points in the above quote. First, to attract *all* children, the three seasons of *Elena of Avalor* make claims to universality. To attract Latinx children the specificity gets messy. This chapter analyzes the built-in tensions in the series, which strives for both universality and specific Latinidad. Second, the finite story arc was predetermined to span three seasons. This classic Disney television strategy is continuous with many three- to four-year narrative arcs. Elena, albeit Latina, functioned within traditional Disney models of animated television content. Gerber's comment informs my understanding of the strategies behind the decisions involved in creating and deploying this animated series, and it also guides many of the questions pursued in this chapter, where I provide the second layer to my circuit of culture approach. In what follows, I investigate the discursive construction of *Elena of Avalor*, through an analysis of ten purposefully selected episodes from the series' three-season run (2016–2020). I develop a continuum of flexibility, where flexibility is categorized according to narrative and contextual weight. Additionally, combining contemporary discourses of Latinidad and postfeminism in mainstream U.S. popular culture helps in understanding the complex approach Disney employs in the construction of flexible Latinidad within the series.

Elena of Avalor was a successful children's television show, with impressive ratings until the end (B. Cantor, 2016a; S. Fox, 2019; TV News Desk, 2016). Not only were the ratings remarkable, but the series secured a handful of awards at various awards ceremonies (e.g., Coffey, 2020; Common Sense Media, 2016). While the success of the series is not the focus of this chapter, I mention the extensive viewership again because it contributes to audiences' cultural universes and to young girls' understandings of Latinidad. *Elena's* animated Latinidad continues to be available through television and is also transmediated via multiple Disney platforms. In a television series, viewership is spread out over time, which is important for understanding the series' significance during the course of four years and three seasons. From an industry standpoint, ratings and awards indicate positive reception for Disney's fantastical Latinidad. Elena, an animated character, represented Latina girlhood for the years of the series. These facts make up the backdrop for understanding the role that *Elena of Avalor* played within the world of Disney, animation, U.S. girlhood, and Latinidad during the time when the series was alive and airing new content via multiple platforms.

This chapter draws on cultural studies and feminist intersectional analysis to interpret how race, ethnicity, nation, age, and gender shape the representations in *Elena of Avalor*. I explore the series in general and ten episodes in particular to identify markers of Latinidad and girlhood. Having viewed the entire series multiple times, and being fully acquainted with all of Elena's iterations, I selected specific episodes based on the following criteria: (1) the episodes focused on frequently used themes (and celebrations) in mainstream media portrayals of Latinxs, (2) the episodes exemplified the type of girlhood that Elena displays throughout the series, and (3) the episodes showcased alternative constructions of Latinidad and girlhood, providing a rupture from previously existing images and representations. Some episodes fulfilled more than one of the criteria required for selection.

To provide an in-depth analysis of the episodes, I develop a continuum to account for the various weights and types of flexibilities of visibilized Latinidad deployed throughout the series. Whereas some episodes rely on highly templated (and already established) tropes, others showcase more unique and refreshing versions of Latina girlhood. After establishing the continuum and the different categories of flexibility within it, I trace the narrative arc of the series and outline character types and tropes. I then analyze four celebrations in *Elena of Avalor* (a total of nine episodes): Día de los Muertos (all four Day of the Dead episodes), the two Navidad (Christmas) episodes, the *quinceañera* and coronation episodes, and the Hanukkah episode, where Disney debuted its first Jewish Latina princess. After the analysis of the celebrations, I highlight negotiations and continuums, followed by the continuities and ruptures, where I include an analysis of the final episode.

A Continuum of Flexibility

I analyze *Elena of Avalor* against the backdrop of contemporary postfeminism, in conjunction with postfeminist sensibilities outlined in the book's introduction. In particular, I heed Gill's call to use the sensibilities as a guide to empirically analyze popular culture (Banet-Weiser et al., 2019). Like Gill (2016), I find in *Elena of Avalor* signifiers of the visibility yet weightlessness of feminism in contemporary U.S. popular culture, which also applies to signifiers of Latinidad. Whereas Gill offers sensibilities, I offer flexibilities. Postfeminism is primarily analyzed and fore-grounded through the lens of whiteness; I expand postfeminist scholarship to investigate whether and how the flexibility of the animated Latina girl expands her visibilization. I achieve this by creating different categories for flexibility, a con-tinuum of flexibility.

Tropes refer to overused themes or representations. They serve to illustrate dis-cursive constructions across gender and ethnicity. Just as there are tropes in U.S. culture that symbolize a visible yet weightless feminism, such as the "you go girl" feminist representation (Gill, 2016) where feminism is used as a "cheer word," but remains devoid of substance, there are also tropes used similarly to represent Lati-nidad. For example, Disney's programming foregrounds celebrations when rep-resenting Latinidad: the most frequently used ones being Día de los Muertos (Day of the Dead) and *quinceañeras* (celebration of a girl's fifteenth birthday), with Christmas appearing often as well (Leon-Boys, 2021a). As explored in chapter 2, the repeated representation of these celebrations in U.S. media flattens differences between Latinxs and Latin Americans, usually conflating the two. This flattening of difference contributes to a hollow and flexible representation of Latinidad that resembles Warner's (2017) theory of "plastic representation," which highlights the issues at stake by relying on quantity of representation over dimensionality. War-ner examines practices common when swapping out racial groups in television remakes without much (or any) adjustment to the narrative. She argues that this creates a superficial change where the performances by nonwhite actors end up coming across as "hollow experiments produced in a laboratory; they feel plastic" (2017). This comparison to plastic experiments is similar to Brüning's (2018) rhe-torical analysis of *Scandal* episodes, where she finds that the lead character, Olivia Pope, serves the interests of white femininity, rendering Black women's experiences invisible. What Gill conceptualizes as weight, Warner theorizes spatially (hollow-ness). I extend their work by bringing Latinidad and postfeminism together in the-orizing representation according to different levels of flexibility.

The flexibility of (and within) the production of *Elena of Avalor* was previously explored in relation to managed prosumerism, the labor of repromotion, and cor-porate social responsibility. In this chapter, I further expand the definition of flex-ibility in terms of representation. I propose a four-part flexibility, in which each layer presents different levels of engagement with actual cultural myths, stories, locations, symbols, cuisines, and narratives. The four layers of the continuum are: weightless flexibility, ambiguous flexibility, hybrid flexibility, and transformational flexibility. Weightless flexibility refers to representations deployed in accordance with what the content creators anticipate their viewers will be familiar with and accept. The simplest way for Disney to achieve this weightless flexibility is via a reliance on easily recognizable tropes dating back to the 1940s, including films such as *Saludos Amigos* (as outlined in chapter 1). Weightless flexibility is similar to stereotypes. However, given the tendency to overuse this term, I distance myself from the concept in favor of one that allows for more complex engagements of issues and tensions.

Ambiguous flexibility is present when authentic sounding narratives and representations have no known origin. Here, it could be a holiday, tradition, location, or food item that is scripted as outside of normative mainstream U.S. culture (it is often characterized this way through language), but without reference to its origin. I attribute this solely to an ambiguity of origin. Valdivia (2020) locates an example of this in the film *Beatriz at Dinner* (2017), starring Salma Hayek. Valdivia argues that in this film, Hayek (who is also a producer) selects difficult Nahuatl words to mark her authentic Latinidad. Hayek's character (Beatriz) explains that she is from Tlaltecuhtli, but Tlaltecuhtli is not a location. She is an Aztec mythical figure. I extend Valdivia's claim to argue that it is through this word, and other similar instances in the film, that Hayek highlights an ambiguously flexible Latinidad that is supposed to be read as authentic. Within the terrain of ambiguous flexibility, no further details about origin are mentioned in the narrative.

Hybrid flexibility can be found in instances that contain mixtures of many specific markers. In other words, an episode or moment that falls within hybrid flexibility might implement various signifiers that pertain to different types of Latinidades, which can often be identified by members of those groups. Here, the Latinidades are named, albeit often used together in ways that do not make sense. For an example of hybrid flexibility outside of Latinidad, we can mention John Ford's *The Searchers* (1956). This Western film features an Indian chief named Scar (played by the German actor Henry Brandon). All the signifiers present during Scar's scenes represent Plains tribes (via teepees, buckskin, types of beads and dress, etc.). However, when Scar is not speaking English, he speaks Navajo. For those of us who are not familiar with the various tribes and their languages, this might not register as messiness, but Native American people would more than likely notice the inconsistencies. Within Latinidades, this type of flexibility is present, for example, when a character is seen referencing Chilean cuisine, making Peruvian drinks, and using vocabulary from Colombia. The character is supposed to represent one identity, yet media makers flatten various elements of Latinidad and package it in one body. Many non-Latinx audiences will not know the difference.

Finally, transformational flexibility refers to those moments that create some kind of rupture within existing narratives. For example, Natalie's character in *The Baker and the Beauty* (2020) is a slightly overweight queer Latina teen, firmly rooted in a Cuban–U.S. cultural specificity, whose non-heteronormative big ideas often inspire significant plot twists that serve to open up possibilities for other characters. Transformational flexibility consists of never before or rarely seen representations rooted in specificity. Beyond ambiguity and flattened hybridity, transformational flexibility proposes a fantastical future that takes us beyond the repetitive, discriminatory, and facile representations of the past and present. This

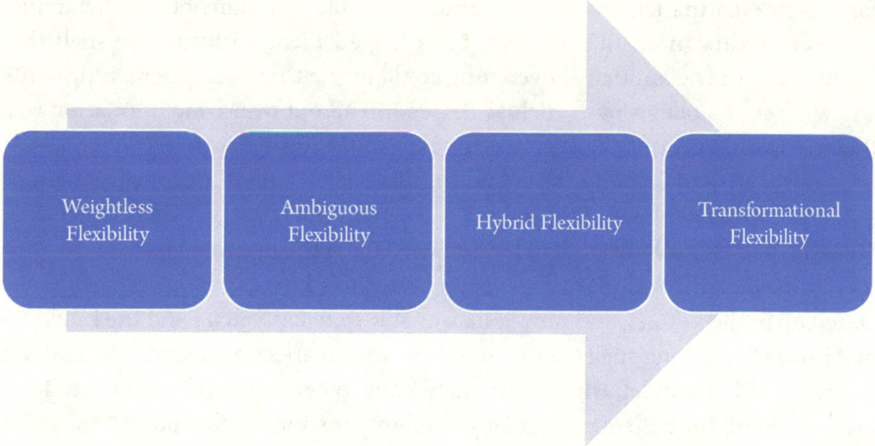

Figure 3. Continuum of Flexibility. Illustration by the author.

extends beyond mere presence, which is not necessarily transformative on its own. Within the transformational category one encounters discourses that allow us to imagine new possibilities within the scope of Latinidad. This, of course, does not mean that they are perfect representations. They are glimpses of the possibility for representations of Latinidad to move in a different direction.

In the three seasons of *Elena*, audiences were exposed to a range of media tactics, borrowing from U.S. media representations of Latinxs at large but sometimes also stepping away from these. Disney employed flexible specificity simultaneously with ambiguity and hybridity. Additionally, the flexibilities overlap with postfeminist sensibilities that showcase a can-do princess guided by discourses of domesticity. Within the series are different degrees of flexibility and a few instances that function as symbolic ruptures (Molina-Guzmán, 2010) of previously existing tropes used to represent femininity and Latinidad. Molina-Guzmán (2010) proposes the term "symbolic rupture" to make sense of audiences' digital reception of media content, arguing that audiences often disrupt the media's hegemonic practices. I adapt her concept to think through ruptures within the media texts themselves (independent of audiences) and further engage with Valdivia's (2021) "flashpoints of intersectional visibility" to explain the moments when mainstream media move away from the more weightless tropes, albeit only for a "flash," through "short-lived presence" (p. 139). The *Elena of Avalor* series illustrates a few of these instances.

The "True" Latina Comes Out Of the Amulet: Narrative Arc

As mentioned in chapter 2, Elena owes her existence to Sofia, from Disney Junior's *Sofia the First*, wherein Elena literally came out of Sofia's amulet. Four months after the debut of *Elena of Avalor*, Disney premiered *Elena and the Secret of Avalor* (November 20, 2016) on Disney Channel and Disney Junior to provide the backstory for this new Latina Disney princess. Since Elena literally came out of the amulet that Sofia wears in all the episodes, Sofia helped Elena to break the spell that trapped her in the amulet. Indeed, one could argue that Sofia/Elena represents a new form of a television franchise that is spread out over time in relation to a theme—Latinidad (and its avowal and disavowal). In the five-form typology of synergy outlined by Meehan (2005) and highlighted in chapter 2, Elena qualifies as a form of "redeployment" whereby "the symbolic universe encapsulated in an artifact . . . is both dependent but removed from the original" (p. 125).

Elena and the Secret of Avalor reveals exactly how Elena's parents died, how she ended up in the amulet, and how Sofia was able to release Elena and the kingdom of Avalor from a long spell. In the movie, Sofia embarks on a journey to find out the secret of her amulet, which ultimately leads to her heroic release of the "lost" princess. With the help of a wizard and a mighty instinct, Sofia finds a book titled "The Lost Princess of Avalor." Even though the title of the book is written in symbols (something common with most of the written text in the *Elena* series), we know from the dialogue (and from the subtitles) that this is the title of the book. Sofia thus helps this mysterious, foreign, lost princess escape from the spell that had trapped her in the amulet. The story situates Elena in a "kingdom across the great ocean." The book explains that on her fifteenth birthday (a nod to *quinceañera* celebrations), Elena was gifted an amulet (a red version of Sofia's amulet), which would protect her from harm. When an evil sorceress attempted to kill Elena's parents, Elena tried to take down the sorceress, but her amulet pulled her inside so she would not die. Elena lived inside that amulet for forty-one years, until Sofia rescued her.

In this made-for-television movie Elena's story is revealed, situating her in a faraway kingdom, a mystical place with ancient ruins. Even when Sofia sets out for Avalor with her family, they all refer to the kingdom as a place located far away within the "great unknown." Sofia's story takes place in present time, but audiences are to understand that Elena was trapped in her amulet for over forty years, while Avalor was stuck in a dark four-decade-long period without a ruler. As highlighted in chapter 2, Disney is well known for employing pre-Columbian images and storylines when creating Latin American or Latinx representations, especially animated representations. Therefore, audiences see landmarks, peoples, and traditions that are supposed to be situated in a distant past, removed from modernity. These types of representations are consistent with the tradition-versus-modernity dichotomy (Lerner, 1958), which positions those outside of the United States as "traditional."

Media also often represent these settings or groups of people in rural settings, or outside of urban areas (as in *Coco* and *Encanto*). As these stories often fall within an "unknown" territory, as expressed by Sofia's family in the movie, someone must often set out on a quest to save, rescue, or release the nonwhite characters from the traditions they are rooted in. In *Frozen 2* (2019), for example, the song titled "Into the Unknown" refers to Elsa's curiosity to follow a call that draws her into an "unknown" enchanted forest inhabited by an Indigenous tribe she must rescue. Avalor is set up in a similar way, as remote, foreign, and in need of rescuing by Sofia.

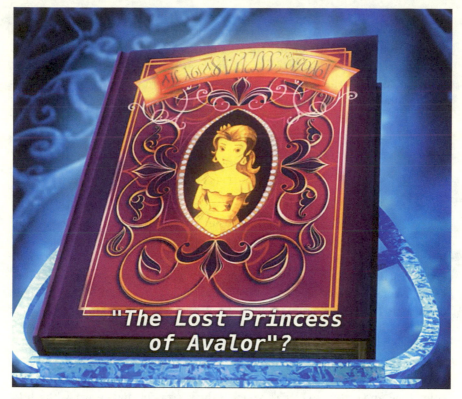

Figure 4. *The Lost Princess of Avalor* book, which Sofia stumbles upon during her quest to find the secret of her amulet in the *Elena and the Secret of Avalor* television movie. The captions are a result of the English subtitles (*Sofia the First*).

These rescue narratives resemble the "rescue fantasy" outlined by Shohat and Stam (1994), although their work positions this fantasy more in line with rescuing women from "dark" men. I extend their work to account for the rescue narratives pertaining to nonwhite groups of people or lands. Also, in line with the center–periphery dichotomy (Latour, 1987), Avalor is firmly situated on the periphery. Latour is interested in science and engineering, but his findings about this dichotomy can be applied to media representations, which center whiteness and push aside the nonwhite other. It is not until the young Sofia comes in that Elena and her kingdom can be set free, but this freedom does not move them out of the periphery. The freedom merely releases them from captivity (in line with the rescue fantasy) and moves them into a fantastical land with a range of degrees of flexible Latinidad.

The *Elena of Avalor* series consists of seventy-seven episodes, but some are divided into multiple parts. There are also three series of shorts (for a total of fifteen shorts) available on Disney+: *Adventures in Vallestrella*, *Scepter Training with Zuzo*, and *The Secret of Sirenas*. These shorts are each three minutes in length and primarily highlight Elena's adventures, while some also focus on the role of her sister, Isabel, within these. The seventy-seven episodes of the series follow princess Elena on her quest to become queen of Avalor. The series begins when Elena is sixteen and culminates on her twentieth birthday, with the coronation finale. The three seasons trace her leadership journey as she communicates with ghosts, learns to deal with rulers from other kingdoms, celebrates many holidays, solves conflict after conflict within her kingdom, wards off power-hungry villains, learns about the many traditions and legends of Avalor, and teaches those around her powerful lessons about love, happiness, and family.

CHARACTER TYPES

Elena does not tackle the challenges in the series on her own. In fact, she is almost always guided by the help of those around her, although the final victories are usually attributed to her. In the series, Elena has a support team of seven characters. Both the promotional materials and the last scene from the introduction to the series visually highlight the following seven characters: Abuelo, Abuela,[1] Isabel, Elena, Naomi, Mateo, and Gabe. Abuelo and Abuela, both with short gray hair, often try to keep Elena out of trouble. They worry about her taking on too much responsibility for someone her age. Isabel (voiced by Jenna Ortega) is Elena's younger sister, who begins the series as a tween girl. She has about the same light-brown skin tone as Elena, though in some promotional materials her skin tone varies. Isabel's eyes are brown like Elena's, and she also has hair that is similar in color, type, and texture to Elena's, which is thick, straight, and brown, with a little bit of curl at the ends. Isabel embodies the Latina "zany STEM girl" trope (Leon-Boys & Valdivia, 2021) and self-identifies as an inventor. She enrolls in college courses and is quite competitive about her inventions, although they often end up causing chaos and confusion for Avalor.

Naomi is Elena's best friend and a member of the Grand Council of Avalor. She is originally from Norberg and now lives in Avalor. Within the series as well as the promotional materials, she stands out visually because of her fair skin, short spikey blonde hair, and large blue eyes. Naomi is often the voice of reason in the series. She provides Elena with advice not just about royal decisions, but also about her personal life. Elena and Naomi disagree from time to time, but they remain friends until the end. Mateo is the royal wizard of Avalor. He shares the same skin color and hair color (brown) as most of the other Avalorans in the series and is almost always seen wearing his maroon, royal wizard gown. At first, he is just a wizard in training, but Mateo quickly proves he can help Avalor immensely with his knowledge of magic. Mateo is goofy, often clumsy, and relies heavily on his mother's cooking and support. Along with Naomi and Mateo, Gabe rounds out Elena's crew of best friends. Also, Gabe, one of the many characters of Avalor with brown hair, brown skin, and brown eyes, begins the series as lieutenant of the Royal Guard and moves up the ranks to general by the end of the series. Unlike Mateo who is short and thin, Gabe is tall and muscular and always sports his blue, royal guard uniform. He frequently accompanies Elena to protect her from harm on her missions.

In terms of language, the younger characters in the series speak in unaccented English, whereas the older characters, like *Abuela* and *Abuelo*, speak with heavy Spanish-inflected accents. These accents are also prominent among some of the parents in the series, such as Gabe's father. Additionally, the farther away anyone gets from the castle, the heavier the character's accents are. For example, when Elena visits the various villages within Avalor, most of the characters speak with heavy Spanish-inflected accents. Spanish words are also quite prominent in the series. The names of many locations, such as Castillo Park, are spoken in Spanish as well as the names of holidays and foods. These are also almost always pronounced with a Spanish accent, but there are some exceptions (often depending on the voice actors).[2] The use of language in this series serves as one of the markers of its fantastical Latinidad. In addition to language, it is also worth mentioning that many prominent Latinx and Latin American celebrities have performed as guest voice actors for various episodes. Some of these actors include Gina Rodriguez, Cheech Marin, Edward James Olmos, Jaime Camil, Eugenio Derbez, and Constance Marie. The seven characters outlined above, however, are the most prominent in the series.

The Many Celebrations of Avalor

Celebrations, parties, feasts, and holidays are great events to sprinkle into series, films, and any other types of mediated content. Plot-altering narratives often take place during large parties or during the events leading up to the parties themselves. In other words, highlighting celebrations via mediated content is not new. However, Avalor takes parties to another level. Out of the seventy-seven *Elena of Avalor* episodes, over twenty highlight large parties, holidays, celebrations, festivals, or celebratory sporting events. Some of these include ambiguous flexibility contained within the fantastical realm of Avalor, such as the fictitious "All Kingdom's Fair," teeming with merchants, artists, and magicians from various kingdoms surrounding Avalor. Others, however, are more specific to Latinidad or Latin Americans, such as the many Día de los Muertos celebrations. The Avaloran celebrations typically involve party-planning fiascos and plenty of food. In what follows I analyze some of the most prominent celebrations that fall within the selection criteria previously outlined.

Dead Latinxs

The Day of the Dead is the most prominently used celebration in *Elena of Avalor*. This holiday has now become a mainstream trope and refers to Día de los Muertos, a Latin American holiday held on November 1 that celebrates the lives of deceased loved ones by honoring them with altars (among other things). As well as appearing in relation to ambiguous Disney Latinas, such as Miranda in *Lizzie McGuire*

(Valdivia 2008c), the celebration lends itself to visually rich animations used in portrayals featuring Latinx children. Two recent examples of the prominent and overused Día de los Muertos celebration in full-length animated feature films are 20th Century Fox's *The Book of Life* (2014) and Disney Pixar's *Coco* (2017). For an adult example, see the opening scene of the James Bond franchise film *Spectre* (2015), which provides a long, spectacular view of a Día de los Muertos parade in the Zócalo, at the center of Mexico City. Many other films include Día de los Muertos celebrations to signify Latinidad,[3] usually through Mexicanidad. It is important to note, though, that within the terrain of children's animated content, producers often find it challenging to talk about or reference death. When death is referenced, it is not often elaborated upon. In *Elena of Avalor*'s Día de los Muertos episodes, they never actually say the word "death," in English.[4] The closest they get is "passed away," which is said one time. In fact, the series often refers to it as a "festival of love," which is a bit of stretch, though one could argue that most festivals contain some element of love. Latinx culture challenges mainstream narratives about childhood and death because this trope, which is so often used to represent Latinidad in the media, is about death, and death is not part of the iconic markers typically used for children's programming in the United States. In these episodes in the series, the flexibility is contained within the parameters of the taboo. The holiday is carefully curated and transformed into a party for children's television.

Elena of Avalor features four Día de los Muertos episodes during the series, all of which demonstrate the U.S media's (and Disney's) reliance on this celebration to represent Latinidad. No other holiday, theme, or celebration is highlighted as prominently in this Disney series as is Día de los Muertos, which needs to be understood alongside its history of cultural appropriation. In 2013, the Walt Disney Company attempted to trademark the term "Día de los Muertos" to "monopolize its Day of the Dead products and themed merchandise across platforms" (Morales, 2020, p. 42) before the release of *Coco* (2017). Although Disney was not successful in trademarking a cultural tradition (having received quite a bit of backlash), the company continues to (over)use visually appealing Día de los Muertos signifiers with any content related to Latinidad. In doing so, it engages in what appear to be specific representations but within the parameters of previously accepted overused representations, thus rendering them weightless. Part of the weightlessness is also related to the fact that Día de los Muertos is not celebrated as prominently or in the same manner in all parts of Latin America as is represented in U.S. mainstream media. This is reminiscent of the festivities surrounding Cinco de Mayo,[5] which is truly just an afterthought in Mexican culture because it is not our independence day, as suggested in mainstream U.S. popular culture. As previously mentioned, the opening scene of *Spectre* (2015) includes an elaborate representation of a Día de los Muertos parade and celebration in Mexico City's Zócalo. However, this is a situation where life imitates art because *Spectre* was the actual inspiration for the first Día de los Muertos parade in Mexico City, which took place in October 2016. The film's portrayal of the celebration looks as though it could be an authentic celebration held in a historic part of Mexico City, but it was entirely curated by Hollywood and adopted by Mexico City almost a year later.

Whereas *Spectre*, *Coco*, and *The Book of Life* were all well-received in Mexico and Latin America, and *Coco* in particular broke records in Mexico (*Coco*, n.d., 2017; Erazo, 2017), it is important to keep in mind that the most prominent mediated celebration for Latinxs on the screen is one in which they either celebrate death or are dead. In an analysis of *The Book of Life* and *Coco*, Martín-Rodriguez (2019) notes that animated studios are failing at "representing more varied images of Mexico and Mexicans" (p. 356). The most overused images are those that celebrate the existence of a state beyond life, a state peripheral to life. To this, I would add that this approach extends beyond Mexico to Latin America at large. As the studios purport to represent U.S. Latinidad, they are actually portraying Latin America, and within those portrayals they are representing a narrow version of Latin America as Mexico. Martín-Rodriguez encourages readers to ask themselves, "What's with dead Mexicans and Hollywood?" (p. 358). Again, I would extend his claim that Mexicans have been represented in animation as pertaining to the past to Latinxs and U.S. Latinidad (where this is also often the case). Mexicans, Latin Americans, and Latinxs have been portrayed not only as part of the past but also as closer to nature and away from modernity, where they are often lost or trapped: Elena is trapped in her amulet. It is up to others to rescue and bring characters to modernity, away from the periphery (the rescue fantasy mentioned above). Against this backdrop, I analyze *Elena of Avalor*'s four Día de los Muertos episodes.

"A Day to Remember" aired on October 16, 2016, and was the ninth episode of the *Elena* series. Leading up to this episode, Disney Junior aired five different commercials promoting the episode, advertising it as a celebration of Latinx heritage through its focus on Día de los Muertos. The episode was part of Disney Channel's "Monstober," featuring Halloween-themed movies, television shows, and commercials. Therefore, including this episode within a celebration of Halloween further flattens the approach to Latinidad, and highlights its weightless flexibility, as it makes it equivalent to a different U.S. tradition. "A Day to Remember" was the only episode in the Monstober lineup to feature prominent markers of a specific culture—meaning that in the absence of othering signifiers the rest of the texts featured during Monstober represented mainstream (read: white, middle-class) U.S. culture. The ratings for this Día de los Muertos episode speak to how successful the implementation of this celebration proved to be. According to a report on Headline Planet based on the L+SD data, this episode "drew 1.38 million total viewers.[6] The number tops the 1.23 million mark garnered by the previous episode, which aired on 9/30" (B. Cantor, 2016b).

During the twenty-nine-minute episode, two short documentaries aired (one during each break), addressing Latinx traditions and culture. The first focused on Día de los Muertos altars and provided a brief background and history of the tradition. The other consisted of a spotlight on Jenna Ortega, the voice of Isabel on *Elena of Avalor*, and her family. Ortega is of Mexican and Puerto Rican descent and often speaks out about her Latinidad. Ortega's spotlight introduces audiences to her family, where they explain how they make traditional Latinx food. Also, every family member talks about the importance of Latinx pride. In my discussion of the "labor of repromotion" in chapter 2, I explained how Disney recycles its Latinx talent via various platforms to serve as ambassadors for Disney's Latinidad. I briefly drew on the example of the Hispanic Heritage Month interstitials, in which all the child actors from *Stuck in the Middle* had their own mini documentary. Disney's consistent focus on ethnicity and culture in relation to Latinx celebrities but not white ones puts the burden of culture and ethnicity (and, perhaps less visibly, race) on Latinx celebrities and audiences as *other*. This is also a way for Disney to position the talent of these actors outside the boundaries of U.S. American identity by highlighting their foreignness. However, this is not just prominent via Latinx celebrities, but basically any nonwhite celebrity that the channel employs.[7] The commercials advertising this episode, in conjunction with the two documentary commercials during the episode, outline how Disney prominently displayed the Día de los Muertos celebration, perhaps not coincidentally, a few months before it started promoting *Coco*'s upcoming debut on the big screen (Leon-Boys, 2021a).

The episode begins with Elena wearing an ornate dress with a skeleton outline painted on it. The rest of the main characters wear this same type of attire for the duration of the episode. This exuberant clothing, however, is not typical in Latinx cultures, especially as an all-day ensemble. This sartorial statement, a commodified co-optation of a holiday, becomes the foundation from which Elena begins to talk about the reasons to celebrate Día de los Muertos and the importance of honoring dead loved ones. These explanations, however, are brief and fall to the background in comparison to the central conflict of the episode.

Figure 5. Elena and her family at her parents' altar in the "A Day to Remember" episode (*Elena of Avalor*).

To describe Día de los Muertos, Elena notes, "It's like we are throwing a party." Most of the context for the celebration is contained within the short musical number at the beginning of the episode. As is the case with many episodes in this series, this Día de los Muertos episode focuses extensively on food, all of which is discussed using culinary terminology in Spanish. Elena makes *calabaza en tacha*, a Mexican candied pumpkin dessert. Both the *calabaza* and the *pan de muerto* (the traditional Day of the Dead bread) help drive the storyline in this episode. Elena not only helps make the *calabaza* but also must set out to find *pan de muerto* for her parents' altar. Although the characters' attire may seem a bit over the top, the reference and inclusion of the *pan de muerto*, the food, the altar, and the explanations of the significance of these items paint what appears to be a specific representation of this holiday, but the representation falls in line with weightless flexibility because it relies on the trope of Día de los Muertos, without providing more than a minute of context in the episode itself.

The central storyline of this episode involves Elena assisting a ghost in her quest to keep her restaurant from being sold. To do this, though, Elena must venture into the village, away from the castle at the center of Avalor. When Elena meets the ghost's grandchildren, Julio and Carmen, we see a clear difference in the skin tone of the characters. While Elena is tan and her brown skin is darker than most Disney princesses, Julio and Carmen are much darker and could be read as being of African descent. By including these two characters with darker skin tones, within the world of fantastical Latinidad, Disney is slightly breaking away from the typical mainstream media representation of Latinidad as light brown. Disney and many other media creators primarily envision Latinidad as brown, but in this depiction of Carmen and Julio, Disney steps away by providing darker characters, albeit playing minor roles. When conceptualizing Latinidad exclusively through mestizaje or a "brown" lens, many Latinxs are erased in the process. The logic of mestizaje within Latinidad has been critiqued by various scholars (e.g., Dávila, 2008; López Oro, 2016). It appears that through the representation of characters like Carmen and Julio, Disney is creating a small rupture in this logic. However, the rupture is steeped in class narratives. Since Elena is royal and Carmen and Julio live in the town of Avalor, this difference in skin tone could be interpreted as a class marker, a skin color trope commonly used in the media when assigning nonwhite people to different class hierarchies. A common media practice when representing Latinxs on the screen is to cast people with lighter skin tones as royals or wealthy and those who are darker as working class, Indigenous, or of African descent (Molina-Guzmán, 2013). This is consistent in the series as working-class characters who live in the village are usually depicted with darker skin, eyes, and hair.

Once in the village, Elena saves the restaurant by helping Julio and Carmen find a lost recipe book. Elena even helps them cook the most popular dishes, which brings business back to the establishment. Similarly, before taking off on her quest, Elena helps her grandmother prepare the kitchen and make the *calabaza en tacha*. Although Elena's can-do spirit helps her navigate the situation, her domestic duties

and skills are ultimately what end up saving the day. Elena's can-do girlhood coupled with traditional discourses of domesticity demonstrate the complexity of her
character. In this episode, we have an instance where Elena's postfeminist domesticity intersects with a weightless flexibility within Latinidad. The episode provides
what appears to be a specific representation of Latinidad, focusing on a well-known
but highly overused celebration that is ultimately inconsequential to the central
conflict of the narrative. The Latinidad exists through the episode as well as the
commercials, but it is a weightless signifier that does not rupture preexisting (and
overused) Latinidad tropes. The weightlessness of the Latinidad in this Día de los
Muertos episode is indicative of Disney's implementation of various efforts to normalize Latinidad by pushing cultural signifiers into the background to represent
them as everyday aspects of life. In its efforts to normalize the Latinidad, Disney
hollows out signifiers through weightless flexibility.

The second season of *Elena of Avalor* opens with another Día de los Muertos
episode. "The Jewel of Maru" aired on October 14, 2017, almost a year after "A Day
to Remember" and a month before the U.S. theater release of *Coco*. This episode,
however, did not consist of the various Latinx and Día de los Muertos promotional
interstitials and documentary shorts present throughout the previous episode. In
fact, Día de los Muertos in the episode itself falls to the background even more than
in the previous episode and is available mainly behind the scenes via symbols, such
as clothing and sugar skulls. Although five minutes into the episode we do see Elena
decorating her parents' altar (in a musical number) and she continues to wear her
Día de los Muertos dress with the skeleton outline painted on it, the central narrative in this episode is not about the holiday, but rather a big test Elena will soon have
to take to prove she is worthy of becoming a queen. The musical number, which
takes place at her parents' altar, is actually about her desire to make her parents
proud, and not about the holiday. Ultimately, Elena does end up making her parents
proud (something they tell her when they appear to her in ghost form). Elena succeeds in her quest to secure the jewel of Maru, and the episode becomes much more
about the universal storyline of restoring peace to her kingdom than about anything related to Día de los Muertos. Additionally, Elena is triumphant not because
of any physical feats per se, but because she has listened to her heart. It must never-
theless be noted that throughout the episode, Elena does perform plenty of physical
feats, which continues to position her within the realm of embodied (Beltrán, 2004)
can-do girlhood. The physical aspects here, however, are not what lead to her success. Once again, this episode falls within a weightless flexibility.

Similarly, "The Return of El Capitan" (season 2, episode 18), which aired on
October 27, 2018, showcases a Día de los Muertos, which is superficial and weightless. Not only is it a weightless flexibility grounded in an overused marker of Latinidad, but it is only available in visual markers, such as the altars, clothing with
skeleton outlines, and the food (which is specifically Mexican cuisine). Rather than
focus on Día de los Muertos, this episode is much more prominently about the universal theme of friendship. The episode follows Elena and her *abuelo* as she helps
him complete an old mission for his two friends who have died. As usual, Elena

succeeds in helping her grandpa assist his dead friends, yet before offering her full assistance she is hesitant about the journey. Perhaps this hesitation is because she wants to protect her grandfather from injury or pain. Her protectiveness of her grandfather becomes more central to the storyline (caregiving—feminine affect). Once the mission is completed and *abuelo*'s deceased friends are satisfied and can return to the spirit world, the episode shifts to focus on the Día de los Muertos celebration, but only for about a minute. The final shift in focus back to Día de los Muertos is a quick and subtle reminder of the holiday, which overall falls to the background of the episode, creating a weightless flexibility without many reference points. This once again exemplifies Disney's efforts to strip Latinidad of its cultural signifiers and situate it within an overused representation with which audiences are more than likely familiar. Also, in this episode we see a combination of Latinidad weightless flexibility with domesticized, caregiving postfeminism.

The final Día de los Muertos episode in *Elena of Avalor* aired on October 16, 2019. "Flower of Light," the eighth episode in the third season, highlights Elena's journey as she travels to the spirit world with an old childhood friend who requests her help. This episode is not only reminiscent of *Coco* in terms of the visuals and the colors, it also showcases the narrative of crossing over into the spirit world. Elena's childhood friend, Feli, learns that Elena can see ghosts on Día de los Muertos (a central theme of the other Día de los Muertos episodes), so Feli asks for help crossing over into the spirit world to see her late husband, Ricardo. Feli is much older than Elena, given that they were friends before Elena was trapped in the amulet and frozen in time. Feli is in her fifties while Elena is a teenager. Regardless of the age difference, Feli and Elena instantly bond once again.

As with all the other Día de los Muertos episodes, Elena wears her skeleton outline red dress as she navigates them to the spirit world. Once they make it to the spirit world, through a portal that leads them to a land almost identical to the land of the dead in *Coco*, chaos ensues when some mystical creatures close the portal to the spirit world.

After Feli is reunited with her late husband she realizes, with Elena's assistance, that she must help open the portal by dancing flamenco. Through the narrative, audiences learn that Feli used to be a famous flamenco dancer who stopped dancing after her husband passed away. As soon as Feli starts dancing, everyone in the spirit world is overcome with joy, happiness, and love. Earlier, Feli had realized that only love could open the portal, so she decided to let go of her resolve not to dance to bring everyone love and joy. It is through her body and her craft that Feli, with the help of Elena's advice and dancing, opens the portal and saves the day.

Showcasing the Latina body through dance is a common media practice (Peña Ovalle, 2011). Incorporating a combination of song and dance has become a trademark of Elena as she sings, dances, and plays her guitar in almost every episode. All Disney princesses sing, of course, but not all of them sing, dance, and play instruments at the same time (Valdivia, 2020). Outside of animation, the Latina body in Hollywood film continues to be portrayed this way. Rita Moreno and Salma

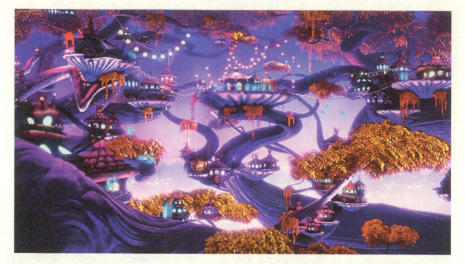

Figure 6. The spirit world from Elena and Feli's perspective in the "Flower of Light" episode (*Elena of Avalor*).

Figure 7. The Land of the Dead in Disney's *Coco* (2017).

Hayek, two of the more prominent, well-known Latina actresses, are often shown dancing, either as a central part of the narrative or just as an added layer to their characters. This focus on the Latina body moving, performing, singing, and providing joy through femininity to save the world is a way in which the series uses femininity and Latinidad to counter (and make kid and family friendly) the overused trope of the Latina spitfire who is almost always seen dancing in sexually suggestive tones. Once again, we see an example of the Latina body signing in as a site for social struggle.

It is important to note that Feli dances flamenco, much more in line with the Spanish influences in Elena (discussed in chapter 2), such as Elena dancing flamenco in the Disney corporate social responsibility reports and the Spanish wrought iron and tile in the *Elena of Avalor* infographic. However, Disney positions flamenco within the realm of the fantastical and flexible amalgamation of

Figure 8. Elena and Feli dancing as the portal, which connects Avalor and the spirit world, begins to slowly open behind them in the "Flower of Light" episode (*Elena of Avalor*).

Latinidad. In this last Día de los Muertos episode of the series, audiences see a slightly more pronounced focus on the holiday, but again this representation focuses on a holiday that is overused by the media to represent Latinidad, a weightless flexibility. The series, in fact, significantly contributes to this overrepresentation by including four Día de los Muertos episodes. Whereas the overrepresentation of the holiday is apparent in a quick glance at the episode selection, the actual significance of the celebration is hardly the focus of the episodes. The holiday functions more as a vessel for Elena to see spirits and communicate with dead people, which drives the narrative in all the episodes. The overrepresentation of Día de los Muertos in this series is consistent with the media's fascination for portraying Latinxs and Latin Americans as links or bridges to the world beyond this realm (the spirit world). It is also an injection of magical realism, which extends to more recent representations like *Encanto* (2021).

NAVIDAD

The Navidad (Christmas) theme, while not as common in U.S. media as the Día de los Muertos narrative, is popular in Disney and mainstream media portrayals of Latinidad. The most common occurrence during the Navidad-mediated instances is the celebration of the *posada*, the reenactment of Mary and Joseph's journey to find shelter before Jesus's birth. Despite the fact that *posadas* are most traditionally celebrated in Mexico, U.S. media producers often highlight them as central to the Navidad episodes, even when these occur outside of Mexico. Dating as far back as the mid-twentieth century, Disney included the animated *Las Posadas* (1945) of *The Three Caballeros*. Moreover, both Día de los Muertos and Navidad associate Latinidad with religiosity, in particular a pagan Catholicism. The *Elena of Avalor* series features two Navidad episodes.

"Navidad," the first of the two episodes, premiered on December 9, 2016, as the eleventh episode of the first season. Like "A Day to Remember," "Navidad" centers on the celebration of a holiday. For this celebration, the people of Avalor gather to showcase how they each celebrate Navidad. Almost all the characters explain that they tie their celebrations to their culture, and all but one of the families present here is Avaloran. Additionally, the only way in which characters refer to Christmas in this episode is by saying "Navidad." In this sense, the creators of the series assume that their audience has insight or knowledge about what the term means or, since other signifiers of Christmas are so strong, they need not translate that one keyword.

However, when the episode is viewed with Spanish audio, the characters do not refer to it as "Navidad." Instead, the event is referred to as "fiestas," thus removing the cultural and religious specificity of the actual word that is present when audiences view the episode in English. "Fiestas," however, is not always used to refer to or replace "Christmas" in the Spanish-speaking world. "Fiestas" simply means parties. The use of this word perhaps points to an acknowledgment that in Latin America not everyone celebrates Christmas. This also points again to Disney's flexible Latinidad. As with "A Day to Remember," food becomes an important topic of conversation and a major marker of Latinidad in "Navidad," especially as the characters get ready to host their Navidad parties. In the first scene, Elena wears a bright red dress in the kitchen as she makes *buñuelos* (a fried dough dessert popular in some parts of Latin America) and reminds those around her that it is almost Navidad, a holiday that she says is very special to her because of its significance (though she never elaborates on what that significance is). Elena also explains that there will be a piñata (a papier-mâché decoration filled with candy and treats) following castle tradition. The incorporation of the piñata continues the Latinx references and themes, though in this episode it is decontextualized from its more frequent association with birthdays. The use of "fiestas" in the Spanish version of the episode and the incorporation of the piñata serve to flatten parties and celebrations.

Halfway through the episode, when the citizens of Avalor display how they celebrate Navidad, a series of events driven by competition lead to the accidental setting alight of a Christmas tree, which causes a fire followed by many fights between the secondary characters. Elena is the one who puts out the fire, metaphorically and literally. She jumps, runs, and swings through the Navidad displays as she puts out the fire wearing her heels and yellow Navidad dress (different from her trademark red dress, which she wore earlier). Elena joins the postfeminist wave of Disney princesses who save the day through a courageous physical feat while never losing their beauty or femininity (Forman-Brunell & Hains, 2013; Hains, 2014; Kennedy, 2018). Further, Elena's Latinidad blends with her can-do talents and positions her within a trope of physically tough Latinas in Hollywood action films (Beltrán, 2004). Elena's physical strength intersects with her community leadership skills, which position her as the caring and nurturing knowledge keeper who takes care of the community and gently provides the answers and advice that save the day—the authentic postfeminist subject who leads *and* cares. This is exactly what happens in "A Day to Remember," when Elena helps save the restaurant in a caring and nurturing way, mostly through cooking.

Shortly after Elena puts out the fire, she once again displays her community-building and leadership skills by bringing everyone back together through a *parranda*. Elena clarifies to another character that a *parranda* is very similar to a *posada*, during which you walk from house to house singing carols. Again, this episode assumes that audiences are familiar with *posadas*, and for those who are not, the episode serves as a marker of the supposed authenticity of the series. The word "parranda" has different meanings throughout Latin America. For example, in Mexico, Colombia, and Chile, it simply means a large party, and in Puerto Rico it refers to musical festivities during the days leading up to Christmas. When viewing with Spanish audio, however, Elena refers to it as a "recorrido,"[8] with the English captions calling it "caroling." By using a Spanish word with different meanings in different Spanish-speaking locations, the series deploys a hybrid flexibility that is supposed to encompass the different lived experiences of a vast population but proves to be potentially messy, confusing, and challenging to translate for normative U.S. white audiences.

With the *parranda*, music, and dancing, Elena unites everyone in Avalor through what appears to be a culturally specific tradition, but, in reality, is not. The last scenes of the episode show Elena leading the village in dance and song, to the sound of mariachis and guitars. Elena stresses that the importance of the holiday centers around love more than anything, thus allowing the holiday to once again take a backseat. This is like the Día de los Muertos references to a "festival of love." Also, just like "A Day to Remember," "Navidad" provides brief explanations for the cultural significance of the event, contributing toward what could appear to be a specific representation of Latinidad, but instead is hybrid flexibility, as it mixes many Latinx markers resulting in a somewhat messy holiday. Also, this hybrid flexibility does not include any references to the religious significance of the holiday. The lack of religious exposition in these episodes is perhaps a way to avoid alienating viewers who have different religious beliefs, practices, or affiliations. However, we will see later that Disney does not always take this route when representing religious holidays. The episode demonstrates a strategic ambiguity in relation to ethnicity, along with an "unambivalent structure of ambivalence" (Valdivia, 2020, p. 73) in that its inclusion of cultural traditions from different Latin American countries flattens the Latinidad while simultaneously bringing in some specific elements that can be recognized as authentic to various nations, thus falling in line with the hybrid category I outline. Simultaneously, in true postfeminist fashion, the episode displays Elena's physical abilities, but what ultimately saves the day is her ability to bring the people of Avalor together through music and dance, very similar to the way Feli opened the portal to the spirit world by dancing flamenco.

The second Navidad episode of the series, "Snow Place Like Home" (season 2, episode 20), premiered on November 24, 2018. The episode focuses on the chaos

Figure 9. Elena singing with her guitar and poinsettia dress in front of a Christmas tree in the "Snow Place Like Home" episode (*Elena of Avalor*).

that unfolds when two wizards unleash a huge snowstorm on Avalor. The opening scenes show Elena in her white poinsettia dress, which is actually very similar to her traditional red dress, but in red and white. When her sister, Isabel, tells her she is going into the village with her grandparents to deliver a gift to her friend, Elena makes sure to remind them to be home before "Noche Buena."[9] In a musical number, where she plays her guitar and dances to a type of hybrid flamenco music, she explains that she just wants "to be home for *Navidad* with my *familia*," saying these keywords in Spanish without any translation. In the song she also notes that this is her favorite season and proceeds to name food items that make the season so special to her. She references "ponche navideño," a "sweet tamal," "pasteles," and "buñuelos."[10] The food references here, yet again, create a type of fantastical authenticity that unites three popular Mexican Christmas treats and a vague reference to cakes. This episode also falls within the hybrid flexibility category, but is a bit closer to ambiguous flexibility than the *Navidad* episode.

Following the musical number, the episode shifts its focus to highlight two fugitive wizards, who conjure up a snowstorm to escape the royal guards. The snowstorm is so bad that Elena and her friends become trapped inside the castle. Naomi, Mateo, and Esteban (Elena's cousin) are trapped inside the home and, similarly, Isabel and her grandparents cannot make it back to the castle because of the storm. Everyone is distraught because they yearn to be home for Christmas. Mateo worries that he will miss the tradition of making a gingerbread house on Noche Buena with his mother. Audiences see a reference to a non-Latin American or Latinx tradition (making a gingerbread house) within the traditionally scripted Latinidad markers of Navidad. This is one instance that positions the episode closer on the continuum to ambiguous flexibility than the previous Christmas episode, while still falling more or less within hybrid flexibility. This Christmas representation potentially appeals to many audiences. Throughout the episode, Elena works arduously to make everyone feel better. She tries to lift their spirits mostly by making and serving food (*ponche navideño*, *tamales*, and *dulces*). Audiences once again see Elena engaging in a more traditional version of normative femininity by cooking and trying to cheer everyone up.

The last scenes in the castle show Elena leading everyone back to happiness through a song about the importance of being with family during Navidad. Again, family and love become central components of celebrating this holiday. Both Navidad episodes in this series highlight a holiday or celebration commonly used to represent Latinxs and Latin Americans on the screen. With a few references to Mexican food sprinkled throughout the narrative, Disney paints a picture that it hopes will create a vision of authenticity, which does not extend beyond food. The fantastical Navidad narratives exist alongside a can-do Elena who, resourceful as she is nurturing, attempts to bring happiness to her loved ones mostly through food and dance.

QUINCEAÑERA STORIES

The *quinceañera* celebration, like Día de los Muertos, is overused in U.S. media representations of Latina girls (González 2019; González-Martin 2016; Leon-Boys, 2021a; Leon-Boys & Valdivia, 2021; Valdivia 2011, 2020). This elaborate coming-of-age party takes place on a girl's fifteenth birthday, and although the tradition originated in Mexico, it is now widely celebrated by Latinxs in the United States as well. *Lizzie McGuire* (2001–2004), *Wizards of Waverly Place* (2007–2012), *The Fosters* (2013–2018), *Stuck in the Middle* (2016–2018), *One Day at a Time* (2017–2020), *Ashley Garcia: Genius in Love* (2020), *Jane the Virgin* (2014–2019), and *Team Kaylie* (2019–2020) all featured young Latina characters who at one point in the series celebrate this coming-of-age event. This list of series only touches on some of the numerous mediated *quinceañera* representations available. Many other movies, such as *McFarland USA* (2015), *Quinceañera* (2006), and *Crazy/Beautiful* (2001) also use *quinceañeras* to signify Latinidad as a cohesive thread juxtaposing the family and tradition-centered Latinxs in relation to the implicitly atomized and unhappy Anglo protagonists. In both live-action films, the cultural tradition functions as a salve to heal emotionally injured Anglos on their way back to normalcy. This Latina cultural rite resonated enough with mainstream media that in 2016 TLC even devoted an entire reality television series to exploring various *quinceañeras*. *Sweet Fifteen: Quinceañeras* follows Latina girls all over the country as they prepare for this rite of passage. A year later, in 2017, HBO released an almost identical series titled *15: A Quinceañera Story*. In fact, *quinceañeras* compose a subgenre within Latina Chick Lit, with one of the best sellers, *Once upon a Quinceañera* (2007), penned by the famed Latina author Julia Alvarez. As with the other two celebrations, Disney stays within accepted, well-known representations of Latinidad, only this time in a gendered ritual.

"My Fair Naomi" (*Elena of Avalor*, season 1, episode 18), premiered on May 6, 2017, after the "King of the Carnaval" episode, which centered around a festival in Avalor. The festival implicitly resembled Rio de Janeiro's Carnival, with characters dressed in vibrant colors as they prepared for and hosted a large parade. Rio's Carnival, however, is never explicitly referenced in the episode and the title "carnaval" is spelled in Spanish rather than Portuguese. Following this vibrantly colored and festive episode, the kingdom of Avalor prepares to host another large celebration, but this time the party is for Naomi. As previously noted, Naomi is Elena's best friend and stands out physically because she is fair skinned with blonde hair and blue eyes. Other than her parents, who appear a few times throughout the series, Naomi is the only character with light phenotypic features. Additionally, Naomi is from Norberg and happens to live in Avalor. Referring to Disney's hybrid live-action and animated *Enchanted*, Tasker (2011) highlights how "such fictional, yet plausibly named magical kingdoms, are a common feature of Hollywood's princess preoccupation" (p. 67). A kingdom named Norberg serves as a stand-in for the non-Latinx universe, implicitly Norway, usually coded as a source of pure whiteness.

When Elena finds out that Naomi did not have a *quinceañera*, she explains that this is an Avaloran tradition and insists that Naomi have a belated celebration. Naomi's sixteenth birthday is fast approaching, and Elena plans on celebrating then, positioning the *quinceañera* as a flexible celebration in terms of age. Other than the fact that it is an Avaloran tradition requiring a great deal of planning, the remainder of the episode does not provide any further explanations about the celebration, its origin, or its significance. While providing substantial information about the significance of *quinceañeras* via this thirty-minute episode might be difficult, more engagement with the significance of the celebration would not be impossible. The central conflict in the narrative involves Naomi's becoming too involved with the party planning and turning into a stereotypical bridezilla, implicitly drawing on U.S. tropes about weddings. Naomi expels Elena and her friends from her court of honor (the *quinceañera*'s closest friends, who dance the main waltz with her), and even hires professionals to replace them during the main dance. This behavior is not typical of Naomi, who throughout the series not only functions as a lighthearted, kind character but also is often the voice of reason guiding the main characters on their many quests. In fact, Naomi is the one who solves one of the most challenging conflicts in the series.[11] This time, however, she becomes so wrapped up in her attempts to have a perfect celebration that, according to Elena, she forgets what the party is supposed to be about—friends, family, and fun.

A *quinceañera*, however, has much deeper cultural significance related to a young girl's coming of age, extending well beyond the dances and the dress, two of the most prominent visual elements in mediated *quinceañeras*. Instead of focusing (even minimally) on the significance of the event, Disney provides a representation that falls between weightless flexibility and ambiguous flexibility. Although the celebration falls in line with the overused representation of *quinceañeras* in the media (weightlessness), it also contains elements of ambiguous flexibility in that

Figure 10. Elena and Naomi dancing together in the final scene of the "My Fair Naomi" episode (*Elena of Avalor*).

Naomi is the one celebrating. The celebration presented in this episode honors the only non-Avaloran in the series. Disney does not explain the coming-of-age event, beyond indicating that it is a large celebration (although most audiences will more than likely recognize it as a Latinx celebration). Instead of focusing on the significance of the *quinceañera*, Naomi and Elena argue over the color scheme, clothing, and dances. We see the struggles of femininity played out through the planning of the *quinceañera*. Eventually, Naomi becomes more preoccupied with the size of her dress than with the meaning behind the celebration. This Disney *quinceañera* adds to the spectrum of inclusion presented in Leon-Boys and Valdivia's (2021) findings of a practically nonexistent Latinidad within Disney's *Stuck in the Middle quinceañera*-themed episodes, in which other issues come to the forefront, usually clothing related, and obfuscate the rich cultural significance of the event. The findings are extended to an analysis of the *quinceañera* in preschool children's television. Again, I find that the celebration is portrayed as a large birthday party, falling between weightless and ambiguous flexibility.

Elena helps Naomi realize that a *quinceañera* celebration as well as being an Avaloran mean putting family and friends first. The episode culminates with dancing and singing at Naomi's *quinceañera* celebration. "My Fair Naomi" contains barely *thirty* seconds of explanation about the significance of the event being celebrated. In addition, it is important to note that the celebration is for Naomi and not Elena, despite that most *quinceañera* celebrations honor Latina/Latin American girls. It could also be that the *quinceañera* has reached a level of generalizability and flexibility in U.S. culture such that is accepted as a Latina event that can be celebrated by anyone. Or it could also be that thirty seconds of explanation is enough explicit pedagogy given that it is a show for young audiences.

Through this representation of a *quinceañera* that falls between weightless and ambiguous flexibility, Disney attracts Latinx audiences, while retaining its broader white audiences. This television episode allows Disney to soothe and smooth over fears about difference, in line with the practice that Joseph (2018) calls "strategic ambiguity" (p. 21). In this series, strategic ambiguity works alongside the blending of can-do girlhood discourses with Elena's domesticity and ability to nurture.

Although not exactly a *quinceañera* celebration, Elena's coronation is a momentous occasion in Avalor and marks a significant transition that she has been working toward throughout the series. Elena's "Coronation Day" (season 3, episodes 29, 30, and 31) concludes the series and is divided into three episodes that aired on August 23, 2020. This series finale showcases Elena working her way through a journey during which where she must prove by completing multiple tasks that she is worthy of becoming queen of Avalor. As the quote from Craig Gerber at the opening of this chapter indicates, Elena's story was written as a coming-of-age tale from its inception. According to Gerber, from the moment they began working on the series, it was understood that Elena would undergo a transition throughout the narrative that would ultimately lead to her becoming queen, leaving behind the realm of princesshood. Elena's transition from princess to queen can be understood in comparison to the symbolic transition, which takes place during the *quinceañera* (the passage from girl to woman). Elena transitions from princess to queen at the age of twenty (Elena's twentieth birthday coincides with her coronation day), leaving behind princesshood as well as her teenage years.

Episodes leading up to the coronation show Elena struggling with the thought of becoming queen. She wrestles with many conflicting feelings about whether she is ready for such an enormous role. Elena must complete a series of tasks to prove that she can handle being a queen. This plotline is consistent with other *quinceañera* or coming-of-age narratives in which there is a pivotal moment for the girl signaling her growth or readiness to take on a new role in life. As is typically the case, Elena showcases her fears and emotions through the musical numbers. The inclusion of self-doubt in the narrative ultimately comes down to her fear that she will not live up to her late parents' wishes or that she will not rule as well as they had. Elena is unsure of how to rule or fit the specific role of queen. This is in harmony with other coming-of-age princess tales in which the girl/princess must learn to exist in a new capacity by going through a postfeminist tween makeover journey, during which one of her ultimate tasks is to stay true to herself as she transitions into her new role (Kennedy, 2018).

After an action-packed scene in which Elena tries to defeat an evil force in Avalor, she is transported to the spirit world (an occurrence that is not limited to just the Día de los Muertos episodes). Elena must undergo the ultimate test with the Grand Macaw, the ruler of the dark side of the spirit world, who will allow her to be granted access back to Avalor. The Grand Macaw is having a large party when Elena and Ash (the antagonist) arrive. To the beats of a hybrid reggaeton and tribal music in the background, the Grand Macaw informs Elena and Ash that he will send one of them back after they face one another in a round of olaball (the Aztec-inspired game referenced in the introduction to this book). During the game, Elena realizes that to successfully rule Avalor she must let go of her desire to avenge her parents' murder. When Elena returns to Avalor after having successfully completed the challenge, she is finally ready for her coronation. Through her journey to the spirit world, she learned how to rule, how to love, how to forgive, and most importantly, how to harness these changes from within. After Elena forgives her cousin Esteban for his role in her parents' death, she tells Cahu (another antagonist in the series), "We may not be able to change the past, but if we can change ourselves, we have the power to change the future." This culminating message resonates with Banet-Weiser's (2015) "neoliberal capitalism" (p. 190) solutions, where girls must resolve a crisis through individual (instead of social) solutions. With this culminating neoliberal message of individual change, the audience is transported to the actual coronation celebration, which is almost identical to mediated *quinceañera* celebrations in popular culture.

The coronation is the actual embodiment of Elena's personal growth and individual change. During the ceremony, she dances her first dance with her *abuelo* (almost identical to the *quinceañera* father–daughter dance), is crowned on the throne (like the *quinceañera* changing of the shoes), and includes her family and friends as central components in the ceremony (again, similar to a *quinceañera*).[12] This family-oriented celebration is actually much more like a *quinceañera* than Naomi's *quinceañera* in the first season. The coronation clearly acknowledges and celebrates a huge transition for Elena, unlike the Naomi *quinceañera* episode. Although originally it seemed as though we would not see Elena celebrate her *quinceañera*, the coronation episode contains all the characteristics of most mediated *quinceañera* celebrations, particularly the coming-of-age narrative and the culminating dance-filled celebration. However, the event never calls out or references *quinceañeras* and is malleable enough to stand in for any type of coming-of-age celebration. The coronation episode thus falls under the category of ambiguous flexibility on the continuum.

HANUKKAH

The last celebration in this celebration analysis is Hannukah. Hannukah is not one of the most prominent celebrations used to represent Latinidad in the media, but in "The Festival of Lights" (*Elena of Avalor*, season 3, episode 17, December 6, 2019), Disney includes it within the world of Avalor. A few months before this episode premiered, Disney and other outlets reported that Disney would soon introduce its first Jewish Latina princess (and first Jewish princess for that matter).[13] Reports noted that Rebecca would be voiced by Jamie-Lynn Sigler (Stump, 2019) and that this would be Disney's first showcasing of a royal Jewish character (Kaplan, 2018). The episode centers on the story of a royal family that becomes shipwrecked off the coast of Avalor as they are trying to make their way to Galonia, their kingdom, for their Hanukkah celebration. When Elena and her family rescue them and hear their story, they ask what Hanukkah is. Rebecca immediately explains the holiday and many other terms and traditions that go along with it. The episode serves a pedagogical purpose for its young viewers, who learn about the holiday and the religion. The carefully constructed explanations surrounding Hanukkah are like those surrounding Día de los Muertos in "A Day to Remember" (the first Día de los Muertos episode). The explanations about the holidays are done through song and performed by the princesses. Disney uses the same template for both holiday songs. The explanations provided in "The Festival of Lights" are a bit lengthier, and the explanations about the Yiddish words are also more prominent than those for Spanish words, almost always used in the series without any translation. In so doing, Disney attempts to normalize Latinidad by hollowing out its signifiers. Disney presents these signifiers in deterritorialized contexts yet articulates them to a princess whose Latinx signifiers are messy. Nonetheless, in this episode Disney attempted a transnational and transreligious episode, a moment of rupture wherein Latinidad was allowed to be pan-religious.

The episode and the character of Rebecca were advertised as Disney's first Latina Jewish portrayals, but the episode focuses on Hanukkah and detaches Jewishness from Latinidad. While viewers are supposed to understand Avalor as Latinx, we know from the first five minutes of the episode that this family is not from Avalor, but instead from a kingdom that Elena does not seem to know much about. In this way, the series positions Galonia and the Jewish Latinx community that potentially lives there as foreign to Avalor. The plot revolves around the preparation of yet another holiday celebration—Hanukkah. Rebecca explains how sad she and her brother are because they will not be able to give their grandmother (referred to as "Bubbe" throughout the episode) the Hanukkah celebration she deserves. Elena, of course, is determined to host an elaborate celebration in Avalor to honor this holiday (which she seemingly knows nothing about). Disney explains the meaning of the celebration, along with songs, dances, and terminology. In fact, throughout the episode, Rebecca and her brother educate Elena on the meaning of Hanukkah and its layered significance for Jewish people. They also translate many Yiddish words. While these explanations are important for educating non-Jewish viewers, within the grand narrative of the series, these extensive explanations for just one holiday create a normalization of Latinidad and an othering of Jewishness (as if these were always separate entities). Further, this attempt to normalize the Latinidad and detach it from any deep meaning (in terms of rituals, holidays, and celebrations), stretches Mexican, Latin American, and Latinx signifiers, thinning them out and not providing as much reverence, care, and exposition for them.

Once again, food becomes a driving force in this episode, and Elena's *abuela* quickly learns how to make *bimuelos* and latkes for the event.[14] When Rebecca tries *abuela*'s *bimuelos* she immediately approves. When Elena tries them, she notes that they taste "kind of like our buñuelos," to which Rebecca replies, "and sound kind of like them, too." Rebecca demonstrates that she does not know what *buñuelos* are, thus signaling a moment at which Disney could have stepped in to bring together her Jewish heritage along with her Latinidad, to display an intersectional representation of Latinidad where it is explicit that Rebecca is a Jewish Latina and

Figure 11. Elena and her family celebrate Hanukkah with Rebecca's family in "The Festival of Lights" episode (*Elena of Avalor*).

not just a Jewish person who is unaware of the existence of different types of Latin American foods. Even though many of the details do not fall into place as perfectly as Rebecca would have liked them to, *Bubbe* is quite pleased with the result of the Hanukkah celebration and with her new Avaloran friends. The last scene of the episode shows both families celebrating Hannukah together at the table, with the sunset behind them.

Although I initially categorized this episode within transformational flexibility, I rethought my categorization after reading about the backlash it received. It is important to note how positionality comes into play in these types of analyses. Not only am I not Jewish, I am also not entirely familiar with Jewish traditions and celebrations. After viewing the episode three times, I felt as though it was indicative of a rarely seen representation of Latinxs as Jewish. After examining various opinion pieces about the episode, though, I realized the representation was a bit more complex than that. In an article for *The Jewish News of Northern California*, for example, Eilath (2019) notes that "Disney blew it with their first Jewish princess." The most prominent points made here are about the use of terminology and language. Eilath notes that given the series' reference to Galonia, it would make sense for Rebecca and her family to be Ladino-speaking Sephardic Jews. However, the terminology the characters use is Yiddish. He explains that "it's disappointing to see that the writers of the show did not attempt to incorporate Ladino or Judeo-Arabic into the languages introduced on the show, and that they defaulted to what has unfortunately become the norm in America of using Yiddish as the catch-all Jewish language" (2019). Eliath's observation is reminiscent of many instances throughout the series where Disney flattens difference by using Latinx stereotypes. The episode also mixes Sephardic (*bimuelo*), with Ashkenazi (latkes) Jewish traditions.

The Jewishness in *Elena of Avalor* is flattened, like so many elements of Latinidad in the series. Other opinion pieces similarly note that many Sephardic Jews were upset by the Yiddish terminology used in the episode, although they did appreciate the representation (Aroeste, 2019; Stevenson, 2019). It is also important to note that despite its messiness (and perhaps inaccuracy), this representation is only available via a "flash," as Valdivia (2021) puts it. Rebecca and her rich Jewish traditions form part of one twenty-two-minute episode of one Disney series. Following this episode, Rebecca appears in a few other episodes elsewhere in the series, but only briefly, in a flash. Given the uniqueness of the Jewish Latina princess and the mixture of so many Jewish markers within the episode, "The Festival of Lights" exists between hybrid flexibility and transformational flexibility.

NEGOTIATIONS AND CONTINUUMS

I began this chapter operationalizing flexibility through a continuum to indicate that flexibility is not stagnant but rather always in motion. Sometimes the flexibilities that I highlight fall squarely within one of the categories on the continuum, while at other times they are located between two. It is important to mention that the flexibilities present in the series reside within an animated program targeting a preschool audience. Often, I locate instances where the series does not dig deeply into the significance of an event or holiday. However, we must step back here and ask ourselves how much of this can be included in a series for preschool children, a series that does not purport to be educational programming. Many moments obfuscate the rich significance of cultural events, but how can content creators highlight these in more layered ways within children's programming? How can this be done within the scope of a thirty-minute (or less) episode? What elements must be negotiated?

One of the key strategies that I found in this series is that the stories often default to the affective mode. Instead of highlighting the intricacies of the events celebrated or the rich histories that make up the holidays, the series highlights themes of family, friendship, love, happiness, and fun. In fact, many of the celebrations turn into a "festival of love." While most festivals contain some element of love to a certain extent, this strategy makes it challenging to locate specificities of the celebrations. By incorporating these strategies, I argue that through *Elena of Avalor*, Disney promotes what Joseph (2018) calls "strategic ambiguity" (p. 21) by engaging patterns of representation that vacillate between weightless specificity and ambiguity, with a stronger emphasis on the ambiguous ethnic image, and sometimes sprinkling in a rupture or flashpoint. The conglomerate can therefore court multiple audiences and soothe fears about difference, especially by relying on highly overused representations to stand in for specificity. Joseph (2018) asserts that strategic ambiguity involves "foregrounding cross-over appeal, courting multiple publics . . . and smoothing and soothing fears of difference" (p. 3). *Elena of Avalor* serves all these purposes by highlighting a brave Latina princess whose Latinidad is not contextualized, but rather flexibly deployed along a continuum. Although

Joseph conceptualizes strategic ambiguity as a type of performance by racialized women to court many publics, Disney similarly uses this tactic to create a Latina princess and other nonwhite characters.

Additionally, as noted in chapter 2, Disney reinforces the supposed Latinx setting and further signifies Elena's Latinidad outside of the series. Disney Channel's YouTube channel, for example, features dozens of videos explaining the inspiration for cultural representations in the series. Most of these clips contain some type of mention of or reference to Latinidad, Latinx culture and heritage, Hispanic influence, and Latin America, used interchangeably. Using these interchangeably, however, points to Disney's ambivalence about ethnic representation, as highlighted by Valdivia (2020) when she notes that "Disney produces an *unambivalent structure of ambivalence* within its narratives and global marketing through representing some characters and situations as ethnically ambiguous and simultaneously unambiguously ethnic" (p. 74; emphasis in original). I argue that through *Elena of Avalor* Disney achieves this structure within one series. The company does this not only by conflating Latinidad, Latinxs, Latin America, and Hispanic culture but also by including various types of flexibilities in the episodes, which leads to the construction of a strategically ambiguous character and kingdom that will attract many publics.

In this animated series, Disney's overused Latinidad celebrations work hand in hand with postfeminist girlhood representations. Disney created Elena to be a leader and a role model for children (Amatangelo, 2016). By experiencing many challenges and adventures, Elena learns to rule her kingdom as she comes of age. Disney thus positions her as a member of the third stage of spunky can-do Disney princesses. Elena exhibits no interest in finding a romantic partner, develops leadership skills, and performs impressive physical feats that fall in line with can-do girlhoods and popular feminism (Banet-Weiser et al., 2019). Elena is constructed as a "flexible and self-realizing" princess (Harris, 2004, p. 2). The series also highlights the zany can-do postfeminist STEM girl through the character of Elena's sister, Isabel. Drawing on Harris (2004), Leon-Boys and Valdivia (2021) find that the "can-do girl has morphed into a postfeminist neoliberal tween and pre-tween protagonist, whose individualist exertions function within a domestic and adolescent social space" (p. 220). Kapurch and Smith (2018) theorize "make-do" girlhood in popular culture as oscillating between girls/princesses. They note that this girlhood is represented in ways that showcase physical strength and intelligence, while foregrounding their primary activities as domestic, including "household work, gardening, and the care of animals" (p. 69). A version of the "make-do" girl is present through both Elena and Isabel. Elena's postfeminist can-do (and "make-do") spirit is highlighted via a reduction of feminist ideals grounded in weightless feminism often located within discourses of domesticity and caregiving.

CONTINUITIES AND RUPTURES

Although *Elena of Avalor* contains plenty of moments that fall in line with stereotypical representations of girlhood and Latinidad, the series also highlights many instances that veer away from these. After all, the series is supposed to highlight a princess who is "ready to rule," and not one who is ready to find a romantic partner. These examples showcase Elena's positioning far away from the less agential princesses of decades past. Two of the most prominent instances that offer an alternative construction of girlhood and Latinidad are the Hanukkah celebration, located close to transformational flexibility, and the existence of Isabel as a girl inventor, a representation within the zone of transformational flexibility. Albeit not entirely groundbreaking, these instances and the discourses that follow them throughout the series provide small ruptures in mainstream representations of Latinidad. As previously discussed, I interpret these moments to be a type of "symbolic rupture" (Molina-Guzmán, 2010), but I employ this term to refer to the media text, separate from any type of audience interpretation. By doing so, I also call upon Valdivia's (2021) "flashpoints of intersectional visibility" to account for the moments in the text itself where mainstream media inch away from the more weightless tropes, although only momentarily, through a "short-lived presence" (p. 139). The *Elena* series provides a few such instances.

The Hanukkah episode provides an image of Latinidad unlike the ones we get through the Día de los Muertos skeletons or the Navidad posadas. Here we see a Jewish Latinidad, which is not prevalent in media representations. Similar to Disney's attempts at showcasing a Latinx family through the live-action series *Stuck in the Middle* (Leon-Boys & Valdivia, 2021), the Jewish Latinidad in this Hanukkah episode does not live beyond the advertisements and promotional materials. Rebecca's Jewishness appears to be detached from her Latinidad. We see Elena's family and Rebecca's family functioning alongside each other as different, with no points of intersection (other than affection and food sharing). In this way, the episode provides both continuities and ruptures. The Jewish faith is othered, while the Latinidad (and implicit Catholicism) is normalized.

Like this representation of Jewish Latinidad, *Elena of Avalor* also provides some divergent instances of tween can-do girlhood. These instances, however, are more than mere flashes and appear throughout the three seasons. While it can be argued that Elena herself is the epitome of the can-do girl, she is often in need of rescuing. When she needs help, Elena is rescued by her best friend Naomi, the royal wizard Mateo, her grandparents, or one of the royal guards. She frequently thanks them and makes it very clear (through the dialogue) that they saved her. Also, as previously explored, Elena consistently displays markers of traditional femininity, which end up taking center stage over her strength and physical abilities. Unique to the series, however, is the character of Isabel, Elena's younger (tween) sister. Although not publicly thanked as often as the characters mentioned above, Isabel often ends up saving the day more subtly. It must be noted, though, that many of the times when Isabel comes to the rescue, it is because she messed something up originally or one of her inventions ruined something for Elena or the kingdom.

Isabel's character presents a rupture because the can-do girlhood here resides within a younger child, a tween. Isabel, voiced by Jenna Ortega, forms part of a more recent Latina girl trope, the zany can-do STEM girl (Leon-Boys, 2021a; Leon-Boys & Valdivia, 2021), although this trope resides almost exclusively within teenage girl-hood (not among women or tweens). Within the terrain of teenage girlhood, this representation has almost entirely transitioned from rupture to trope. In this series, though, since Isabel is much younger than the usual teenage STEM inventor, she provides a rupture. Isabel's character is almost identical to Jenna Ortega's role in the Disney live-action series *Stuck in the Middle* (2016–2018). Isabel is an inventor, skilled at both math and science. In fact, in the second season of the series, Isabel secures a position as a student at Avalor's prestigious Science Academy, where she is the youn-gest person in attendance. Throughout the three seasons of the series, Isabel is either creating new inventions or working on existing ones. Although she does create quite a lot of chaos with her inventions, they often end up saving everyone.

The first episode of season 3, "Sister of Invention" features Isabel attempting to prove that she is old enough to aid Elena and her crew in their various missions to take down two villains, Ash and Carla. Isabel is often ignored or overlooked due to her age, but in this episode, she is determined to prove that she is worthy of being included. From the first few seconds of the episode, Isabel's intelligence is highlighted as the family toasts her because she has just completed her (college-level) engineering class with honors. As Elena, Mateo, Naomi, and Gabe prepare to go to a cabin in the woods to set a trap for Ash and Carla, Isabel pleads with them to let her join. She argues that she can help them because she has just com-pleted a college course and her inventions could prove useful. After Elena denies her request, Isabel changes into a green jumper, packs her bags, and hides under the carriage. Elena changes into her adventure jeans and once the team arrives at its destination, Elena becomes upset when she realizes Isabel has sneaked onto the carriage and joined them. Not only does this upset Elena, but Isabel's presence is what ultimately prevents the rest of the crew from capturing Ash and Carla.

Although Isabel gets in the way at the cabin, she soon finds remnants of a blue pumice, which she informs them only grows in Xotep, a volcano in central Avalor. The name Xotep is reminiscent of a major train station, Xotepingo, in Mexico City. This practice is consistent with the series' quest to strive for authenticity through naming. Often, names are firmly situated within Mexico or Mexican references rather than any other parts of Latin America. When Isabel shares her findings with everyone, they realize that the villains must be hiding in Xotep and decide to set out in that direction. Elena is still upset with Isabel but realizes they must bring her with them because taking her back to the castle would be too time consum-ing. The blue pumice sighting is like many situations in the series. Often, Isabel clumsily destroys things because of her inventions, but this havoc causes other (more pressing) issues to come to the forefront. Isabel's finding the blue pumice, albeit a subtle ten-second scene, is what leads the team to the villains' lair.

Once they all arrive, everyone but Isabel goes to Xotep to find Carla and Ash. Isabel is under strict orders not to leave the carriage, but again she disobeys these orders and makes her way inside. As soon as she is inside, Isabel trips Mateo and ruins his spell. Because of this small incident, Elena is left dangling from a cliff,

Figure 12. Isabel showing Naomi, Mateo, and Gabe the equations to her latest catapult invention in the "Sister of Invention" episode. (*Elena of Avalor*).

with nothing but lava between her and the rest of the crew. With not much time to spare, as Elena hangs on by the tips of her fingers, Isabel figures out how to make a catapult (out of rocks) to bring Elena back to the other side. She frantically jots down some equations on a piece of paper and shows the others her latest invention. Without missing a beat, Isabel creates the invention that allows Elena to work her way back to safety.

As she often does, Isabel saves not only Elena but also the rest of the team and allows them to get to the villains once and for all. This and similar instances throughout the seasons make up a large part of the storyline and are perfectly exemplified in the "Sister of Invention" episode. This representation of girlhood might seem weightless given that Isabel's zany antics often make her appear clumsy and underprepared, but beneath the clumsiness is a brilliant tween child who often saves those around her with her creativity and STEM expertise. Perhaps placing Isabel's brilliance inside a clumsy package allows the character to be more digestible to larger, mainstream audiences, but Isabel also provides a rupture that is more than momentary. It is a rupture in terms of both girlhood and Latinidad. In the culminating scene of "Sister of Invention," Elena finally agrees to let Isabel join the royal team and Isabel provides her much-needed assistance for the remainder of the third (final) season.

"Sister of Invention" highlights a moment at which Isabel's help and expertise are publicly praised. As noted earlier, Isabel often performs uncredited labor. The emotional and material labor performed by Isabel is like that performed by Naomi. Both characters often solve major issues for which they are seldom recognized. This division of labor falls in line with the postfeminist tendency to obscure labor in favor of beauty, dance, and performativity. We see instances of this as well when Elena supposedly solves a major issue, problem, or feud by singing and dancing. Before the dancing, though, many unacknowledged events take place that allow for a resolution. Additionally, the events or instances are often led by either Isabel or Naomi.

The episodes analyzed in this chapter highlight prominent themes and storylines in *Elena of Avalor*. Following the analysis of the production components of the series, the chapter has addressed the middle ground between production and consumption—the televised text. Elena and the other characters perform Latinidad through celebrations (which have now become tropes) and a complex, sometimes internally contradictory set of signifiers, which expand the narrative through a continuum of flexible Latinidad. The flexibility deployed throughout the series is often templated. The coronation episode, for example, is templated in accordance with *quinceañera* celebrations. The *quinceañera* is never explicitly referenced, but the episode contains all the markers of one. The same can be said for the Hanukkah musical numbers being templated in accordance with the Día de los Muertos musical numbers. Templates help ensure continuity. There are also moments when the templates extend beyond Latinidad to include postfeminist sensibilities, mostly situated within domesticity and caregiving. These overlap with the layers of flexible Latinidad as a way to understand the complex world of *Elena of Avalor*.

In addition, some moments within the narrative highlight newer versions of girlhood and Latinidad, which do not necessarily appear to be templated. Some of these are brief, while others are accompanied by ebbs and flows: sprinkles of flashpoints and some backward steps. As Valdivia (2020) reminds us when thinking through the possibilities for the future of Latinx media and the (im)possibility of a Latinx media utopia: "But then, this futurism is part of the definition of utopia—an ideal place always deferred, never reached: no place. This is not to say that gains have not been made, but that these are part of the implicit utopian road" (p. 157). As previously noted, moments of symbolic rupture and symbolic colonization will continue to be part of the process. Such moments are prevalent in *Elena of Avalor*. Long before the series' inception, Disney had high hopes for it. Indicative of these hopes, Disney allowed Elena to debut at Orlando's Magic Kingdom Park in August 2016, just weeks after the beginning of the animated television series. Unusually, Elena's placement and debut at the park occurred before Disney could gather solid data on the reception of the princess on the small screen. In the following chapter, I conclude my circuit of culture analysis by providing case studies of *Elena of Avalor* at the two U.S. Disney theme parks. The studies provide insight into the reception of this princess on the ground and how Disney positions this commodity within its various theme park spaces.

CHAPTER 4

On-Site Performance of Latinidad from East Coast to West Coast

Tengo una sobrina que le encanta todo lo de Elena. Pasan su programa allá en el Netflix de Sonora en español. Dice Ximena que le encanta porque es la primera princesa Mexicana. Voy a tener que llamarle a Ximena por el FaceTime para que vea que si habla Español también aquí en Disneylandia.

(I have a niece who loves everything about Elena. They show the series in Spanish on the Netflix in Sonora. Ximena says that she loves her because she is the first Mexican princess. I am going to have to call Ximena on FaceTime so she can see that she also speaks Spanish here in Disneyland.)
> —*Disneyland Park guest, summer 2018*

My grandmother asked me to practice my English today because we are in Cinderella's Kingdom.
> —*Princess Elena at Disney World's Magic Kingdom, summer 2019*

On February 8, 2021, shortly after the Tampa Bay Buccaneers won Super Bowl LV, Tom Brady and Rob Gronkowski exclaimed, "We're going to Disney World!" in a four-second clip uploaded to the Disney Parks Twitter page. This popular Disney marketing slogan has been used by Super Bowl champions and other athletes since 1987. The Walt Disney Company makes payment arrangements with the athletes well before the games (Wasko, 2020). As part of his Super Bowl LV victory celebration, Rob Gronkowski partook in a parade around Disney World's Magic Kingdom the following day, bringing together Disney and NFL fans. The Tampa Bay Buccaneers official Twitter page uploaded a picture of Gronkowski on a float with Mickey and Minnie with the caption: "The most magical place on earth" (Tampa Bay Buccaneers, 2021). To say that the cultural significance of Disney World (and Disney theme parks) is vast is an understatement. The theme parks are cherished places for many people around the world. As Fjellman (1992) notes, Disney World is "the most ideologically important piece of land in the United

States" (p. 10). Whether it is an NFL star celebrating on a float with Disney characters during a global pandemic or a critically ill child fulfilling their last wish via the Make-A-Wish Foundation, the Disney theme parks play a significant role via not only popular culture but also U.S. American culture at large.

Disney theme parks compose an essential part of the company's synergistic circulation of cultural properties. In December 2020, the conglomerate revealed its new plan to disclose key metrics differently beginning in February 2021. Accordingly, reports since February 2021 break down metrics in line with a new structuring system, which is organized under two main businesses: (1) Disney Media and Entertainment and (2) Disney Parks, Experiences, and Products (Walt Disney Company, 2020). With only those two categories, the theme parks carry significant weight in terms of generating revenue and must be understood and analyzed in this context. As large revenue-generating entities, they must further be understood in the context of the conglomerate's major revenue losses attributed to COVID-19, most of which fell under the category of theme parks and experiences (Scribner, 2020; Whitten, 2021). Given these major losses, Disney continues to be ever vigilant about theme park operations.

Theme parks offer guests a unique opportunity to encounter animated characters in live form in character meetings. Both children and adults can enjoy a temporary corporeal experience with their favorite animated characters brought to life by real performers. Aside from the rides and parades, this is one of the most popular and sought-after aspects of the Disney parks experience. In fact, some of the lines for the character meet and greets are just as long as those for the rides. Next to the iconic Cinderella Castle, the most popular photograph locations for Disney PhotoPass holders are the character meet-and-greet sites (Delpozo, 2019), at which park guests can chat with characters, take pictures, and enjoy their company for a short time. Although all the characters provide different experiences (in terms of location, conversations, and picture poses), the overall opportunity to interact with a Disney character at the park is very popular, unique, and highly sought after.

From 2016 until the COVID-19 theme park closures in March 2020, Elena held "meet and greets" with Disney park guests at both U.S. theme park locations.[1] Her appearance at both parks immediately after the launch of the *Elena of Avalor* television series illustrated Disney's ambitions for this princess. These objectives may very well have been backed up by focus group data before the debut of the princess on the small screen. However, at the level of the theme parks, the hopes came to a halt with the 2020 COVID-19 closures. Following the July 2020 opening of the Florida parks, Elena's only appearance was as part of the Royal Princess Cavalcade, a parade at Magic Kingdom featuring various princesses. A year later, after the California parks opened post-COVID, Elena was rotated from time to time through the new ten-feet-apart meet and greets with characters.

Having analyzed the animated series along with its most prominent production practices in previous chapters, we now move to the third node in the circuit of culture: reception. This chapter provides an analysis of Disney's control of the identity and lived transactional space of the princess in the zone where the company allows real-time interaction with audiences. I trace how people at the park interact with this cultural product (Elena). We know that Elena is part of Disney's strategic attempts to increase revenue and expand its audience through the representation of a nonwhite princess. But what do we know about how Elena interacts and engages with audiences in the live theme park setting? How is gendered Latinidad quite literally embodied in the California and Florida theme park spaces? What do these embodied representations simultaneously reveal about local and global understandings of gendered Latinidad? Further, how are audiences responding to this princess in the flesh? I address these questions by sharing my modified situated ethnographies, conducted at both Disneyland in California and Disney World's Magic Kingdom in Florida. In this chapter, I present my findings and highlight the significance of place in relation to the strategic choices that Disney makes about its theme park assets (most notably characters).

Modified Situated Ethnography

Conducting research at theme parks is no simple feat, especially when trying to capture the evanescent interaction between theme park guests and cast members. To trace various elements surrounding the inclusion of Elena at the parks, I had to develop a nimble methodology, consisting of a mixture of methods, which included pre- and post-digital analyses as well as on-site ethnography. This innovative method allowed me to analyze on-site performance of Latinidad by Elena princesses at both Disneyland and Disney World, alongside audience reactions to and interactions with the princess. Comparing the embodied location of the princess at the parks in relation to her digital park presence, this method engages a three-stage process conducted at both parks. Physical visits to the theme parks and two stages of digital data collection supplement this analysis. The process combines photodocumentation (Suchar, 1997), participant observation (Emerson et al., 1995), and critical technocultural discourse analysis (CTDA) (Brock, 2016) to study frequency and patterns at the theme parks, both digitally and on the ground. The study spanned the course of 4 days at both theme parks, along with 120 days of digital data collection. Elena's physical presence at the park, in conjunction with her digital representation through the Disney Parks mobile applications, illustrates how a major media conglomerate commodifies and tames complex hybridity in real time and in accordance with the *Elena* paratexts.

The first stage of my three-stage process consisted of extensive research on what I call the *representation of possibility*. At this stage, I analyzed *Elena of Avalor's* appearances via the Disney Park mobile applications, where I logged all of the princess's appearances, locations, and descriptions every day for a thirty-day period before my visit to the parks. During this period, I tracked how the mobile application represented the possibility of encountering Elena at each park, and once on the ground, I was able to trace whether these representations were consistent.

Tracking and logging these data also allowed me to understand the brief virtual discourses surrounding the princess.[2] I thus engaged in a type of virtual ethnography, where I adapted traditional ethnographic processes to online spaces (Hine, 2015; Kozinets, 2010). Studying theme park settings, now more than ever, necessitates analyzing the digital technologies that accompany the theme park visits, especially as these continue to play a more dynamic role before, during, and even after the theme park experience (Williams, 2020).

The second stage took place at the physical theme park, for twenty hours at Disney World's Magic Kingdom and twenty-five and a half hours at Disneyland, where I immersed myself in the theme park setting as a guest. During this portion of the analysis, I interacted with the mobile application, the princess, the park, guests, and other attractions simultaneously. Given my role within this project as an active park guest, I must also acknowledge my identity as a Disney fan. Like many media scholars before me, I approach this study as a scholarly critic and a fan. Further, part of my process in producing a self-reflexive theme park ethnography requires that I frame this study, and this chapter in particular, within the context of my role as mother to a young Latina girl (who accompanied me on both of these research trips). Given that central to my method was the task of remaining unobtrusive to protect my access at the theme park, I outwardly navigated my experience there as a fan and guest. I wore Disney clothing (a different Disney T-shirt every day), stood in line with other park guests, and attended the Disneyland park with my daughter and mother and Disney World with my husband and daughter. I should also mention that during the first day of the Disneyland trip, my cousins from Tijuana, Mexico, joined us for a few hours. These details inform my experiences and findings at the park. Further, I must note that I did not conduct any formally structured interviews or plan any part of my participant observation. My experience at both parks was organically guided by the events that unfolded on the ground. Additionally, my shared observations from the parks do not reveal the identities of any unknown individuals.

The third and final stage took place after my theme park visits and consisted of tracking Disneyland and Disney World's *representation of possibility* for *Elena of Avalor* for thirty days, to ensure a full circle of preproduction, production, and postproduction of Elena at the parks and virtually. This stage was meant to be a replication of the first stage. However, following my first theme park visit (to the California park) I was able to modify my strategy given my observations there. This modification consisted of tracking the *representation of possibility* multiple times a day, instead of once.

While there is extensive research on Disney theme parks (e.g., Bryman, 2004; Eco, 1986; Fjellman, 1992; Leon-Boys & Chávez, 2021; Mittermeier, 2020; Project on Disney, 1995; Wasko, 2020; Williams, 2020), this chapter examines how a specific character comes to life at the park and the types of discourses the character engages in as she communicates with park guests. It also takes into consideration how park guests react to the princess and her discourses during the character meet and greets. Research has demonstrated that audiences often read media texts differently from the ways that scholars do (Hall, 1980; Morley, 1993). Building on the existing body of work in audience studies, this chapter provides much-needed empirical evidence of how theme park audiences engage with the live embodiment of Latinidad at the two theme parks in the United States and how Disney implements differing strategies on the ground at each theme park location.

My ability to conduct fieldwork at both U.S. Disney parks gave me the opportunity to adapt my methodological approach. This strategy allowed for an empirical demonstration of Disney's positioning of Elena at both parks during the summers of 2018 and 2019. Further, my experiences at the parks were informed by my digital data collection via both parks' mobile applications. The distinct method also uncovered key differences at the two theme parks in terms of production, representation, and audiences. The themes highlighted below emerged from observations, conversations, and experiences with the princess, as well as noting her location and frequency of appearances. I selected the themes based on their frequency (i.e., the conversations or instances I discuss happened more than twice as many times as others) and to highlight the differing discourses between the Florida park and the California park. The ethnographic material presented in what follows demonstrates that the performance of the princess varies drastically from coast to coast. This finding suggests that the inclusion of the princess and Latinidad at the parks is malleable and ever changing, varying according to geographic setting, and dependent on other factors, which the conglomerate does not disclose.

DISNEY THEME PARKS

Disneyland opened its doors in Anaheim, California, on the morning of July 17, 1955. Sixteen years later, on October 1, 1971, Walt Disney World Resort in Orlando, Florida, welcomed guests on its opening day. Although Walt Disney died almost five years before Disney World opened, his brother Roy took over the creation of the Florida park and remained true to Walt's vision. Throughout the years, Disney themes parks have proved incredibly successful and have generated significant income for the company. Currently, U.S. ticket prices stand at $133 per ticket (for one-day, single-park visits during the week), though the prices have occasionally dropped since the Florida parks reopened after the COVID-19 closures. Further, in 2017, Disneyland admissions were above 18,300,000 visitors (Theme Index and Museum Index, 2017). The 2019 Annual Investor Report revealed that by September 28, 2019, "Parks, Experiences, and Products" had generated US$26.7 billion. The report notes that "increase in theme park admissions revenue was due to an increase of 8% from higher average ticket prices" (Walt Disney Company, 2019). The Walt Disney Company Annual Reports document that Disney parks are lucrative, which prompted the company to expand, first nationally and then globally. From Disneyland's inception, this theme park experience was meant to be financially different from other parks of the time. Before the opening of the Disney parks, amusement park visitors would pay for rides and other activities separately, at parks with no entrance fee for visitors (Mittermeier, 2020). Disney revolutionized the theme park experience by charging a flat fee to enter the park (a fee that continues changing as the years go by). It is against this financial backdrop that the following analysis unfolds. In particular, the ethnography in this chapter focuses on U.S. theme parks.

Disney theme parks have always been, first and foremost, commercial spaces. As Wasko (2020) notes, "Disneyland was designed to recycle existing Disney stories and characters in another commodified form" (p. 171). Every experience and sensation at the park is a commodity. Here, visitors pay admissions and patronize shops, restaurants, and hotels. As Bryman (2004) contends, consumption is integral to the Disney experience and "to become a full participant, the visitor needs to consume" (p. 156). The entire theme park layout is carefully constructed so that park guests can consume and purchase along every step of the way. In ultimate neoliberal fashion, Disney disguises the commercial enterprise as fantasy, allowing visitors to believe they are playing while they are in fact constantly purchasing. Of course, this is not to say that the park guests are passive theme park visitors, but the strategic choices employed by the park creators ensure that park guests partake as consumers at every turn.

Although primarily consumption sites, Disney theme parks perform significant ideological work as well. Upon entering the park, Disney guests are exposed to a carefully constructed and sanitized version of the past, what Fjellman (1992) terms "distory." Here, historical unpleasantries are erased and stories of the past are told in a carefully (and commercially) remythologized form. Given that the original target audience for the U.S. Disney theme parks was primarily domestic (Colt, 2015b), the parks served as spaces in which U.S. tourists could collectively participate in the imagined community of the nation (Anderson, 1983). Of course, the target audience changed as Disney began to expand nationally and internationally, but the original goal of a cohesive U.S. vision is still central to the park experience (Leon-Boys & Chávez, 2021).

THE MAGICAL LABOR AT THE PARKS

Through the process of creating "distory," the Walt Disney Company controls the re-creation of the past, present, and future. The control extends beyond the creation of the "distory," however. The parks offer guests the ability to interact with their beloved characters in what seem like organic and unscripted moments, but every occurrence at the parks is strictly monitored and controlled (O'Connell, 2014). Everything inside the Disney parks' property is planned, nothing is a coincidence.

When visitors enter the park, they become "guests," a term that is part of the Disney parks' internal language and culture. Additionally, Disney employees are referred to as "cast members." For the remainder of this chapter, I use the Disney terminology. Disney cast members (everyone from the barista at the Main Street USA Starbucks to the meet-and-greet characters) are highly scripted and must follow performance and behavior rules (O'Connell, 2014). Therefore, the labor they perform on behalf of the company is invisibilized and rendered "magical" (Bryman, 2004). The invisibilization of the cast members' labor is highlighted by the use of seemingly unscripted moments between Disney characters and park guests. Here, lines are blurred between cast members and the characters through a process of "dedifferentiation" (Wasko, 2020), and this becomes a coveted component of the Disney park experience. Disney carefully creates a fictitious world in which the cast members never stop performing for the company (Project on Disney, 1995). Their constant performance is coupled with the affective and emotional labor necessary to sustain all that is expected of them by park guests as they become immersed in a make-believe world. If ever in doubt, cast members can consult their pocket "tell a cast" booklet with answers to frequently asked questions or theme park dos and dont's (such as instructions on how to wave or where to go if you become ill in front of a guest).

As previously mentioned, Disney placed Elena at both of its U.S. theme parks although it had little to no data about the success of the series. Placing Elena in the theme park after her presence on the small screen is a form of recirculation, as per the synergy typology developed by Meehan (2005) referenced in chapter 2. Elena's royal debut at Disney World's Magic Kingdom featured appearances by Cinderella and Girl Scouts USA, thus linking the character to Disney princess history and to a mainstream can-do girl organization that highlights girl power. Elena's royal theme park debut took place on the Cinderella Castle stage, which is reserved for prominent Disney events. The live debut featured Craig Gerber, the executive producer and creator of *Elena of Avalor* and *Sofia the First*, who mentioned, "It was very important for us that in creating Disney's first Latina princess that we create a fairy tale that was very relatable, that was based on authentic culture, that Latino audiences could watch and feel like they were represented" (Mauney, 2016).

The theme park location allows for park guests to have direct interaction with Disney characters and commodities. However, given that this experience includes actual human beings in person, the situation at the park is dynamic and relational. Building on the two previous case studies, this theme park chapter interrogates how Disney controls its products and their meanings at the theme parks. When guests interact with characters in real time, the conglomerate implements unique strategies in each of its theme park locations. In California, Disney deploys an Elena imbued with consumer femininity in relation to her Mexican identity and Spanish pedagogy, though for a limited time. While in Florida, Elena exists for extended periods of time, but avoids cultural specificity and promotes assimilation discourses. Using these tactics, Disney manipulates a character at the parks so that she is "relatable . . . based on authentic culture" yet appealing to all park guests.

Disneyland's Domestic, Spanish-Speaking, Mexican Princess

As I waited in line for *Elena of Avalor* to make her first appearance on July 22, 2018, at Disneyland's Fantasy Faire Courtyard, I met a family of three young adults from

Sonora, Mexico. The two sisters and their brother, all in their early to mid-twenties, chatted with me as we waited in line to interact with Elena at her designated location beside the purple umbrella by the Royal Hall. The first quote at the beginning of this chapter came about after one of the sisters explained to me why it was important for them to see Elena on this trip. Immediately after she overheard Elena speaking to other park guests in Spanish, she loudly told her family, "¡Miren! ¡Si habla español!"[3] Although throughout her account she made sure to tell me various times that she was waiting so that she could take a picture for her little cousin, Ximena, I got the impression that she was quite eager to see Elena herself. As she talked about Elena's bravery, the series' uniqueness, and the importance of a "princesa Mexicana,"[4] I could see that Elena was significant for her as well, not just for Ximena. The three siblings from Sonora, however, were not the only ones to refer to Elena as the "princesa Mexicana." I heard this statement multiple times during my two days at Disneyland.

This is not necessarily surprising given that California has a large Mexican and Mexican American population (U.S. Census, n.d.). According to the U.S. Census Bureau's data specific to the greater Los Angeles area, of the 48.5 percent "Hispanic" people in the region, 36.8 percent categorized themselves as Mexican, 0.5 percent as Puerto Rican, 0.4 percent as Cuban, and 10.9 percent as "Other Hispanic/Latino" (U.S. Census, 2020). Additionally, Disneyland is located just a little over 100 miles north of the United States/Mexico border and receives quite a few park guests from Mexico, such as the siblings from Sonora with whom I interacted in line. Disneyland sits outside of the Los Angeles metropolitan area, a region where white residents are the minority. Home to people from over 140 countries who speak 224 languages, Los Angeles has a significant Latinx population, at 49 percent (U.S. Census, 2020). My experience at the park for two days in 2018 illustrates how Disney incorporates its Latina princess into a geographical setting with a large Mexican population, a setting situated on the western coast of the United States, where a large part of the population is politically liberal (e.g., McGhee, 2020; Nelson, 2020; Sarasohn, 2018).

At Disneyland during the summer of 2018, Elena lived in the Fantasy Faire, which is nestled in the Fantasyland portion of the park, immediately to the left of Cinderella's castle (arguably the most iconic Disney landmark). Fantasyland depicts medieval Europe and the Fantasy Faire is a picturesque village that looks as if it came out of a storybook, though not specific to any one fairy tale. As is the case with Disney's thematic efforts throughout the parks, the goal is to achieve an emotional and affective response to the space, where the land (in this case Fantasyland) "exists for the time period during which the visitors inhabit that space" (Leon-Boys & Chávez, 2021). In this circular region, you can meet princesses at the Royal Hall, watch performances at the Royal Theatre, shop for princess trinkets at the Fairy Tale Treasure Shop, or take a picture in front of Rapunzel's tower. The Royal Hall is the most advertised portion of the Fantasy Faire and the one with the longest lines. It is a large, dimly lit building, where park guests take turns going inside to meet princesses. Elena, however, was not located inside the Royal Hall,

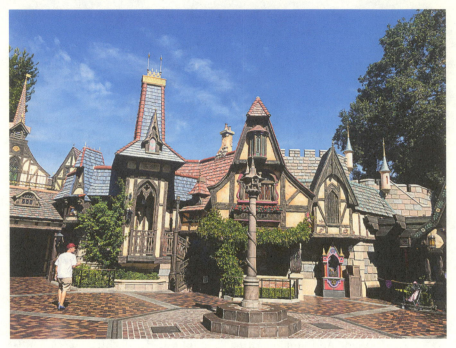

Figure 13. Disneyland's Fantasy Faire. Photo by the author.

Figure 14. View of Disneyland's Fantasy Faire including the blocked off Royal Hall due to COVID-19 protocols. Photo by Christopher Chávez.

but outside of the building, underneath a purple umbrella. She made appearances (advertised on the mobile application as five-minute sessions) under this purple umbrella a few times a day.

La Princesa Mexicana

Out of all the cultural texts analyzed in this book (production materials, television series, and theme park spaces), the California theme park was the text with the most prominent positioning of Elena as a specific version of a Mexican Latinidad rather than the all-encompassing pan-Latinx/Latin American character represented in the animated television series and promotional materials. Over the course of my two days at the park, I observed Mexican cultural specificity in the character of Elena, the references to her make-believe kingdom of Avalor, and how audiences reacted to her. The park location as a setting did not provide the same back-and-forth culture mixing that occurs throughout the series and its promotional texts (as analyzed in chapters 2 and 3). All too often the media implement various degrees of flexible Latinidad, as outlined in chapter 3. Nonetheless, the number of Mexican identities represented in mediated fictional settings is greater than other Latinx identities represented on the screen, and this resonates with the actual demographics in this country, where Mexicans make up the largest population (about 62 percent) of Latinxs living in the United States (Krogstad & Noe-Bustamante, 2020). Whereas the televised Elena incorporates other Latinidades, her embodiment at the California park does not allow room for much else other than Mexicanidad.

Elena at Disneyland was bilingual and communicated in Spanish anytime a guest initiated a conversation in Spanish. On our first day at the park, my daughter and I had a lengthy interaction with Elena during her first appearance of the day. Our conversation that morning concluded with my daughter asking Elena what she enjoyed most about being Disney's first Latina princess. Elena said, "Estoy muy orgullosa de compartir mi cultura, mi idioma, y mi comida."[5] As soon as she mentioned food, she turned to my daughter and asked her, "¿Te gustan los tamales o las enchiladas, princesita?"[6] These references to Mexican food serve to reinforce the findings from chapter 3 about food, media, and Latinidad. Although people in other parts of the world are familiar with, and consume, tamales, enchiladas, and even *pan de muerto*, these foods are considered Mexican staples, and the Elena at the Disneyland theme park articulates her Mexicanidad by referencing these Mexican foods at length, consistent with the television series. After my daughter answered her question, Elena explained, "Pues a mi me encantan las enchiladas y los tamales. Son mis comidas favoritas."[7] Not only does the Elena at the park reference Mexican foods, but she explains that they are her favorites.

During Elena's first appearance that day, she mentioned food on four separate occasions, and every time she referenced tamales and enchiladas. In the last instance, she mentioned a churro as well. I was not able to listen to all her conversations, but Mexican food was prominently mentioned, and almost every time, usually immediately after she mentioned the Mexican food, she explained that Avalor was teeming with "culture." She mentioned this to Spanish speakers and non-Spanish speakers alike. During one of her conversations in English with a young girl and her caretaker, both of whom spoke to her in English, Elena said, "I love teaching young girls about where I am from and how beautiful Avalor is. We have so many traditions that a lot of people do not know about." I was not able to hear how the young girl responded to Elena, but Elena cut her off by exclaiming, "¡Exactamente! Muy bien!"[8] She said this in Spanish, although it was not clear whether the young girl spoke Spanish.

In these conversations, Elena marked her status in Disneyland as an outsider. By positioning her culture as something she liked to "teach" others about, it is implied that the park guests do not share that culture. Within the Disneyland universe, Elena positions herself as an eternal foreigner, which is a common media practice when representing Latinx characters (e.g., Aparicio, 2003; Flores-González, 2017; Valdivia, 2020). Through Elena, the eternal foreigner status is tied to food and culture, which are firmly rooted within Mexicanidad.

Park guests also highlighted Elena's Mexicanidad. The Sonora siblings mentioned earlier were the first ones who referred to Elena as the "princesa Mexicana" that day. We had a long conversation as we waited in line for Elena that morning. When they told me they were from Sonora, Mexico, I asked if they watched *Elena of Avalor* in Sonora. One of the sisters immediately responded by saying, "¡Claro que si! La vemos en Netflix Latino America y esta en Español."[9] I also overheard another guest saying that she had never seen *Elena of Avalor*, but she knew she was the first Mexican princess. The following day at the park, when a different cast member was playing the part of Elena, a young girl was brought to tears during her encounter with the princess. I heard the young girl say, "Los regalos son de Mexico."[10] The young girl was wearing an Elena dress and had a small bag with gifts for Elena. From where I was standing, I could only see one of the gifts, a yellow bracelet. This instance provides yet another link between Elena and Mexicanidad: the young girl chose to bring her something from Mexico. Whether she was bringing Elena a gift from her home, her family's home, or a recent vacation location, she made a strategic choice to gift her something from Mexico.

Aside from the frequent references to Mexican cuisine and their constant use of Spanish, I also noticed that every cast member playing Elena incorporated Spanish phrases that are typically used in Mexico, phrases that some might even consider Mexican slang. During one interaction on my first day, one of the adults in a group of picture-takers asked Elena a question that I was unable to hear. Elena looked surprised and responded by saying "a poco?" "Poco" means little, but the phrase is commonly used in Mexico to mean "oh, really?" This is typically said in response to something unexpected or surprising. This was part of a conversation that had taken place solely in Spanish. In another instance, a young girl shared with Elena that she had ridden Space Mountain twice already, to which Elena replied, "¡Qué padre! Para la próxima me invitas!"[11] The literal translation for "padre" is father, but people use this phrase in Mexico to mean "how cool!" or "how awesome!" I overheard Elena use "¡Qué padre!" a few times during my park visit. These examples illustrate how the Elena at Disneyland speaks a specific type of Mexican Spanish, rather than neutral Spanish or another type of Spanish found in Latin America.

Not only was Elena communicating (quite prominently) at Disneyland in a language other than English, she was doing so primarily by relying on Mexican Spanish. As Llamas (2020) argues, Netflix Mexico productions are incredibly white, middle- and upper-middle class. Representations of Mexico tend to favor light-skinned upwardly mobile people and similar to this growing Netflix trend, representations of Latinxs tend to center on Mexicans and Mexican Spanish. This finding is not new (e.g., Dávila, 2001), but we continue to see an extension of it even on Netflix Latinoamérica. What we see happening with Elena at the California park is similar to how the media at large tend to represent Latinidad (as fixed Mexicanidad with olive skin). Furthermore, on the days that I was at the park, the women playing Elena had dark eyes and olive skin (in addition to the dark-brown Elena wig), thus reifying typical representations of Latinas. Though there have been recent representations that step away from this model (e.g., *Gentefied, One Day at a Time, Diary of a Future President*), the tendency to represent Latinidad as Mexican (with a very specific look) has a long history, and Disney incorporates this strategy at its California park. Here, the company acknowledges the majority present in the region and simplifies the performance of the princess within Latinidad.

Elena as Spanish Pedagogy

As previously noted, the Elenas at Disneyland spoke fluent Spanish and were eager to speak to guests in Spanish, even when it was clear that the guests did not understand what they were saying. In this way, Elena served as an educator at the Disneyland theme park during the times when I was there, representing the Spanish language in an easily consumable form. Although the women playing Elena are real human beings, the Spanish references they made are contained within the land of Avalor and the Disneyland theme park. Disney cautiously implements these strategies at their park locations, perhaps to gauge audience reception of the Spanish language, particularly at a point in our nation's history when Spanish is readily condemned (Reuters, 2015). However, it is important to keep in mind the location of Anaheim within the United States. As previously referenced, this theme park is nestled within majority liberal politics, which frames the decisions Disney makes about including Spanish at the parks. The location of each park contributes significantly to the decisions made within the park gates. It is highly probable that Disney conducted focus group analyses before bringing the princess to the park locations, and the conglomerate more than likely has continued to carry out this type of research following her establishment as a character at the park. This hypothesis is further strengthened by comparing Elena's use of Spanish in California versus Florida.

Shortly after my visit to California, I stumbled upon a YouTube video by Leo Camacho titled "Speaking Spanish with Elena of Avalor." Most of the content on Camacho's YouTube channel focuses on Disneyland. In this video, Camacho explains, "We are finally getting some representation on that royal front" (Leo-Camacho, 2017), referencing Elena's Latinidad and Disney's much-awaited representation of Latinx royalty. As soon as Camacho meets Elena, she tells him that she is learning how to rule her kingdom. Her strategies for being a good ruler involve being "kind and funny" along with "eating tres leches."[12] She concludes her royal tips by telling him that a final strategy for ruling properly is to "always practice your Spanish, too." She looks at Camacho seriously and says, "Spanish is very important," and then begins speaking to him in Spanish. She tells him that he must practice and gives him a basic Spanish lesson including how to say hello and introduce himself: "Hola. Mi nombre es Leo."[13] Their interaction concludes with them taking a picture. Once he leaves Elena, Camacho explains to his followers how important it is that she embraces her culture and allows others to embrace it as well. Camacho equates culture to language, and shares that he is determined to continue practicing his Spanish following his encounter with Elena at the park.

Although Camacho's experience with Elena was recorded, uploaded to YouTube, perhaps rehearsed, and even edited, I encountered incredibly similar experiences during my two days at Disneyland. In our first encounter with Elena, on July 21, 2018, she initiated her conversation with us in Spanish. Given that we were speaking Spanish quite loudly, it is possible that Elena had heard us. Instead of saying "hello," Elena looked at my daughter and asked, "¿Hablas español? ¿Si? ¡Igual que yo! ¿Como te llamas?"[14] We conversed for about one minute fully in Spanish, and then I asked her "¿Cual es tu parte favorita de ser princesa?"[15] She replied: "Compartir mi cultura y mi idioma."[16] The Elena we encountered at the California park highlighted her culture and language as central to her princess role. Additionally, she is the first Disney character at a U.S. theme park location to engage in full conversations with park guests in a language other than English.

Previously, when exploring her Mexicanidad, I highlighted a conversation during which my daughter asked Elena to explain her favorite part of being the first Latina princess. My daughter specifically asked the question as it related to Elena's Latinidad, and not princesshood in general. In answering this question, Elena highlighted her joy in sharing her "culture, language, and food." Language forms a central aspect of not only how Elena identifies herself in California but also how she identifies her importance within the Disney universe. Like Leo Camacho, Elena often conflated Spanish with culture, as she explained to other park guests her role within the theme park and Disney at large. In addition to positioning her as an outsider, Elena's Spanish is also used to highlight her "authenticity," consistent with Valdivia (2020) and Leon-Boys and Chávez's (2021) findings that language plays a significant role in the creation of mediated authenticity, even in theme park settings. By incorporating words, or brief non-English phrases, the media render characters and locations as "exotic" or "authentic," but always falling outside of the U.S. national imaginary.

By conversing in Spanish as well as by consistently using Spanish phrases, such as "gracias," "excelente," and "adios,"[17] Elena solidifies her roles as a pedagogical tool for non-Spanish speakers, and at the same time performs authenticity through language. She does not necessarily fulfill the role of educator for those of us who speak Spanish, but rather highlights a connection or a similarity. Even when she is addressing Spanish speakers in Spanish, Elena not only showcases her ability to communicate with us in our mother tongue but also provides a safe display of the language for people who do not understand it, consistent with Disney representational production strategies.

Although Disney has officially included Spanish at the California park, the conglomerate is able to minimize its use, or take it away, at any given moment. Consistent with Urciuoli's (1996) findings of Spanish use in inner and outer spheres, Elena's safe, consumable Spanish becomes a commodity at the Disneyland theme park location. Urciuoli notes that "languages other than English become ethnically safe when used in carefully scripted contexts: print and electronic media, emblematic language in festivals and parades, waiters with accents at ethnic restaurants" (p. 55). Urciuoli further explains that in the inner sphere, language (specifically Spanish) is messy and accepted mostly among members of the in-group. Language in the outer sphere, however, is highly policed and structured. As part of the outer sphere, the Disneyland theme park showcases Spanish through its only Spanish-speaking princess. The fact that the Spanish-speaking Elena is contained within the park, where Disney can mold her in real time, makes sense as a corporate strategy to avoid risk. Further, it positions a character who communicates in Spanish within the outer sphere of language policing.

Additionally, when Elena says, "Sharing my culture and my language," as her favorite part of being a princess, she is relating her role as a princess to her actual function at the park, beyond the role assigned to her on the screen. Therefore, Elena is explaining her role as a pedagogical tool employed by Disneyland to educate audiences (in this case, the guests at the park), about a specific culture and language, which are both understood to form part of a reality that is far away. This is an extension of the assertion of her authenticity through difference. This is unique to Elena, and Disney's first engagement with Latinidad in princess form, because she is one of a few princesses (if not the only one) to position her culture as her "favorite" aspect of being a princess, which she repeatedly states at the California park.

FEMINIZING LATINIDAD

During a meet and greet with a young woman from Tijuana, Elena spent about two minutes explaining to her how to pose for their picture. She suggested that the young woman pose with one hand on her hip and a slightly bent knee in front of her. She modeled the pose for her a few times and, after a few failed attempts, said, "Asi. Bien linda."[18] even though the guest did not model the pose exactly as it had been demonstrated. This young woman from Tijuana was my cousin and before we parted ways so she could head off to Adventureland, she mentioned that she did not understand why Elena was so invested in that specific pose. It was not until my cousin made note of Elena's insistence on the pose that I realized how often the character had done that with other young women and girls.

During that same meet and greet when my cousin was repeatedly asked to model Elena's pose, Elena complimented my daughter on her outfit and asked her if she owned any of her clothes. Elena asked, "¿Tienes ropa mia?"[19] My daughter interpreted that to mean clothing from the series or clothing featuring Elena on it, so she immediately responded by telling her that she had an Elena dress, Elena shoes, a scepter (the magic wand-like device that Elena uses to cast spells and perform magic), and a set of pajamas. The rest of their conversation focused on my daughter's dress, her accessories, and other articles of clothing that she owns, Elena- and non-Elena specific. Elena concluded the conversation by asking my daughter if she owned a lot of shoes.

Many of Elena's conversations focused on physical appearance and attire. Once again, on our second day at the park, Elena (played by a different cast member) asked my daughter about her clothing. Following a short exchange about my daughter's dress collection, Elena asked what her plans were for the rest of the day. Elena suggested that the next time my daughter came to the park, they could meet her sister, Isabel, and go to the Bibbidi Bobbidi Boutique. Elena did not specify what they would do at the boutique, but this is the location where young children (typically girls) undergo princess makeovers. According to the Disneyland Resort website, "With the wave of a wand, Bibbidi Bobbidi Boutique offers head-to-toe pampering for budding bluebloods suitable for even the most castle-worthy occasion" (Disneyland Resort, 2018b). Packages range from $64.99–$450.00 (plus tax). Elena's performance of femininity is clearly inflected by upper-middle-class consumer discourses. I further argue that Elena's strong emphasis on feminine consumption at the park frames her Mexicanidad and Spanish-speaking abilities in a package that is easier to consume. This is often the primary way in which corporate America understands and frames Latinxs: via our role as present or future consumers.

Lightly placing her hands on her chest might not seem to be such an extraordinary gesture, but when the gesture occurs repeatedly it is most likely not a coincidence but part of something larger. Both cast members playing Elena at the California theme park engaged in this gesture during almost every encounter with a park guest. Elena performed this rehearsed and staged position when displaying emotions of love or admiration for something or someone. This body language was identical for all cast members. In addition to the delicate positioning of her hands on her chest, she also engaged in a similar gesture when she lightly placed her hands under her face. These gestures create an aura of delicacy, a delicacy in her character that is not as readily visible via the version of princesshood we see in the series or the promotional materials. Elena's gestures and poses are almost identical to those described by Goffman (1976) as "the feminine touch" and "self-touching." Goffman notes that in advertisements it is more often women who are showcased delicately using their fingers to provide a "just barely touching" (p. 29) effect, evident when witnessing Elena barely placing her fingers under her face. Further, the "self-touching" that Goffman describes is supposed to convey "a sense of one's body being a delicate and precious thing" (p. 31), which seemed obvious when witnessing Elena lightly placing her hands on her chest.

Elena's body language and posture distinguish the princess at the park from the princess on the screen while aligning her with other Disney princesses through an emphasis on traditional femininity. The television Elena is much more in charge and ready to fight. She often engages in daring physical feats, battles enemies, and casts spells on villains. At the theme park, however, Elena does not reference these moments or engage in such physical challenges (the latter would probably prove difficult in a meet-and-greet setting). This differs drastically from characters such as Rey or Vi Moradi at Disneyland's *Star Wars: Galaxy's Edge*.[20] Elena's body language emphasizes traditional femininity (McGladrey, 2014), and much like the other Disney princesses at the park, Elena also uses a sweet, high-pitched voice. She sounds rather rehearsed and scripted as she talks about clothing, accessories, and sometimes about baking. Disney adds another layer of identification to Elena's Spanish and her overall Latinidad through this unambiguous, economically privileged femininity. The Elena at the park talked about cooking and taking care of her sister and constantly asked the young girls who greeted her about the clothing and accessories they were wearing. She also often encouraged the young children to shop or visit certain stores at the park. In this way, Disney positions Elena's prominent use of Spanish alongside a palatable, nonthreatening version of consumer femininity that highlights "domesticity" (Haralovich, 2017). Disneyland's Elena does not present the same qualities that mark her as strong and fearless in the series, proving that she is not a consistent figure of girl power in all her various iterations.

Although Elena's performance of femininity was consistent with those of other princesses at the park, such as Cinderella and Snow White, it was not consistent with the performances of femininity by the newer wave of princesses, like Moana or Merida, who often talked about bravery and courageous acts during their meet and greets. I argue, then, that one of Disney's most prominent strategies for achieving a safe and sanitized inclusion of Latinidad at Disneyland is by connecting Elena to traditional femininity and middle-class consumerism.

OVERREPRESENTATION OF POSSIBILITY AND UNDERREPRESENTATION OF PRESENCE IN CALIFORNIA

Feminization may not be enough for Disney to minimize economic risk in presenting its newest princess at the California park location. The above themes must be understood in relation to the frequency and number of Elena appearances at that park. During my time there, it became obvious that Disney limits and suppresses Elena's appearances, but the only way to fully understand how this works is through immersion in the Disneyland mobile application. As previously noted,

I tracked Elena's appearances both digitally and on the ground. Tracking and log-ging these data from the mobile application allowed me to perform a thorough analysis of Elena's appearances throughout the summer of 2018. During the first stage of my process, I tracked the *representation of possibility* for the princess. How-ever, when my digital findings from the previous thirty days met the theme park setting, a new situation unfolded.

I call Disney's strategy of featuring Elena at the park *the overrepresentation of possibility and the underrepresentation of presence* because through a perusal of the Disneyland app at the beginning of the day (early morning), Elena's appearances were overpromised, but after tracking the application I found that a significant number of her appearances were removed throughout the day, which was not con-sistent with my tracking of other princesses (such as Rapunzel). After gathering data during my initial trip to Disneyland in California, I found that Elena did not make as many appearances as the mobile application promised. Before my trip, I logged Elena's appearances at the park every day for thirty consecutive days. I only logged onto the mobile application in the morning (9:00 a.m., central standard time) and obtained my information once a day. Given my experiences at the park, I modified my approach after my return and began logging on multiple times a day. This modified strategy allowed for an empirical demonstration of Disney's positioning of Elena at the California park during the summer of 2018 and at the Florida park during the summer of 2019.

Working in tandem with the suppression of Elena's times at the park and also forming a part of the underrepresentation of her presence is her actual location at the park when she does make an appearance. Before arriving at Disneyland, I knew Elena's appearances would take place at the Fantasy Faire Courtyard, but it was not clear from the description on the app what section of the courtyard she would inhabit. The most popular princesses are the ones typically allowed to appear inside the Royal Hall. During my time at the California park, Ariel, Snow White, and Cinderella greeted guests inside the hall, and when I asked the royal attendants if Elena would move to the hall and when, one of them said that she makes appear-ances inside the hall "on rare occasions." Otherwise, on that day and most days, Elena greeted guests beside (or under) the purple umbrella outside of the Royal Hall.[21] Elena's existence next to the purple umbrella speaks to her underrepresen-tation at the park. Rather than living inside the Royal Hall all day with the most popular princesses, Elena is not only eliminated from the princess rotation on mul-tiple occasions but also relegated to the princess periphery (literally) next to the Royal Hall. Beyond her actual location at the park, Elena's appearances are virtu-ally overrepresented but physically underrepresented there. I noticed this during my first day at the park, before her first scheduled showing, and continued to notice it for the duration of my time there.

Once I returned from my California trip, my modified approach consisted of checking the application multiple times a day. When I engaged this strategy, I noticed a trend emerge. During ten of the thirty days, all but Elena's 10:00 a.m. appearances were removed. During five of the thirty days, her appearances were removed following her 11:30 a.m. appearance. Finally, during three of the thirty days, solely her 4:00 p.m. appearance was removed. Out of a total of thirty days following my Disneyland visit, the Disneyland application consistently featured Elena as a meet-and-greet character for twelve days, without altering or removing her times. This means that Elena made her advertised scheduled appearances less than half of the times throughout the end of July and most of August 2018.[22] This trend seems to further solidify my observations from the park concerning her underrepresentation in the flesh. On any given day, Elena might be advertised as a set meet-and-greet character (appearing four times a day), but she is overrepresented virtually and underrepresented in the live space at the park. I argue that Disney implements this strategy as it tries to figure out whether and how to permanently add Elena (and all that she represents) to the Disney park universe. During the summer of 2018, Elena's existence at the California park was dynamic. It consisted of an inclusion *and* an exclusion. The princess minimally lived outside of the Royal Hall, but she was unconstrained. Below, we will see how the inverse took place in Florida, where Elena prominently lived inside the Royal Hall, but was permanently constrained.

The Production and Consumption of Latinidad in Florida

Although the results of the 2020 presidential election were contested by Donald Trump and many of his followers, one fact that remained uncontested by parties on both sides was Florida's presence as a majority Republican state. Here, Trump won by over 51 percent (Calvan, 2020). This did not come as a surprise to most, but what appeared to shock many people was the Latinx vote in this state. In Miami-Dade County, for example, Trump "took 61% of [the] 482 majority-Latino precincts, up from 26% of them in 2016" (Tartar et al., 2020). Miami-Dade is almost 70 percent Latinx and the most common language spoken here, other than English, is Spanish. A large proportion of this Latinx population comes from Cuba and Venezuela (Miami-Dade County, 2020). Following the election, many headlines indicated surprise and shock that the Latinx voters had supported Trump (e.g., Medina, 2020; Navarrette, 2020; Torregrosa, 2020). The headlines and voting trends during the 2020 election are indicative of the fact that Latinxs do not represent a monolith. The Latinx vote is just as complex as are the various identities composing Latinxs in this country. Florida contains a very powerful Latinx assimilationist presence, of which the majority is conservative. As a new Florida resident, I have experienced a type of conservativism I had never encountered before living here (and I should note that I grew up in Texas, which is another incredibly conservative state). In terms of global theme park visitors, I must also account for the fact that unlike Los Angeles, where park guests often drive up from Mexico, Disney World attracts visitors from Latin America more broadly. Florida airports are often the gateway from Latin America into the United States.

It is worth mentioning as well that within the past fifteen years, Central Florida has become quite diverse. A 2014 Pew Research Center report that outlined clusters of cities in the United States with the largest Hispanic populations noted that "Miami-Fort Lauderdale-West Palm Beach, FL" was third with 42.9 percent of the Hispanic population identifying as Cuban, 9.3 percent as Colombian, and 9.3 percent as Puerto Rican (Hispanic Population and Origin, 2016). The same report shows that the numbers in Orlando look quite similar. The numbers fluctuate every so often, but the distribution remains consistent. Therefore, it is clear how Disneyland and Disney World are situated in vastly different Latinx spaces. In addition to the Latinidad present in Florida and the park guests coming from Latin America, I must also note that Disney World attracts a wide range of park guests internally from the United States as well. Situated on the East Coast of the United States, and firmly within the Deep South, Florida's cultural and political makeup is vastly different from California's. There are shifts over the years, but the Deep South tends to be politically conservative, although this can often be attributed to gerrymandering and voter suppression (Bullock & Rozell, 2012; French, 2018; Jones, 2019). As Mittermeier (2021) notes in her description of the inception of the Florida park, "The East Coast of the United States drew different demographics than Disneyland on the West Coast, including more international visitors. . . . The Magic Kingdom [then] had to deal with a different audience. This was reflected in its line-up of attractions, however cautiously" (p. 80). As soon as I set foot inside Disney World's Magic Kingdom in the summer of 2019, I was surrounded by accents from South Carolina, Georgia, Alabama, Mississippi, Tennessee, and so on, along with a variety of Spanish accents from all over Latin America. These geographic, cultural, and political settings are the background to the following analysis.

In June 2019, eleven months after my trip to Anaheim, I embarked on a research trip to Disney World's Magic Kingdom Park. I spent two days at the park, just as I had in California, and tracked Elena's appearances through the Disney World mobile application multiple times a day, exactly as I had during my third stage of data collection after my California trip. One of the most prominent differences I noted immediately after I started collecting the digital data for the Florida park was the overrepresentation of Elena in Orlando. According to the mobile application, during the thirty days before my trip, guests could visit Elena *inside* the Fairytale Hall for twelve uninterrupted hours. This stood in stark contrast to her underrepresentation in California the previous summer. Initially, however, I assumed that it was merely a digital overrepresentation (even though, after tracking the app multiple times a day, her appearances remained unchanged). Given the *overrepresentation of possibility and underrepresentation of presence* in California a year prior, I was not convinced that the Elena in Florida would be available for meet and greets for twelve hours every day.

Once I arrived at the park, however, I realized that this overrepresentation was not just digital. Unlike my experience in California the previous summer, in Orlando Elena was prominently showcased for twelve uninterrupted hours, coinciding with my digital findings from the thirty days before my trip. Additionally, Elena's twelve uninterrupted hours took place *inside* the Fairytale Hall, a location reserved for the most prominent princesses. Although the names are different, the

Figure 15. The Magic Kingdom's Princess Fairytale Hall. Photo by the author.

Fairytale Hall in Florida is the equivalent of California's Royal Hall. Elena is the only Disney Junior character that has ever been granted access inside Florida's Fairytale Hall. Typically, animated Disney Junior characters such as Doc McStuffins and Vampirina live in Hollywood Studios, one of the other three parks in Florida's Walt Disney World Resort. The findings from my research in Florida must be understood alongside Elena's overrepresentation and positioning at the park. Elena's presence in Florida, as in California, consists of both inclusion *and* exclusion. Elena is prominently highlighted inside the hall next to Cinderella, but she is constrained. The following outlines Disney's discursive—literal and ethnoracial—practices on the ground when there is a purposeful overrepresentation of Latinidad at the most popular park in the Walt Disney World Resort in Florida.

No Spanish in Cinderella's Kingdom

While I found that California's Disneyland produced a Spanish-speaking Elena, in Florida, Elena did not converse in Spanish or incorporate Spanish phrases into English conversations. Elena was a central park figure in Florida, but she was stripped of her abilities to speak Spanish. Disney provides the cast members playing Elena scripted lines to deliver to park guests about the use of Spanish. I witnessed the different cast members playing Elena delivering these scripted lines on more than seven instances during my two days of fieldwork. On one occasion, a young girl asked Elena if she spoke Spanish, to which Elena replied, "Si princesa, but my grandma asked me to practice my English today because we are in Cinderella's kingdom." A few hours later that same day, another cast member who was playing Elena answered a young girl who asked her a question in Spanish by saying, "I am going to answer you in English because I am practicing my English and practicing takes a lot of work." Most of these conversations centered on the importance of practicing English. These lines were uttered by five of the actresses playing Elena, further demonstrating the highly scripted nature of the theme park experience and Disney's strategic insistence that Elena not speak Spanish in Florida. In addition to the cast members' rehearsed gestures, such as the delicate touch of the face, these lines are part of the constant and repetitive labor the cast members must engage in (Bryman, 2004).

Inside the Magic Kingdom's Fairytale Hall, two Disney princesses stand alongside one another (you can interact with one first and then move on to visit the other) in one section, and the other section features two more princesses. During my two days at the park, and during the other thirty days before and after my visit, for a total of sixty-two days over the summer of 2019, the same princesses existed alongside one another inside the Fairytale Hall. On the right side of the hall, guests could visit Elena and Cinderella, while the left side featured Tiana and Rapunzel. As soon as guests entered the line, they had to decide which side of the hall they planned to visit (but many would visit one and then get back in line to visit the other).

The Fairytale Hall is located directly behind Cinderella's Castle in Orlando. The hall usually has some of the longest wait times in Fantasyland, often competing with *It's a Small World* and *Peter Pan's Flight* (both rides). Even during the park's Magic Hours, the Fairytale Hall usually has over an hour wait.[23] Yet again, Elena is a prominent attraction as part of the Florida park's Fairytale Hall. However, she is a prominent attraction who does not speak any Spanish, even when she is asked to speak the language by park guests.

During another instance on my second day at the park, a family of five waited in line in front of me. During their fifty-five-minute wait, I was able to hear them telling another family that they were visiting from Honduras. While they waited, they only spoke Spanish to each other, so I was eager to see how they would interact with Elena. Once they reached the princess, they not only spoke to one another in Spanish but also addressed Elena in Spanish: "Hola, Elena. Mucho gusto."[24] Unlike the Elena in California, this cast member did not respond to the family in Spanish. She responded by saying "Hello, everyone!" It was obvious after a few seconds that the family did not speak English. Given that the Disney parks attract a wide variety of international visitors, the cast members are more than likely trained regarding how to respond to and interact with guests who do not speak English. Elena continued to speak short sentences in English while taking pictures with the family and instructing them how to pose. Before they said their good-byes, Elena pointed at one of the young girls' shoes and exclaimed, "Beautiful shoes!" Then she slightly lifted her dress to show her shoes and said, "Look at mine!" With those closing remarks, Elena waved farewell to the family, not once having spoken to them in Spanish, but instead reinforcing the girl's presumed, shared femininity as the primary similarity between them. She had thus attempted to manufacture a positive interaction without relating on the level of race, ethnicity, or language.

Like the Elena in California, Elena in Florida was always eager to talk about girls' wardrobes or accessories. However, she never spoke a word of Spanish, and even when she was asked about the language, the different cast members playing the part delivered similar lines expressing that they would not communicate in Spanish and why. At the Florida park, Disney actively minimizes difference between Elena and the other white, traditionally feminine princesses and therefore between Elena and the heteronormative (often conservative) white audiences. The conglomerate does this not only by positioning her within traditional markers of femininity (much like in California) but also goes an extra step by eliminating her Spanish-speaking abilities. My analysis demonstrates that when Disney provides an overrepresentation of Latinidad at the theme parks, it produces a princess who is not scripted to speak Spanish and foregrounds stereotypical discourses of celebrations, which leads to a flattening of Latinidad. Although Florida is teeming with Latinxs, Disney strategically made the decision to constrain Elena's Spanish-speaking abilities.

Latinxs are not homogeneous. Voting patterns, politics, and cultural differences are vast within Latinx populations, particularly as they relate to views on assimilation. Focusing on an educational setting, Rosa (2019) traces the discourses surrounding language shifts from Spanish to English and notes that they are interpreted as signs of progress. He finds that "the goal for racially minoritized subjects is to supplant or supplement their perceived home language practices. These efforts toward the modification of racially minoritized individuals' linguistic practices are rooted in a troublesome accumulation-based theory of change that promotes the acquisition of cultural and linguistic capital" (p. 6). These popular discourses demonstrate how Latinx difference, and the racialization of Spanish, is linked to anxieties about race that are connected to language. To ease some of these anxieties, Disney produces a princess who is vocal about how much she practices her English, signaling linguistic progress and assimilation, to prove that she is a worthy guest in Cinderella's kingdom.

Florida, in particular Orlando, has a significant Latinx population and has become one of the top U.S. destinations for Puerto Ricans (Silver, 2013). The fact that Disney prevents Elena from speaking Spanish in Florida reflects larger politics of race and space. After all, it was just in 2015 that then presidential candidate Donald Trump chastised Jeb Bush, the former Florida governor, for speaking Spanish on the campaign trail. Trump said that Jeb "should set the example by speaking English while in the United States" (Reuters, 2015). Perhaps Trump's condemnation of a Florida man speaking Spanish was part of the backdrop influencing Disney's decision on whether and how to include a Spanish speaking princess. The stigmatization of the Spanish language in the United States goes back well before the Trump years, though.[25] As a foreign language, Spanish is often viewed as an asset or a commodity when taught as a second language. It is highly sought after in terms of improved global opportunities and marketability on the job market. Yet when spoken by native speakers it is often discouraged and becomes a threat or a marker of difference (Aparicio, 1998). Cepeda (2010a) perfectly explains this race- and class-based differentiation when she notes that "within this hierarchical framework, any usage of Spanish on the part of an upper-class, Anglo is hailed as a sign of cosmopolitanism, whereas Latino linguistic practices are deemed unsophisticated" (p. 32). Cepeda draws on Urciuoli's work to distinguish between the scripted/unscripted and the inner/outer sphere uses of Spanish (discussed above in relation to Disneyland).

Similar linguistic politics exist in California, but these are framed differently. The California park assumes that guests will be amenable to Spanish, but it does not allow the Spanish to appear for more than forty-five minutes out of an average fourteen hours, and this Spanish is strategically positioned on the periphery (outside of the Royal Hall). At both U.S. park locations, Elena's Spanish, or lack thereof, frames her as an outsider. Additionally, her use of Spanish is highly scripted and regulated. During the fall following my fieldwork in Florida, Elena was not featured as prominently at Disney World. Between September and November 2019, Elena sometimes did not appear for two or three weeks at a time. This demonstrates that Disney's inclusion of Elena, Spanish, and Latinidad at the parks is malleable. Further, the Florida park was closed from March 2020 to July 2020 due to COVID-19 restrictions. When it reopened in July 2020, the character meet and greets inside the Fairytale Hall had been canceled and were later replaced with the Royal Princess Cavalcade, which consisted of prominent princesses making their way through the streets of Disney in a socially distanced manner[26].

CELEBRATIONS IN ANOTHER KINGDOM

Elena's overrepresentation at Disney World is constrained within an overrepresentation of celebration discourses. Although this was also a recurring theme at the California park, the instances when Elena referenced celebrations were much more prominent in Florida.[27] During every one of my experiences interacting with and waiting in line for Elena (this included hearing conversations between other guests and the princess), I observed Elena mentioning or making reference to some type of celebration. Most of the celebrations that she mentioned took place in her kingdom or, as she would often say, "where I am from." Keeping in mind that Disney parks are often a place for celebration, this could influence why Elena mentions celebrations so often. However, this is not something I witnessed with any of the other princesses I visited at the Florida park (Cinderella, Tiana, and Rapunzel). Further, by explaining that these celebrations take place "where I am from," Elena confirms her existence as an eternal foreigner (Valdivia, 2020) in the kingdom of Disney, Florida, and the United States at large, just as she did in the California park.

The overrepresentation of the celebration discourses through Elena highlights the highly scripted reality of the theme park cast members. *Every one* of the women playing Elena in Florida during my fieldwork referenced celebrations. For example, during my first visit to the Fairytale Hall, Elena immediately asked, "What are you celebrating today, your majesty?" I responded by saying that yesterday had been my birthday, so I was celebrating "the day after my birthday." Elena wished me a happy birthday and said, "Celebrations are very important in my kingdom. We usually have gigantic celebrations when it's someone's birthday." Later that same day, another cast member playing Elena complimented a young girl on the bows she was wearing. Following her compliment, she said, "You know what would be fun? If we had a festival where everyone wears bows! Where I come from, we love festivals and all kinds of celebrations!" The following day, yet another cast member playing Elena referenced celebrations when she said to a young boy from Brazil: "Oh, you're here from far away too? Did you come all the way here to celebrate something? In my kingdom we have so many celebrations!" Sometimes Elena's references to celebrations seemed a bit out of place (e.g., a festival of bows) but were consistent with her frequent mention of celebrations in her "faraway" kingdom.

During my last interaction with Elena at the Florida park, I became aware of a conversation that happened with the guests in front of me in line. When Elena asked the guests what they were celebrating, they did not have a specific answer. They responded that they were there to "have fun" and a few of them talked over each other as they tried to explain what they were celebrating. Elena quickly jumped in and said, "Where I am from you can celebrate just about anything! Every day is a celebration! Our celebrations are so big!" Even though Elena's comments here resembled celebration overkill, minutes later she concluded her interaction with the guests by saying, "If you all ever come to visit me in Avalor we can have a big celebration with Avaloran chocolate cake for everyone!" This statement made two things very clear: (1) Elena enjoys and is a proponent of large celebrations (for just about any occasion), and (2) Elena is from a faraway kingdom, outside of the Disney theme park. However, the celebrations are not situated in Mexico or within prominent markers of Mexicanidad as they were in California. Instead of referencing *tres leches* cakes or churros as she often did when talking about desserts in California, the Elena in Florida offered no references to any type of Latinidad in her food choices. Instead, she kept it generic with a flavor known around the world (chocolate), although with historic roots to ancient Mesoamerica.

This discourse of celebration in faraway kingdoms did not take place during any of my visits with Cinderella, who occupied the other side of the Fairytale Hall. After every time that I visited with Elena, I would take a few steps to the left and begin my visit with Cinderella (this was the process for every other park guest as well). Cinderella also spoke at length about guests' clothing (especially with young girls) and asked the guests what they had done at the park that day. Sometimes she would talk about her mice or ask if anyone had seen her stepsisters outside. At no point, however, did I hear her mention celebrations or living in a faraway kingdom. Park guests are to understand that Cinderella's kingdom *is* Disney. After all, her castle is but a few feet away from the entrance to the hall. It is Elena who is a guest inside the hall. Elena must therefore prove she is a worthy guest via her assimilationist ideologies regarding language and place.

These examples are only a few of many instances where Elena (all the cast members playing the part) highlighted the importance of celebrations in her kingdom or "where I am from." By doing this, Elena not only reduces Latinidad to festivals and celebrations, a common media trope used to represent Latinidad (Dávila, 2001), but she also positions herself on the periphery, as an outsider in the kingdom of Disney. This could be a strategy used by Disney to flatten Latinidad to appeal to various nonwhite guests who also come from "far away." However, it must also be understood alongside Disney's long history of representing Latinxs and Latin Americans. Celebrations have always been a central component of Disney's representations of those south of the border, even dating back to *Saludos Amigos* (1942) and *The Three Caballeros* (1945). The plot for *The Three Caballeros*, for example, is a celebration for Donald Duck's birthday, consisting of multiple celebrations within each of the presents he receives from his "friends" south of the border. As Donald receives each present box, he hops inside and is transported to a new celebration. Such strategies to represent Latin Americans as friendly and nonthreatening (Goldman, 2014) continue to be reproduced many decades later.

In keeping with the tradition of celebrations and festivities, even in the animated series, Elena is often organizing celebrations or joyously dancing through the streets of Avalor. As noted in chapter 3, showcasing the Latina body through dance also falls in line with prominent representations in mainstream media, particularly in Hollywood productions (Peña Ovalle, 2011). Given that the Florida theme park attracts a large share of international tourists (many of whom are from Brazil), showcasing an Elena who loves celebrations provides a risk-averse strategy on behalf of Disney as the conglomerate continues to play with Elena's malleability at its U.S. theme park locations. At one point, when a young boy asked Elena (in Spanish) if she spoke Spanish, Elena said, "Yes, I do. My grandma says it is very important to learn a lot of languages so we can communicate with everybody. We have a lot of people here visiting from Brazil, so I am trying to learn Portuguese, too." Elena did admit that she spoke Spanish, but she did not even utter the word "Spanish" in her response to the young boy, and instead focused on another language (which the young boy had not asked about).

Just as was the case in California, the Elena at the Florida park is both included in and excluded from normative Disney discourses. In Florida, Disney forbids Elena to communicate in Spanish, but she is prominently showcased as a main attraction (that produces incredibly long lines). She is inside the Fairytale Hall yet constrained. In California, the princess is outside on the periphery, yet unconstrained by language. Further, if we understand the Disney kingdom as a stand-in for normative culture, Avalor falls outside of this terrain. By referring to her kingdom as external to Disney World and Disneyland, Elena contributes to her own "othering" within the theme park. Othering "is a strategy that reinforces the mainstream by differentiating individuals and groups and relegating them to the margins according to a range of socially constructed categories" (Valdivia, 2017, p. 133). Elena further solidifies her position at Disney World through her discourses on the importance of "practicing English in Cinderella's kingdom." Elena not only proves that she is a worthy guest in Cinderella's kingdom but also highlights the importance of "hard work" in maintaining a linguistic unity in this kingdom through English only and assimilation. By limiting her identification with Latinidad and simultaneously feminizing her, Disney World presents a nonthreatening, easily consumable Elena. The overrepresentation of her traditional femininity (practiced using consumerist narratives) and her frequent references to celebrations allow her to occupy this nonthreatening zone.

At all the theme park locations, Disney personnel are aware that many of the experiences at the parks can be unpredictable, and because of this, the conglomerate implements as much control as it can. It maintains tight rules and regulations for cast members to follow and conducts ample research at each of the theme park locations. Additionally, the conglomerate is not shy about ejecting guests who do not comply with the park regulations (e.g., Bartiromo, 2020; Brito, 2018; Roy, 2019). Disney executives often boast about their ample audience data. In fact, as part of the Disney Investor Day 2020 report on December 10, 2020, Bob Chapek (the current CEO) frequently referenced the "wealth of data" and "unique access" the conglomerate has to "consumer touchpoints across all businesses." In the same report, Kareem Daniel, chairman of media and entertainment distribution, also explained that the company uses all its consumer data "with the goal to maximize both audience engagement and commercial impact" (Walt Disney Company, 2020). The beauty of the theme park setting is that Disney can alter cast member decisions in real time, without adjusting too much (or any) of its media content. For instance, the conglomerate can adapt or change the language spoken by a certain character or adjust the script depending on the data obtained. Disney can even go as far as removing the character(s) altogether. The theme parks constantly go through updates and adjustments based on the data that Disney is eager to explain that it has, but never actually discloses.

The Walt Disney World Resort and Disneyland are both central components of the conglomerate's "Disney Parks and Experiences" business operations. As large revenue-generating portions of its operations, executives are careful about the decisions they make at these parks. At a superficial glance, the Florida and California locations might seem to be the same park operating on different coasts of the nation. However, this is not the case. Each park was created differently and operates within the cultural, geographic, and political landscapes present in its respective state. These discourses are further influenced by the types of tourism that each of the locations attracts (locally and internationally). My analysis here demonstrates that at the Florida park, Elena's existence and the discourses she perpetuates differ from her presence at the California park. Such findings allow us to understand that the inclusion of the princess at these parks is malleable, situated within specific geographic settings, and dependent on various unpredictable social and cultural factors. Further, the inclusion of the princess at the parks is best understood as part of Disney's recent efforts to include Latinidad across business sectors. Through a three-stage ethnographic approach focusing on frequency and patterns, despite key differences between the production and consumption of Latinidad at these two parks, this case study reveals a consistent positioning of this princess as an outsider in relation to the world of Disney.

Disney's creation of a flexible Latina on the periphery is not careless. The conglomerate is aware of the potentials and challenges of including the first Latina princess. Through my theme park analysis, I was able to back up Valdivia's (2020) claim that "introducing a new set of characters with relational attributes that do not take away from the moral high ground represented by whiteness yet expand tired stereotypes proves to be a difficult task" (p. 111). Indeed, the difficult task of whether and how to include Elena as a prominent park figure continues to plague the conglomerate. Following the COVID-19 park closures and the modification of the character meet and greets in accordance with evolving Centers for Disease Control and Prevention guidelines, Elena's appearances fluctuated more than ever. Elena's future existence within the world of Disney is even more questionable given that the series has ended, and she is no longer a princess, but a queen. Will Elena continue to have a presence at the parks for years to come now that episodes are no longer being created and produced? Perhaps the COVID-19 theme park modifications aided in the phasing out of the princesa of the periphery from the theme park lineup.

Conclusion

A PRINCESS FOR ALL IS A PRINCESS
WITHOUT A HOME

In February 2020, I began planning a trip to France after seeing many videos of *Elena of Avalor* at Disneyland Paris's Princess Promenade, and of Sofia from *Sofia the First*. In these videos, the princesses danced through Main Street USA to various songs from their respective series. Shortly after coming across all these videos on YouTube, Instagram, and Twitter, a friend of mine in Illinois mentioned that she had just spent three weeks in Spain over the winter break. When in Spain, her daughter started watching *Elena of Avalor* with her cousin (who lived in Spain), and the cousin understood Elena as *the* Spanish princess. Elena's presence at Disneyland Paris, along with my friends' comment about the princess in Spain, prompted me to plan a research trip to see how Elena was deployed and understood by audiences in Europe. The plan was to visit Disneyland Paris for three days in early April 2020. However, as we all know, the state of the world changed drastically just weeks before my anticipated trip.

In March 2020, Disney parks around the world closed their doors due to COVID-19. When Disney World (in Orlando) reopened in July 2020, Elena was not originally part of the reopening plans, which included a variety of safety precautions based on Centers for Disease Control and Prevention guidelines. The first phase of the reopening plans did not include character meet and greets for the initial few months. Since then, however, character meetings have slowly been reintroduced in the mix of attractions at both theme parks. At Disney World, for example, Elena appears from time to time during the Royal Princess Processional Cavalcade, a parade in which Disney princesses ride around the park on a float while waving at guests. A few weeks after Disney World's reopening in July 2020, the *Elena of Avalor* series came to an end with the culminating episodes of the princess's coronation. Now that Elena is no longer a princess, but a queen, her future existence within the Disney princess universe is unclear.

The Animated Girl as Outsider

This book has demonstrated that *Elena of Avalor*, as analyzed through production, text, and audiences components, is marginalized from the U.S. mainstream. In my three case studies, I tease out various moments of complex negotiations by Disney, producers, and audiences as they navigate flows of culture. The research here has charted a unique course for other scholars looking to engage in intersectional analyses of mediated Latinidad as well as for those interested in considering the dynamics of neoliberalism and postfeminism in the lives of young Latina girls. The case studies demonstrate that the princess and parts of her narrative might appear front and center on promotional materials, but her existence is tangential to Disney's normative vision of princesshood. Not only is her future within the Disney universe unknown, but so is her place of belonging. For my friend's niece, Elena and her kingdom represent Spain, for others she is a Mexican princess, and for some she is a mixture of a fictitious Latinx land. This flexibility allows a larger audience base to identify with her. This is precisely what Disney hoped for—a transnational representation that would appeal to a multitude of nonwhite girls and children. The princess at the Florida parks, though, makes it very clear that her home exists outside of Disney and this is also evident in the production and text components analyzed here. It appears that Disney planned for the transnational character and storyline to fall outside the scope of the "normative." This multilayered analysis of Disney's approach to mediated Latina girlhood interrogated the complex relationship between the largest U.S. ethnic minority and the global conglomerate that stands in for U.S.-America on the global stage. The analysis demonstrates how Elena's existence within the Disney universe is indicative of the overall presence of Latinxs in popular culture, media, and the nation. Not only do Latinxs continue to be portrayed as foreigners or outsiders, but these representations actually fall much more in line with peoples of Latin America and the Iberian Peninsula. As a narrative franchise, Elena is a perfect example of our existence on the periphery, eternal foreigners without a place to call home.

Although Disney worked hard to promote this princess as its "first Latina princess," Elena and her kingdom reside firmly within Latin American narratives and implicit geographic locations. Thus, not only is Elena marginalized from the U.S. mainstream, but the research in this book indicates that she is not a "Latina" princess. U.S. Latinxs and Latin Americans are not the same, yet the media conflate us to create an easily digestible and recognizable image for non-Latinx viewers. Whether at the theme parks, on the mobile applications, through the merchandise, on the screen, or via the corporate reports, it is to be understood that Disney is not Elena's home. In EPCOT, for example, Elena's merchandise lives only in the Mexico Pavilion. On the Disney parks mobile application, Elena's biography notes that she "finds inspiration in her culture and traditions," expecting audiences to understand that her culture does not fall within Disney culture, which stands in for normative U.S. culture. This book has showcased a key example of how Disney carefully produces a version of animated Latina girlhood that is intended to court domestic Latinxs as well as global nonwhite audiences, while not alienating normative white audiences.

This research intersectionalizes girls' media studies by extending feminist media scholarship to examine the intersection between age, gender, and race in relation to the study of girls and the media by focusing on a Disney text. Various iterations of this Disney text reveal a girl and her kingdom as external to normative culture. As girlhood studies scholars have previously argued, if girls' bodies stand in for larger cultural and social anxieties (Gonick, 2006; Harris, 2004; Mazzarella, 2020; Projansky, 2014), Elena and her fictious kingdom are representative of the larger discourses present during the time when Disney produced these episodes. This book should be read with that context in mind. To obtain a more holistic understanding of how this research fits within larger societal discourses, readers (especially those reading this text years after it is published) should situate the analyses alongside discourses present in the United States (and beyond) from 2015 to 2021.

LATINA GIRLS' MEDIA STUDIES THROUGH THE CIRCUIT

This book weaves together multiple disciplines, addressing issues in girlhood studies, Latina/o/x studies, Disney studies, media studies, and even childhood studies. I foreground two identity categories that are understudied—pre-tweens and Latina girls. Within this, I focus specifically on animated content aimed at attracting a young girl audience. Within childhood studies, specifically cases focusing on media, investigations surrounding nonwhite children and nonwhite characters continue to exist within the category of the "child." That is, there is almost no separation between girls and boys at the pre-tween stage. However, a separation in the research would make perfect sense considering that media (and consumer culture in general) target girls and boys in drastically different ways. Media attempt to attract girls and boys differently through programming, clothing, accessories, and basically anything that can be purchased. So, why not conduct research in a way that separates young girls from young boys? Additionally, the research in this terrain, which focuses on Latina girls is quite limited and almost nonexistent. This book extends, and continues to carve out the space for, the scant scholarship within Latina girls' media studies (Leon-Boys 2021a, 2021b; Leon-Boys & Valdivia, 2021). I productively push this subfield forward to examine the terrain of animation and pre-tween programming.

Taking a circuit of culture approach proved most useful for understanding how a transnational media giant deploys Latinidad at different levels pertaining to one narrative franchise. Rather than focus on various texts that purport to represent Latinidad, focusing on one narrative franchise, paying special attention to almost all its iterations, allowed for an incredibly in-depth study of Disney's latest negotiations and attempts to represent animated Latina girlhood over a four-year period. The circuit of culture approach, as explained in the introduction, allows media scholars to "understand the conditions by which capitalist-produced cultural forms are lived and read" (Durham et al., 2021). This model illustrates the complexity of cultural artifacts and the interrelated nature of culture and power found within the various nodes of the "circuit." Although I studied only three of the nodes via the three case studies, these provided plenty of support for my argument surrounding Elena's peripheral placement and how this placement reflects the discursive location of U.S. Latinidad more broadly. My case studies have provided a way to engage major cultural processes for understanding how Disney represents Latina girlhood and the intricate negotiations taking place between the conglomerate, producers, and consumers. By engaging the circuit of culture model, this book broadly explores how marginalized people are represented in the media by providing an analysis of a narrative franchise, which highlights Latina girlhood. The project here explored how a transnational media giant reinforces a flexible and ambiguous Latinidad to its economic advantage. To advance its economic goals, the Latinidad produced and disseminated is not Latinidad, but rather Latin Americanness, and most often a narrow version of Mexicanidad.

THE FUTURE OF (WOKE?) DISNEY

I cannot conclude this book without acknowledging how it felt to hear mariachi music behind the iconic Disney castle before *Coco* began playing at the movie theater or how it felt to watch a television series (*Elena of Avalor*) with my daughter in which the main characters talk about *buñuelos* and *pan de muerto*. This is quite different from anything I experienced growing up. I appreciate these representations; I appreciate the increased visibility. However, as countless media scholars have noted, visibility is not enough. And even within the terrain of presence and visibility, we have yet to see an actual representation of animated Latina girlhood from within the Disney family, although *Elena of Avalor* and *Encanto* (2021) claim to accomplish this goal. Both representations (as well as *Coco*) are grounded and situated within Latin America, which *should not* be conflated with U.S. Latinx experiences.

I have encountered countless posts on social media of parents showing off their children (mostly girls) with Elena at Disney theme parks. Many of the captions state something about representation, often including the hashtag #representationmatters. I reiterate that it does matter, but it is just a first step to achieving equity on the screen and beyond. What happens when that representation is situated as an outsider? What does it mean for young children who will grow up with the visibility on the screen accompanied by narratives about that character's eternal state as an outsider? As Báez (2018) finds, "contemporary Latina/o media representation presents a paradox" (p. 137). This paradox of hypervisibility in conjunction with stereotypes extends into the realm of Latina girlhood. Although Báez's findings pertain to adult women, we can see some of the patterns she traces present within animation and children's television content. The hypervisibility element is what I think media scholars and media consumers in general ought to be cautious about. Hypervisibility is not the only result we want to strive for. Drawing on Foucault, Blue (2017) analyzes the visibility of teenage girls in Disney Channel programming and finds that the hypervisibility of girls on television can be a "strategy for disciplining and silencing" (p. 191). Blue reminds us that the images we see are developed, deployed, and managed by the "mouse machine" (p. 190), and I thus follow in her footsteps and interrogate what could seem to some as a recent surge in Latin American (and wrongfully labeled) Latinx representations. We should be ever so vigilant about what these representations say to our children, not just how many (if any) are available.

In my Disney classes, I hear time and time again how far Disney has come, and some students have even gone as far to say that Disney is "woke." This statement has also been echoed in various headlines praising Disney's recent efforts to remove some terribly racist images and narratives from the parks. This is not just in terms of race, though. A student in one of my Disney classes explained to me how as a queer person she found it especially significant to see Disney theme parks selling pride merchandise and showcasing queer characters through live-action and animated representations. As Wasko (2020) reminds us, though, this is part of Disney's revision efforts. As a massive media enterprise, Disney must continue to shift and adjust its strategies in response to the times. The types of princesses that appealed to parents (and young children) in 1950 are not the same as the ones that appeal to large segments of the population today. This is partly why I noted earlier that this book must be read with an understanding of the time period around 2015–2021, not just in terms of what was happening in the United States and internationally, but also in relation to Disney's strategies, goals, and ownership. It is significant that *Elena of Avalor* debuted a year before the theatrical release of *Coco* (2017), a year before Disney showcased its first-ever openly gay child character in a live-action series (the character of Cyrus in *Andi Mack*), a year before the Disney parks removed the bridal auction from the *Pirates of the Caribbean* ride, and a few years before the removal of references to *Song of the South* from the theme parks. All these moments help compose a holistic picture of the time period during which this series, including its multiple iterations, existed and thrived in real time.

Although the research in this book took place from 2016 to 2021, a few months before it went to the press, Disney released its *2021 Corporate Social Responsibility Report*. While the report falls outside of the scope of my analytical time frame for Disney's corporate social responsibility (CSR) efforts, it is worth mentioning how the report falls in line with "woke" Disney. This report, unlike any before it, positions diversity front and center through the "World of Belonging: Diversity, Equity, and Inclusion" section, which is ten pages in length and the first major section of the report following fiscal year numbers. The "Letter from Our Chief Executive Officer" even opens with a statement about the importance of diversity and the introduction of Disney's "Diversity Dashboard," where the conglomerate will report workforce diversity in an attempt to be more transparent. Not long after this CSR report was released, though, Chapek found himself tangled up in an equity nightmare. Disney employees, fans, and critics took to social media to denounce the company's support for politicians who backed Florida's "Don't Say Gay" bill.[1] After having been the target of much criticizing, Chapek publicly came out in opposition to the bill. Although the details of the bill, Disney employee walkouts, and the company's support for conservative politicians are outside the scope of this book, it is important to note these broad details and their ties to Disney's ongoing struggle to be seen as "woke."

I would caution not to necessarily think about Disney as "woke" but rather as going through a revision process, as Wasko (2020) calls it. Disney is driven by the profit motive before all else. The prioritization of profit over any other element is abundantly clear when one looks at the company's website, where stock performance is prominently displayed and updated every fifteen minutes on the homepage. This takes center stage on the website before social responsibility or recent Disney news. This is how the company operates. This is how it thrives. By keeping this goal in mind, audiences and consumers of Disney products can more accurately gauge how and why these revisions are taking place within the mouse machine. What Disney claims it is doing must always be weighed against a boots-on-the-ground engagement with products, audiences, and production practices.

A FEW COMMENTS ON MISSED OPPORTUNITIES

Perhaps the future of (woke) Disney involves digging into missed opportunities where the company employs weightless flexibility as opposed to transformational flexibility. Valdivia reminds us time and time again that if we are looking for the revolution, we should not look to the mouse machine. I am often left wondering, though, where Disney will go next. What type of flexibility will the company employ as it continues attempting to promote the brand as socially conscious and "woke"? Many times throughout my experience in viewing the *Elena of Avalor* series I was left hoping for more layered representations of certain holidays, celebrations, terms, and even cuisine. I would finish the episode and think to myself that it was a missed opportunity. I wondered why, for example, the episode did not do a bit more to explain what a *quinceañera* celebration is and why it is important, in terms of both culture and religion. I had similar feelings when watching the "Lead Like Elena" Girl Scouts videos. Instead of framing these issues as individual problems that girls can solve by having bake sales, wouldn't it have been useful to include more references to systemic changes the girls could advocate for? The closest example of what I was hoping for was the one-minute video called "Lead Like Elena: Girl Scout Olivia—Be Inspired," in which Olivia writes a letter to the mayor of her city asking for help in fixing her neighborhood park. Although the mayor does help with the one park, more examples of girls' leadership through less individualistic frames would help Disney fill in the holes with these missed opportunities. I had many similar feelings after all my theme park visits. Why couldn't we see an Elena that cares less (or not at all) about clothes, accessories, and traditional markers of femininity? There was not a single instance when the cast members playing Elena did not comment on my daughter's clothing. Of course, these were some of the missed opportunities that readily came to *my* mind as a scholar pursuing issues of Latinidad, childhood, and gender. I am certain that people who occupy other positionalities have noticed other types of shortcomings.

What is the alternative though? When one provides four episodes (under thirty minutes each) focusing on the same holiday (Día de los Muertos), you cannot expect a history lesson in every episode or even a review of the quick background content that was provided in the first episode. In fact, most animated content that highlights Día de los Muertos glosses over the actual death component and fails to delve into the roots of the holiday. How does one provide more layered content in children's animated television programming? How can the mouse machine or other media giants produce representations that do not showcase a weightless flexibility, but instead at least acknowledge the significance of a cultural celebration? The 2021 Netflix dramedy *The Chair*, starring Sandra Oh, features a small instance where a mainstream media streaming giant incorporates a flashpoint of intersectional visibility showcasing the roots of not only Día de los Muertos but also La Catrina. Halfway through episode 4 of the first season, Bill helps young Juju (Sandra Oh's adopted Latina daughter in the series) with her class project on Día de los Muertos. Juju is supposed to be the "cultural ambassador for *Día de los Muertos*" at her school and Bill (a white, male professor) takes on the role of her mentor for this project. He quizzes Juju in preparation and asks her "Who created La Calavera Catrina?" For those audience members who do not know, they can see on his computer screen that La Catrina is the famous fancily clad skull that has become a Día de los Muertos icon. Juju rests her head on the kitchen counter as she reluctantly answers Bill's questions, bored out of her mind. Bill follows up his initial question by asking, "And whom was he making fun of?" To which Juju groans, "rich people." After a few more questions, Bill explains that "Posada was making fun of Mexico leader Porfirio Díaz because even though Díaz modernized Mexico, his reforms really only benefitted the ruling class." Juju interrupts him and says, "My name's Bill, and I'm so boring." After Bill pretends to cry and Juju asks, "When is recess?" this fifty-second scene is over. Although it truly is just a flashpoint, this brief scene provides more nuance than audiences typically receive with any Día de los Muertos–related content or any content featuring the skull drawings and paintings.

Although referencing the Porfiriato and delving into issues of lampooning the social elites is far too much to include in a thirty-minute animated episode, this is more in line with the type of content that I hope to one day see (even if only briefly) in children's programming.[2] Media are only a fraction of a cultural ecosystem, in which parents, guardians, schools, and peers also play large roles. I do not expect children's entertainment programming to educate children on every aspect of all cultures, but if a series is to purposefully highlight one celebration time and time again, we should expect a little more than skeleton outline outfits in the background. Perhaps part of the missed opportunity also involves showcasing other holidays or narratives as central celebrations. The Hanukkah celebration is a great example of this. Although not a perfect celebration episode (especially according to a lot of Jewish people), it breaks away from the tradition of representing Latinx series, films, and characters firmly within Catholicism. According to Disney, Princess Rebecca is a Jewish Latina, a representation that young audiences would benefit from seeing more of.

Whether we are media scholars, youth media literacy advocates, or any kind of educator, we must continue to study children's entertainment media from various angles and seriously explore the implications of the content. We must continue to ask questions about how media are produced, by whom, and to serve what interests. We must continue to interrogate the content we see on the screen. And we must ask questions about how audiences are interpreting the various images and storylines available. In chapter 3 of this book, I propose an architecture of flexibility, a flexibility that Disney employs to represent Latinidad. The architecture that I provide can be adapted and utilized to interrogate mediated representations of various underrepresented populations. Flexibility is not fixed; it varies and consists of different degrees. It is part of a continuum. Almost all the missed opportunities that I highlight above—and those that I often think about as I interact with the various iterations of *Elena of Avalor*—fall more squarely within the weightless flexibility that I outline in the continuum. Weightless flexibility is a simple template that media makers can use to keep risk at a minimum. But is it what Latinas, in particular Latina girls, crave? Do Latina girls want to see more representations of *quinceañeras* on television? Do media makers, particularly those from underrepresented groups, have enough agency to propose and carry out anything other than weightless flexibility? Although this book did not set out to answer those questions, it sets the groundwork for others to do so. Elena wears a very heavy crown on her head, having been tasked with representing an incredibly large group of people including U.S. Latinxs, Latin Americans, and Spaniards to a broader nonwhite audience. Although I critically analyze and dissect the many flexibilities present in almost every iteration of this text, how can we possibly expect Elena to do it all? Flexibility also has limits. After all, if you stretch a rubber band too far, it snaps.

Acknowledgments

I keep a list of all the people who, in one way or another, have helped shape this book into what it is. I began writing about Elena in the summer of 2016 and always had a feeling this project would turn into something big. I have been keeping my list since the day I first heard about the series. Now, brace yourselves! This list is long.

This research would not exist if it were not for my advisor at the University of Illinois, Angharad N. Valdivia. I made the journey from Texas to Illinois to work with Anghy and it is one of the best decisions I have ever made. Anghy not only helped pave the road for scholarship like mine to exist but also helped guide me through the academic process in a way that is unlike any I have ever heard of before. I am so lucky to now call her a mentor *and* friend. While at the University of Illinois I also received invaluable support from faculty members like Cameron McCarthy (who was the guiding light behind my ethnographic research), Isabel Molina-Guzmán, John Nerone, Rolando Romero, Jonathan Inda, James Hay, Kevin Wise, Anita Say Chan, and Amanda Ciafone. During the incredibly isolating time of writing, I also received support from many doctoral students at the university. Megan McSwain became my ultimate sounding board for issues of identity, representation, and absence. Thanks for inspiring my work in so many ways! Morten Stinus Kristensen, my cohort best bud, thank you for believing in my work. Thanks not only for being an amazing academic support but also for being a close friend to me and my family. Rhiannon Bettivia, my amazing scholar-mama buddy. Thank you for all the support you provided through so many wonderful writing sessions full of delicious meals, teas, coffees, and snacks. You will forever be my and Zoila's snack queen! And to all the writers at Anghy's writing retreat—thank you for making the writing process much more fun than I ever imagined it could be! I still miss sharing that space with all of you and learning from your work.

The University of Illinois allowed me to meet these people, but it also provided the stimulating intellectual environment I needed to begin this project. I owe a great debt of gratitude to the Institute of Communications Research (ICR), the

Department of Latina/Latino Studies, and Gender and Women's Studies. I learned so much from my time in all these spaces, both as a student and as an instructor. These spaces helped shape this book. I also received generous financial support from both the ICR and the Graduate College, which allowed me the time to begin the long writing process.

I was also very lucky to have had the support of many academic voices outside of Illinois while I worked on this project. Myra Washington, Sarah de Los Santos-Upton, Jillian Báez, María Elena Cepeda, Mary Beltrán, Christopher Chávez, Hector Amaya, Arcelia Gutiérrez, Bryce Henson, Sharon Mazzarella, Rebecca Hains, Morgan Blue, M. Cristina Alcalde, Mary Celeste Kearney, Emilie Zaslow, Janet Wasko, Claudia Bucciferro, Litzy Galarza, and Matt McAllister, thank you for believing in my work and for providing feedback (verbal and written) on various parts of this manuscript. Morgan Blue, in particular, provided not only an immense amount of encouragement but also incredible editorial assistance at almost every stage of this project (in addition to a fabulous index).

Although I began this book long before arriving at the University of South Florida, this institution provided support in more ways than one. To all my colleagues in the Department of Communication, thank you for always being mindful of this book project and protecting my time as a junior scholar in the department. Two graduate student research assistants helped me with this book—Camille Ruiz Mangual and Glenda Vaillant Cruz. I thank both of you so much for all your hard work and attention to detail! Readers will also notice that throughout the book I include many examples from my Disney courses. The undergraduate students in these classes have helped shape this book in more ways than they will ever know. They helped me rethink and fine-tune some of my questions. A special thanks to Maya Quiñones and Nicole Coppage for all your critical questions, comments, suggestions, and Disney intel!

And now a big thank you to my family! You all will always be the most important component of any acknowledgments section I may ever write. Jason, I am eternally grateful for everything you do for our family. Thank you for believing in my scholarship from the day we met. Your excitement about my work fuels my passions in a way I can't explain. Thank you for all those weekends and evenings of writing time when you would take Zoila to pick up trash in the woods. Thank you as well for waiting in line with me to meet Elena at Magic Kingdom more than a dozen times, for taking pictures of all the princesses at the park, and for watching countless episodes of the series with me. My mother also helped me throughout this process in many ways, but most importantly she traveled with me to Anaheim in July 2018. She not only served as my daughter's sole caretaker (on the first day for fifteen hours at the park in mid-July heat), but she also helped point out aspects of Disney I had never thought of before. Mil gracias! And finally, to the girl who inspired this work—gracias, Zoilita! You are my inspiration and my hope for the future. You always tell me how proud you are of me, and I hope you always know the feeling is mutual. I could not have asked for a more amazing daughter. This project has literally grown alongside you, and as you've grown into an amazing young girl, you've allowed me to ask questions about girlhood that I would never have considered asking before. This book would not be what it is without you.

Finally, this research was supported with generous funding from the University of Illinois Distinguished Fellowship, the University of Illinois Institute of Communications Research Block Grant Fellowship, and the University of South Florida Humanities Institute Summer Grant. What an honor to have these institutions believe in and support my work. Although I have listed many people who have helped make this project what it is, any remaining shortcomings are my own.

Notes

1. I use quotes to highlight that this is not a claim I am making, but rather the term used by Disney.

2. I use "Latinx" instead of "Latina/o" to allow for more gender flexibility through the use of the "x" instead of the "a/o" binary. Though I recognize that many find the *x* problematic, particularly for linguistic reasons, it is the term I will use in this book if the gender is not specified. However, given my study's focus on girls and gender, I use "Latina" quite prominently as well to refer to the unique experience of gendered Latinidad in the United States.

3. Although the term "Latinidad" is defined in different ways by many scholars, I use it to mean the state or process of being Latinx. It refers to the shared experiences of people of Latin American descent living in the United States.

4. The fictitious sport of olaball appears to be inspired by the Aztec game of Ōllamalitzli, where players attempt to get a ball into a hoop on the wall. The game has been experiencing revivals throughout various states in Mexico for over ten years now.

5. Two of many examples post 2020 include the inhumane treatment of immigrants in detention centers across the U.S.–Mexican border, along with the Trump administration's family separation policy. Unfortunately, these examples are not solely post-2020 issues. They are caused by deep structural issues that date back far longer than 2020 and are ongoing.

6. Ashley Garcia in Netflix's *The Expanding Universe of Ashley Garcia/ Ashley Garcia: Genius In Love* (2020), received her PhD in rocket science at the age of fifteen.

7. Like "postfeminism," "neoliberalism" does not have a straightforward definition. My work understands "neoliberalism" as a shift within capitalism, periodized by the Reagan/Thatcher moment, where the state stepped in on capital's behalf. Further, when the state passes neoliberal policies, it paves the way for capital at the expense of laborers. Under neoliberalism, individuals are supposed to take care of themselves and alleviate any issues through the marketplace. In this sense, privatization is justified by emphasizing personal responsibility (e.g., people should work rather than receive welfare), although this personal responsibility does not take into account systemic imbalances.

8. To be fair, of all industrialized countries the United States also has the highest teenage pregnancy rates across all ethnicities and socioeconomic classes.

9. I purposefully refer to the man as Walt rather than Disney to clearly mark a distinction between references to the person and references to the company, although they are so interrelated that sometimes there is overlap.

CHAPTER 1 — FROM BLACK-AND-WHITE MOUSE TO "LATINA" GIRL

1. Otherwise known as *The Alice Comedies*, this series was a hybrid of live-action and animated shorts, in which a young girl named Alice and an animated cat embark on a series of adventures. This was also the inspiration for what would later become *Alice in Wonderland* (1951).

CHAPTER 3 — ANIMATED LATINA GIRLHOOD
AND THE CONTINUUM OF FLEXIBILITY

1. The terms "abuelo" and "abuela" mean grandfather and grandmother, respectively. In the series they are usually referred to in this way, though their names are Francisco and Luisa Flores.

2. For example, Jane Fonda, who voices the villain Shuriki, often does not pronounce words or names in Spanish.

3. Some of these films include *The Night Crew* (2015), *Once Upon a Time in Mexico* (2003), *Assassins* (1995), and *Under the Volcano* (1984).

4. Though they do say "Día de los muertos" and "muertos" means "the dead."

5. Cinco de Mayo (the fifth of May) refers to the Battle of Puebla where Mexico defeated France in 1862. Although Cinco de Mayo is widely celebrated in the United States, the Battle of Puebla does not mark Mexico's independence from Spain, which took place on September 16, 1810, half a century prior to the Cinco de Mayo battle.

6. L+SD refers to the metrics used to capture ratings. L= live and SD = same day. L+SD includes viewing that occurred both during the live airing of the show and in all playback within the same day that it aired.

7. Disney also featured a few interstitial celebrity spotlights during Asian Pacific American Heritage Month. These included Olivia Rodrigo and Karan Brar, both of whom talk about their family's immigrant journeys.

8. The Spanish word "recorrido" means "route" or "voyage."

9. "Noche Buena" means Christmas Eve.

10. In Mexico, "ponche navideño" is a warm fruit drink, typically served during the Christmas season. In Chile, it is a drink of regular milk, condensed milk, and liquor served during the Christmas season. "Sweet tamal" is a sweet tamale. "Pasteles" are cakes or pastries. "Buñuelos" are fried dough desserts typical in Mexico and popular in other parts of Latin America.

11. In "A Spy in the Palace" (season 2, episode 5) and in "The Rise of the Sorceress" (season 2, episode 7), Naomi is the only one who realizes that something about Rita's presence in Avalor is problematic. The other characters brush this off while Naomi conducts her own investigation to find out why her instincts continue to tell her something bad is about to happen. Ultimately, in "The Rise of the Sorceress," Naomi reveals that Rita is in disguise and is actually Carla, one of the main villains of the series. This instance allows the rest of the story to unfold all the way until the last episode of the series. From the moment Naomi reveals this villain's identity, Elena and her crew continue trying to find her (along with two other villains) until they finally do so in the culminating episodes of the series.

12. The father–daughter dance is a central part of the *quinceañera* celebration. The dance is supposed to signal the girl's first dance as a woman, a dance that she tradition-

ally dances with her father, although within the past twenty years or so, many *quinceañeras* have adapted this tradition to include their dancing with other caretakers or family members. The changing of the shoes is another central component of the celebration when the *quinceañera* changes from flats to heels to visually and sartorially signify her coming of age.

13. Disney claims Rebecca of Galonia from *Elena of Avalor* as its first Jewish princess, although Sarah Silverman claimed via Twitter that Vanellope von Schweetz, the character she voices in *Wreck-It Ralph* (2012) and *Ralph Breaks the Internet* (2018), is the original Disney Jewish princess (March 9, 2018).

14. "Bimuelos," a Sephardic Hanukkah dessert of fried dough and sugar.

CHAPTER 4 — ON-SITE PERFORMANCE OF LATINIDAD FROM EAST COAST TO WEST COAST

1. Elena is played by multiple cast members at each Disney location.

2. Every character featured on the mobile application has a brief character description. During my fieldwork, Elena's said the following, "Elena finds inspiration in her culture and traditions, support from her family and friends, and excitement in every new day as Crown Princess of Avalor."

3. "Look! She does speak Spanish!"

4. "Mexican princess"

5. "I am very proud to share my culture, my language, and my food."

6. "Do you like tamales or enchiladas, little princess?"

7. "Well, I love enchiladas and tamales. They are my favorite foods."

8. "Exactly! Very good!"

9. "Of course. We watch it on Netflix Latin America and it is in Spanish."

10. "The presents are from Mexico."

11. "How cool! Next time you should invite me."

12. "Tres leches" is a sponge cake made with three types of milk. Mexicans often claim that it originated in Mexico.

13. "Hi. My name is Leo."

14. "Do you speak Spanish? Yes? Just like me! What is your name?"

15. "What is your favorite part about being a princess?"

16. "Sharing my culture and my language"

17. "Thank you," "excellent," and "good-bye," respectively.

18. "Like this. Very cute."

19. "Do you have my clothing?"

20. Both characters talk at length about fighting and going on adventures to defeat the First Order. In fact, they often attempt to enlist park guests to join them on their crusade.

21. I was later informed that when it rains, they cancel the appearances under the umbrella.

22. However, I cannot be certain that this translated onto the physical space at the park because these findings were solely digital.

23. Disney Magic Hours are available for guests staying at Walt Disney World Resort hotels. Each day, one of the theme parks opens an hour early and closes two hours later to allow the resort guests to partake in the park experience with fewer crowds.

24. "Hi, Elena. Nice to meet you."

25. Trump was not the first president to make such comments either (Jeb's cousin George W. Bush made similar remarks in 2006).

26. As of spring 2022, the meet and greets inside the Fairytale Hall in Florida have been reinstated. Although this was beyond the time frame of my analysis, I would sometimes

log on to the mobile application and notice that Elena was still featured alongside Cinderella inside the Fairytale Hall.

27. I was able to interact with her much more in Florida, so that should be accounted for.

CONCLUSION

1. This controversial Florida bill (HB 1557/SB 1834) prevents teachers from discussing LGBTQ+ identities and issues in elementary school settings.

2. Porfiriato refers to the time period between 1876 and 1911 when Porfirio Díaz was president of Mexico.

References

Adorno, T., & Horkheimer, M. (1944). The culture industry: Enlightenment as mass deception. In T. Adorno and M. Horkheimer (Eds.), *Dialectic of enlightenment* (pp. 120–167), (J. Cumming, Trans.). Herder and Herder.

Aladé, F., Lauricella, A., Kumar, Y., & Wartella, E. (2020). Who's modeling STEM for kids? A character analysis of children's STEM-focused television in the U.S. *Journal of Children and Media, 15*(3), 338–357. https://doi.org/10.1080/17482798.2020.1810087.

Alper, M., Katz, V. S., & Schofield Clark, L. (2016). Researching children, intersectionality, and diversity in the digital age. *Journal of Children and Media, 10*(1), 107–114. https://doi .org/10.1080/17482798.2015.1121886.

Alvarez, J. (2007) *Once upon a quinceañera: Coming of age in the U.S.A.* Plume.

Amatangelo, A. (2016, July 20). "Elena of Avalor": TV review. *Hollywood Reporter.* http:// www.hollywoodreporter.com/review/elena-avalor-tv-review-912793.

Amaya Schaeffer, F. (2013). *Love and empire: Cybermarriage and citizenship across the Americas.* New York University Press.

American Academy of Child and Adolescent Psychiatry (2020, February). *Screen time and children.* https://www.aacap.org/AACAP/Families_and_Youth/Facts_for_Families/FFF -Guide/Children-And-Watching-TV-054.aspx#:~:text=Screen%20Time%20and%20 Children&text=Children%20and%20adolescents%20spend%20a,spend%20up%20to%20 9%20hours.

American Psychological Association (1993). *Violence and youth: Psychology's response.*

Anderson, B. (1983). *Imagined communities.* Verso.

Anderson, C. A. (2004). An update on the effects of playing violent video games. *Journal of Adolescence, 27*(1), 113–122. https://doi.org/10.1016/j.adolescence.2003.10.009.

Animation Magazine (2016, July 21). *Behind the scenes of "Elena of Avalor"* [Video]. YouTube. https://www.youtube.com/watch?v=3OpgpfttyTo.

Aparicio, F. R. (1998). Whose Spanish, whose language, whose power? Testifying to differential bilingualism. *Indiana Journal of Hispanic Literatures, 12,* 5–25.

Aparicio, F. R. (2003). Jennifer as Selena: Rethinking Latinidad in media and popular culture. *Latino Studies, 1*(1), 90–105. https://doi.org/10.1057/palgrave.lst.8600016.

Aparicio, F. R., & Chávez-Silverman, S. (1997). *Tropicalizations: Transcultural representations of Latinidad.* University Press of New England.

Ariès, P. (1962). *Centuries of childhood: A social history of family life.* Vintage.

Aroeste, S. (2019, December). Disney's "Elena of Avalor" Hanukkah episode is a win for representation. *Times of Israel.* https://www.timesofisrael.com/disneys-elena-of-avalor -hanukkah-episode-is-a-win-for-representation/.

Aubrey, J. S., & Harrison, K. (2004). The gender-role content of children's favorite television programs and its links to their gender-related perceptions. *Media Psychology, 6*(2), 111–146. https://doi.org/10.1207/s1532785xmep0602_1.

Auxier, B., Anderson, M., Perrin, A., & Turner, E. (2020). *Children's engagement with digital devices, screen time.* Pew Research Center. https://www.pewresearch.org/internet /2020/07/28/childrens-engagement-with-digital-devices-screen-time/.

Avery, G., & Reynolds, K. (2000). *Representations of childhood death.* Palgrave Macmillan.

Báez, J. M. (2007a). Speaking of Jennifer Lopez: Discourses of iconicity and identity formation among Latina audiences. *Media Report to Women, 35*(1), 5–13.

Báez, J. M. (2007b). Towards a *Latinidad feminista*: The multiplicities of Latinidad and feminism in contemporary cinema. *Popular Communication, 5*(2), 109–128. https://doi .org/10.1080/15405700701294079.

Báez, J. M. (2008). Mexican (American) women talk back: Audience responses to Latinidad in U.S. advertising. In A.N. Valdivia (Ed.), *Latina/o communication studies today* (pp. 257–281). Peter Lang.

Báez, J. M. (2018). *In search of belonging: Latinas, media, and citizenship.* University of Illinois Press.

Baker, K., & Raney, A. A. (2007). Equally super? Gender-role stereotyping of superheroes in children's animated programs. *Mass Communication & Society, 10*(1), 25–41. https:// doi.org/10.1080/15205430709337003.

Banet-Weiser, S. (2004). Girls rule! Gender, feminism, and Nickelodeon. *Critical Studies in Media Communication, 21*(2), 119–139. https://doi.org/10.1080/07393180410001 688038.

Banet-Weiser, S. (2007). *Kids rule! Nickelodeon and consumer citizenship.* Duke University Press.

Banet-Weiser, S. (2012). *Authentic™: The politics of ambivalence in a brand culture.* New York University Press.

Banet-Weiser, S. (2015). "Confidence you can carry!" Girls in crisis and the market for girls' empowerment organizations. *Continuum, 29*(2), 182–193.

Banet-Weiser, S., Gill, R., & Rottenberg, C. (2019). Postfeminism, popular feminism and neoliberal feminism? Sarah Banet-Weiser, Rosalind Gill and Catherine Rottenberg in conversation. *Feminist Theory, 21*(1), 3–24. https://doi.org/10.1177/1464700119 842555.

Bartiromo, M. (2020, September 16). *Disney World guest without mask is escorted from park while attempting to garner support, video shows.* Fox News. https://www.foxnews .com/travel/disney-world-guest-no-mask-removed-paraphrases-bugs-life.

Baudrillard, J. (1994). *Simulacra and simulation.* University of Michigan Press.

Bavidge, J. (2004). Chosen ones: Reading the contemporary teen heroine. In G. Davis & K. Dickinson (Eds.), *Teen TV: Genre, consumption, and identity* (pp. 29–40). British Film Institute.

Bean, T. (2020, April 8). Report: Disney+ overtakes Netflix as top streaming app of 2020. *Forbes.* https://www.forbes.com/sites/travisbean/2020/04/08/report-disney-overtakes -netflix-as-top-streaming-app-in-2020/?sh=69baf9bb7aa6.

Bell, E. (1995). Somatexts at the Disney shop: Constructing the pentimentos of women's animated bodies. In E. Bell., L. Haas, & L. Sells (Eds.), *From mouse to mermaid: The politics of film, gender, and culture* (pp. 107–124). Indiana University Press.

Beltrán, M. C. (2002). The Hollywood Latina body as site of social struggle: Media constructions of stardom and Jennifer Lopez's "cross-over butt." *Quarterly Review of Film and Video, 19*(1), 71–86. https://doi.org/10.1080/10509200214823.

Beltrán, M. (2009). *Latino stars in U.S. eyes: The making and meanings of film and TV stardom.* University of Illinois Press.

Beltrán, M. C. (2004). Más macha: The new Latina action hero. In Y. Tasker (Ed.), *Action and adventure cinema* (pp. 186–200). Routledge.

Bemis, B. (2020). Mirror, mirror for us all: Disney theme parks and the collective memory of the American national narrative. *Public Historian, 42*(1), 54–79. https://doi.org/10.1525/tph.2020.42.1.54.

Betancourt, M. (2018, February 28). *Listen to Latino film critics explain what mainstream outlets got wrong about "Coco."* Remezcla. https://remezcla.com/film/podcast-coco-reviews/.

Blue, M. G. (2013). The best of both worlds? Youth, gender, and a post-feminist sensibility in Disney's *Hannah Montana. Feminist Media Studies, 13*(4), 660–675. https://doi.org/10.1080/14680777.2012.724024.

Blue, M. G. (2017) *Girlhood on Disney Channel: Branding, celebrity, and femininity.* Routledge.

Blue, M. G. (2018). Girlfriends go green: Disney Channel, corporate responsibility, and girls' citizenship. In M. G. Blue & M. C. Kearney (Eds.), *Mediated girlhoods: New explorations of girls' media culture* (pp. 137–155). Peter Lang.

Blue, M. G., & Kearney, M. C. (Eds.). (2018). *Mediated girlhoods: New explorations of girls' media culture.* Peter Lang.

Boyd, D. (2014). *It's complicated: The social lives of networked teens.* Yale University Press.

Brady, A. (2016). Taking time between g-string changes to educate ourselves: Sinéad O'Connor, Miley Cyrus, and celebrity feminism. *Feminist Media Studies, 16*(3), 429–444. https://doi.org/10.1080/14680777.2015.1137960.

Brayton, S. (2013). Learning to labor with Handy Manny: Immigration politics and the world of work in a children's cartoon. *Social Semiotics, 23*(3), 335–351. https://doi.org/10.1080/10350330.2012.719731.

Breaux, R. M. (2010). After 75 years of magic: Disney answers its critics, rewrites African American history, and cashes in on its racist past. *Journal of African American Studies,14*(4), 398–416. https://doi.org/10.1007/s12111-010-9139-9.

Brito, C. (2018, November 14). *Man kicked out of Disney World after waving "Trump 2020" banner during ride.* CBS News. https://www.cbsnews.com/news/dion-cini-disney-world-spalsh-mountain-trump-2020-banner/.

Brock, A. (2016). Critical technocultural discourse analysis. *New Media and Society, 20*(3), 1012–1030. https://doi.org/10.1177%2F1461444816677532.

Brown, M. (1999). *Infogirl: A girl's guide to the Internet.* Rosen.

Brown, R. (1976). *Children and television.* SAGE.

Brulle, R. J., Aronczyk, M., & Carmichael, J. (2020). Corporate promotion and climate change: An analysis of key variables affecting advertising spending by major oil corporations, 1986–2015. *Climate Change, 159*(1), 87–101. https://doi.org/10.1007/s10584-019-02582-8.

Brüning, K. (2018). Olivia Pope: A black post-feminist subject? Analyzing *Scandal*'s intersecting post-feminist and colorblind discourses. *Feminist Media Studies, 19*(4), 463–478. http://doi.org/10.1080/14680777.2018.1508049.

Bryman, A. (2004). *The Disneyization of society.* SAGE.

Bucciferro, C. (2021). Representations of gender and race in Ryan Coogler's film *Black Panther*: Disrupting Hollywood tropes. *Critical Studies in Media Communication, 38*(2), 169–182. https://doi.org/10.1080/15295036.2021.1889012.

Bui, H. (2019, January 22). *Disney's first Latina princess movie may be in the works with Lin-Manuel Miranda*. /Film. https://www.slashfilm.com/latina-disney-princess-movie -lin-manuel-miranda/.

Bullock, C. S., & Rozell, M. J. (Eds.). (2012). *The Oxford handbook of southern politics*. Oxford University Press.

Burns, W. (2015, June 15). Disney proves that profitable marketing is about brand stories. *Forbes*. https://www.forbes.com/sites/willburns/2015/06/09/disney-proves-that-profitable -marketing-is-about-brand-stories/#59b95cc7227b.

Buschman, B. J., & Anderson, C. A. (2002). Violent video games and hostile expectations: A test of the general aggression model. *Personality and Social Psychology Bulletin, 28*(12), 1679–1686. https://doi.org/10.1177/014616702237649.

Butler, J. (1990). *Gender trouble: Feminism and the subversion of identity*. Routledge.

Cain, K. (2017, July 20). *How Disney's mobile app transformed their park experience*. Business 2 Community. https://www.business2community.com/mobile-apps/disneys-mobile-app -transformed-park-experience-01880714#:~:text=The%20interactive%20GPS%2Denabled %20map,times%20for%20fireworks%20and%20parades.

Calvan, B. (2020, November 4). *President Trump wins Florida, collects 29 electoral votes*. AP News. https://apnews.com/article/election-2020-joe-biden-donald-trump-virus-outbreak -tallahassee-c13067371d409668309fb1f06d8a29d6.

Camil, J. [@jaimecamil]. (2016, October 13). *Don't miss a very special episode of #Elenaof-Avalor THIS SUNDAY night on @disneyjunior AND @disneychannel simultaneously #DiaDeLosMuertos* [Photograph]. Instagram. https://www.instagram.com/p/BLg7zYVj Jtl/?taken-by=jaimecamil.

Cantor, B. (2016a, August 1). *Ratings: "Elena of Avalor" falls in week two, "Girl Meets World" leads Disney's Friday*. Headline Planet. http://headlineplanet.com/home/2016 /08/01/ratings-elena-of-avalor-falls-in-week-two-girl-meets-world-leads-disneys -friday/.

Cantor, B. (2016b, October 18). *Ratings: "Elena of Avalor" viewership rises for Dia de los Muertos episode*. Headline Planet. http://headlineplanet.com/home/2016/10/18/ratings -elena-avalor-viewership-rises-sunday-episode/.

Cantor, J. (2003). Media violence effects and interventions: The roles of communication and emotion. In J. Bryant, D. Roskos-Ewoldson, & J. Cantor (Eds.), *Communication and emotion: Essays in honor of Dolf Zilmann* (pp. 197–219). Erlbaum.

Cardenas, S., & Gerber, C. (Writers), & Bour, E. M. (Director). (2016, December 9). Navidad (Season 1, Episode 11) [TV series episode]. In C. Gerber & J. Mitchell (Executive Producers), *Elena of Avalor*. Los Angeles, Disney Television Animation.

Casas Pérez, M. (2005). Cultural identity: Between reality and fiction: A transformation of genre and roles in Mexican telenovelas. *Television & New Media, 6*(4), 407–414. https:// doi.org/10.1177%2F1527476405279956.

Castillo, M. (2016, November 25). A Latina Disney movie princess? The wait isn't over. *New York Times*. https://www.nytimes.com/2016/11/25/movies/a-latina-disney-movie-princess -the-wait-isnt-over.html.

Castillo, M. (2017, August 8). *Disney will pull its movies from Netflix and start its own streaming services*. CNBC. https://www.cnbc.com/2017/08/08/disney-will-pull-its-movies -from-netflix-and-start-its-own-streaming-services.html.

CBS News. (2015, September 16). *Transcript: Second-tier CNN Republican debate 2015*. CBS News. http://www.cbsnews.com/news/transcript-second-tier-republican-debate-2015 -reagan-library/.

Center for Disease Control and Prevention. (1991). *Position papers from the third national inquiry conference: Setting the national agenda for injury control in the 1990s.* Department of Public Health and Human Services.

Centers for Disease Control and Prevention. (2020, October 28). *About teen pregnancy.* CDC. https://www.cdc.gov/teenpregnancy/about/index.html.

Cepeda, M. E. (2010a). Singing the star-spanglish banner: The politics and pathologization of bilingualism in U.S. popular media. In G. M. Pérez, F. A. Guridy, & A. Burgos (Eds.), *Beyond el barrio: Everyday life in Latina/o America* (pp. 27–43). New York University Press.

Cepeda, M. E. (2010b). *Musical imagiNation: U.S. Colombian identity and the Latin music boom.* New York University Press.

Cepeda, M. E. (2015). Beyond "filling in the gap": The state and status of Latina/o feminist media studies. *Feminist Media Studies, 16*(2), 344–360. https://doi.org/10.1080/14680777.2015.1052005.

Cepeda, M. E. (2017). *The Routledge companion to Latina/o Media.* Routledge.

Cerejido, A. (Producer). (2017, November 17). *It's a small world, after all* [Audio podcast episode]. In *Latino USA.* National Public Radio. http://latinousa.org/episode/its-a-small-world-after-all/.

Chávez, C., & Kiley, A. (2016). Starlets, subscribers, and beneficiaries: Disney, Latino children, and television labor. *International Journal of Communication, 10,* 2616–2636.

Ciafone, A. (2019) *Counter-Cola: A multinational history of the global corporation.* University of California Press.

Coco—Financial information International. (n.d.). The Numbers. Retrieved July 23, 2021, from https://www.the-numbers.com/movie/Coco-(2017)/Mexico#tab=international.

Coffey, K. (2020, May 23). *Disney nominated for 48 daytime Emmys; "Elena of Avalor", "Mickey Mouse" and more!* Inside the Magic. https://insidethemagic.net/2020/05/disney-daytime-emmy-awards-kc1/.

Colt, S. (Director). (2015a). *Walt Disney's early days* [Video]. PBS. Retrieved May 23, 2018, from Kanopy. https://www.kanopy.com/en/product/204925

Colt, S. (Director). (2015b). *Walt Disney's legacy* [Video]. PBS. Retrieved May 23, 2018, from Kanopy. https://www.kanopy.com/en/product/204927.

Common Sense Media (2016, July 19). *Elena of Avalor T.V. review.* https://commonsensemedia.org/tv-reviews/elena-of-avalor.

Cook, D. T. (2004). *The commodification of childhood: The children's clothing industry and the rise of the child consumer.* Duke University Press.

Coombe, R. J., & Herman, A. (2004). Rhetorical virtues: Property, speech, and the commons on the world-wide web. *Anthropological Quarterly, 77*(3), 559–574.

Cortés, C. (2000). *The children are watching: How the media teach about diversity.* Teachers College Press.

Coscarelli, J. (2012, June 5). Disney to stop peddling junk food with Michelle Obama's blessing. *New York Magazine Intelligencer.* http://nymag.com/daily/intelligencer/2012/06/disney-michelle-obama-to-stop-junk-food-ads.html.

Couldry, N. (2000). *Inside culture: Re-imagining the method of cultural studies.* SAGE.

Cox, D. (2000, April 3). The keys to the kingdom: How Michael Eisner lost his grip—Masters' mouse trap fails to catch Eisner. *Variety.* http://variety.com/2000/more/reviews/the-keys-to-the-kingdom-how-michael-eisner-lost-his-grip-masters-mouse-trap-fails-to-catch-eisner-1200461895/.

Croce, P. J. (1991). A clean and separate space: Walt Disney in person and production. *Journal of Popular Culture, 25*(3), 91–103. https://doi.org/10.1111/j.0022-3840.1991.91118.x.

Dávila, A. (2001). *Latinos, Inc.: The marketing and making of a people.* University of California Press.

Dávila, A. (2008). *Latino spin: Public image and the whitewashing of race.* New York University Press.

Dávila, A. (2014). Contemporary Latina/o media: Production, circulation, politics. New York University Press.

Dean, C. (2000). Boys and girls and "boys": Popular depictions of African-American children and childlike adults in the United States, 1850–1930. *Journal of American & Comparative Cultures, 23*(3), 17–35. https://doi.org/10.1111/j.1537-4726.2000.2303_17.x.

de Beauvoir, S. (1953). *The second sex.* Knopf.

Del Barco, M. (2016, December 22). *"Elena of Avalor" takes the Throne as Disney's first Latina princess.* National Public Radio. https://www.npr.org/2016/12/22/505714020/elena-of-avalor-takes-the-throne-as-disneys-first-latina-princess.

Delpozo, B. (2019, July 25). *11 things you need to know about Disney World's PhotoPass.* AllEars. https://allears.net/2019/07/25/11-things-you-need-to-know-about-disney-worlds-photopass/.

Denner, J., & Guzman, B. L. (2006). *Latina girls: Voices of adolescent strength in the United States.* New York University Press.

De Ras, M. (1999). Female youth: Gender and life phase from a historical and sociocultural perspective. *Women's Studies Journal, 15*(2), 147–160.

Disis, J. (2018, November 9). *Disney stock jumps after streaming service news.* CNN. https://www.cnn.com/2018/11/08/media/disney-fourth-quarter-earnings/index.html.

DisneyJunior (2017, May 1). *Lead like Elena: Girl Scouts Maria and Alexa- be inspired | Disney Junior* [Video]. YouTube. https://www.youtube.com/watch?v=qfjgHs9FYYk.

Disneyland Resort. (2018a). *Princess Elena's grand arrival.* Retrieved December 16, 2018, from https://disneyland.disney.go.com/entertainment/disney-california-adventure/princess-elena-grand-arrival.

Disneyland Resort. (2018b). *Bibbidi Bobbidi Boutique at the Disneyland Resort.* Retrieved November 1, 2018, from https://disneyland.disney.go.com/shops/disneyland/bibbidi-bobbidi-boutique/.

Donaldson, K. (2018, January 20). *How Disney buying Fox could affect the Avatar sequels.* ScreenRant. https://screenrant.com/avatar-2-changes-disney-buys-fox/.

Dorfman, A., & Mattelart, A. (1971). *How to read Donald Duck: Imperialist ideology in the Disney comic.* International General.

Douglas, S. (1994). *Where the girls are: Growing up female with the mass media.* Random Books.

Dreier, P. (1982). Capitalists vs. the media: An analysis of an ideological mobilization among business leaders. *Media, Culture, and Society, 4*(2), 111–132. https://doi.org/10.1177%2F016344378200400203.

Driscoll, C. (2002). *Girls: Feminine adolescence in popular culture and cultural theory.* Columbia University Press.

Driver, S. (2007). *Queer Girls and popular culture: Reading, resisting, and creating media.* Peter Lang.

Du Gay, P., Hall, S., Janes, L., Mackay, H., & Negus, K. (1997) *Doing cultural studies: The story of the Sony Walkman.* SAGE.

Durham, A. S., Johnson, W., & Sanders, S. J. (2021). Guest editor's introduction. *Departures in Critical Qualitative Research, 10*(2), 1–6. https://doi.org/10.1525/dcqr.2021.10.2.1.

Durham, M. G. (2001). Adolescents, the internet and the politics of gender: A feminist case analysis. *Race, Gender, & Class, 8*(4), 20–41.

Durham, M. G. (2008). *The Lolita effect: The media sexualization of young girls and what we can do about it*. Overlook Press.

Eagan, D. (2017). Disney Pixar travels to the mythical Land of the Dead cuckoo for *Coco*. *Film Journal International, 120*(11), 34–36.

Eco, U. (1986). *Travels in hyper reality: Essays*. Harcourt Brace Jovanovich.

Eilath, A. (2019, December 17). A Sephardic girl with a bubbe? Disney blew it with their first Jewish princess. *Jewish News of Northern California*. https://www.jweekly.com/2019/12/17/a-sephardic-girl-with-a-bubbe-disney-blew-it-with-their-first-jewish-princess/.

Elena of Avalor [@elenaofavalor]. (2017, October 15). *Celebrating #HispanicHeritageMonth with the team that creates #ElenaOfAvalor! We're going behind-the-scenes to see how tradition and culture inspire the show* [Video]. Instagram. https://www.instagram.com/p/BaRo2XRFbQ2/?taken-by=elenaofavalor.

Emerson, R. M., Fretz, R. I., & Shaw, L. L. (2011). *Writing ethnographic fieldnotes* (2nd ed.). University of Chicago Press.

Epstein, J. (2016, February 12). *"Dream Big, Princess" inspires girls and kids of all ages to realize their ambitions*. Disney Parks Blog. https://disneyparks.disney.go.com/blog/2016/02/dream-big-princess-inspires-girls-and-kids-of-all-ages-to-realize-their-ambitions/.

Erazo, V. (2017, November 17). *Pixar's "Coco" is now the highest-grossing movie in Mexico's History*. Remezcla. https://remezcla.com/film/pixar-coco-highest-grossing-animated-film-mexico-history/.

Exclusive: Inside the magic of Elena of Avalor (2016, July 22). Oh My Disney. http://ohmydisney.com/tv/2016/07/22/elena-of-avalor-feature/.

Fairclough, N. (1995). *Media discourse*. Hodder Education.

Fairclough, N. (2010). *Critical discourse analysis* (2nd ed.). Longman Group.

Faughnder, R. (2020, November 12). Disney+ subscribers hit nearly 74 million as COVID-19 brings big losses. *Los Angeles Times*. https://www.latimes.com/entertainment-arts/business/story/2020-11-12/disney-streaming-covid-pandemic-losses-iger.

Felski, R. (1995). *The gender of modernity*. Harvard University Press.

Fjellman, S. (1992). *Vinyl leaves: Walt Disney World and America*. Routledge.

Flores-González, N. (2017). *Citizens but not Americans: Race and belonging among Latino millennials*. New York University Press.

Forman-Brunell, M., & Hains, R. C. (Eds.). (2013). *Princess cultures: Mediating girls' imaginations and identities*. Peter Lang.

Foucault, M. (1980). *Power/knowledge*. Wheatsheaf.

Fox, M. (2018, February 6). *Disney's Bob Iger: Fox deal on track, even "more encouraged" now about assets*. CNBC. https://www.cnbc.com/2018/02/06/disneys-bob-iger-fox-deal-on-track-even-more-encouraged-now-about-assets.html.

Fox, S. (2019, September 19). *"Elena of Avalor" season 3 begins in October*. Slanted. https://theslanted.com/2019/09/35269/elena-of-avalor-season-3-guest-cast-list/.

Francaviglia, R. (1995). Walt Disney's Frontierland as an allegorical map of the American west. *Western Historical Quarterly, 30*(2), 155–182. https://doi.org/10.2307/970490.

Fregoso, R. L. (1995). Homegirls, cholas, and pachucas in cinema: Taking over the public sphere. *California History, 74*(3), 316–327.

French, D. (2018, July 26). *What democrats don't get about the south*. TIME. https://time.com/5349531/democrats-dont-get-the-south/.

Friedman, K. (2017, July 12). Disney's getting its first Latina princess. *Glamour*. https://www.glamour.com/story/elena-of-avalor.

Fry, R., & Passel, J. S. (2009, May 28). *IV: A profile of Hispanic children*. Pew Research Center. http://www.pewhispanic.org/2009/05/28/iv-a-profile-of-hispanic-children/.

Fürsich, E. (2009). In defense of textual analysis: Restoring a challenged method for journalism and media studies. *Journalism Studies, 10*(2), 238–252. https://doi.org/10.1080
/14616700802374050.

Gamber, F. (2008). Riding the third wave: The multiple feminisms of Gilmore Girls.
In S. M. Ross & L. E. Stein (Eds.), *Teen television: Essays on programming and fandom*
(pp. 114–131). McFarland.

Garcia, L. (2012). *Respect yourself, protect yourself: Latina girls and sexual identity.* New
York University Press.

Gaunt, K. D. (2006). *The games Black girls play: Learning the ropes from double-dutch to
hip-hop.* New York University Press.

Gehlawat, A. (2010). The strange case of *The Princess and the Frog*: Passing and the elision of
race. *Journal of African American Studies,*14(4), 417–431. https://doi.org/10.1007/s12111-010
-9126-1.

Gerber, C. [@CraigGerber_]. (2016, December 28). *Orizaba in "Scepter of Night" was
inspired by the Aztec goddess Itzpapalotl. #ElenaOfAvalor #Sources.* [Image attached]
[Tweet]. Twitter. https://twitter.com/CraigGerber_/status/814130781622771712?s=20.

Gerbner, G. (1990). Cultivation analysis: An overview. *Mass Communication & Society,
1*(3/4), 175–194. https://doi.org/10.1080/15205436.1998.9677855.

Gerbner, G., Gross, L., Morgan, M., & Signorielli, N. (1986). *Living with television: The
dynamics of the cultivation process.* In J. Bryant & D. Zillman (Eds.), *Perspectives on
media effects* (pp. 17–40). Lawrence Erlbaum.

Gill, R. (2007). Postfeminist media culture: Elements of a sensibility. *European Journal of
Cultural Studies, 10*(2), 147–166. https://doi.org/10.1177/1367549407075898.

Gill, R. (2016). Post-feminism? New feminist visibilities in postfeminist times. *Feminist
Media Studies, 16*(4); 610–630. https://doi.org/10.1080/14680777.2016.1193293.

Gill, R., & Scharff, C. (2011). Introduction. In R. Gill & C. Scharff (Eds.), *New femininities:
Postfeminism, neoliberalism, and subjectivity* (pp. 1–17). Palgrave Macmillan.

Gilmore, J. H., & Pine, B. J. (2007). *Authenticity: What consumers really want.* Harvard
Business.

Girl Scouts & Disney Channel. (2017). *Leadership guide* [Brochure]. http://cdnvideo
.dolimg.com/cdn_assets/3dfa69f593c2b26b0e5e0d317a4ae42fa05ba178.pdf.

Giroux, H. A., & Pollock, G. (1999). *The mouse that roared: Disney and the end of innocence.* Rowman and Littlefield.

Goffman, E. (1976). *Gender advertisements.* Harper Torchbooks.

Goldman, K. (2014). *Saludos Amigos* and the *Three Caballeros*: The representation of Latin
America in Disney's "Good Neighbor" films. In J. Cheu (Ed.), *Diversity in Disney films:
Critical essays on race, ethnicity, gender, sexuality, and disability* (p. 23–37). McFarland.

Gonick, M. (2006). Between "Girl Power" and "Reviving Ophelia": Constituting the neoliberal girl subject. *NWSA Journal, 18* (2), 1–22.

González-Martin, R. V. (2016). Barrio ritual and pop rite: Quinceañeras in the folklore-
popular culture borderlands. In F. L. Aldama (Ed.), *The Routledge companion to Latina/o
popular culture* (pp. 279–290). Routledge.

González, R. V. (2019). *Quinceañera style: Social belonging and Latinx consumer identities.*
University of Texas Press.

Goodfellow, M. (2020, April 6). *Disney reboots launch of Disney+ in France after Corona-
virus delay.* ScreenDaily. https://www.screendaily.com/news/disney-reboots-launch-of
-disney-in-france-after-coronavirus-delay/5148825.article.

The Great Courses (2015). *Why did Disney buy Pixar?* [Video]. https://www.kanopy.com
/product/why-did-disney-buy-pixar.

Gramsci, A. (1971). *Selections from the prison notebooks*. AK Press.

Greenberg, B. S. (1982). Television and role socialization: An overview. In D. Pearl, L. Bouthilet, & J. B. Lazar (Eds.), *Television and behavior: Ten years of scientific progress and implications for the eighties* (Vol. 2, pp.179–190). Technical Reviews, National Institute of Mental Health.

Griffin, R. A., & Rossing, J. P. (2020). *Black Panther* in widescreen: Cross-disciplinary perspectives on a pioneering, paradoxical film. *Review of Communication, 20*(3), 203–219. https://doi.org/10.1080/15358593.2020.1780467.

Guba, E. G., & Lincoln, Y. S. (2005). Paradigmatic controversies, contradictions and emerging confluences. In N. K. Denzin & Y.S. Lincoln (Eds.), *The SAGE handbook of qualitative research* (pp. 191–215). SAGE.

Gunter, B. (1994). The question of media violence. In J. Bryant & D. Zillmann (Eds.), *Media effects: Advances in theory and research* (pp.163–211). Erlbaum.

Hains, R. C. (2014). *The princess problem: Guiding our girls through the princess-obsessed years*. Sourcebooks.

Hains, R. C., Thiel-Stern, S., & Mazzarella, S. R. (2011). "We didn't have any Hannah Montanas": Girlhood, popular culture, and mass media in the 1940s and 1950s. In M. C. Kearney (Ed.), *Mediated girlhoods: New explorations of girls' media culture* (pp. 113–132). Peter Lang.

Hall, S. (1972). *Encoding and decoding in the television discourse*. Centre for Cultural Studies, University of Birmingham.

Hall, S. (1980). Encoding/decoding. In M. G. Durham & D. M. Kellner (Eds.), *Media and cultural studies: Keyworks* (pp. 163–173). Blackwell.

Hall, S. (1997). The work of representation. In S. Hall (Ed.), *Cultural representations and signifying practices*. SAGE.

Halter, M. (2000). *Shopping for identity: The marketing of ethnicity*. Random House.

Hamilton, B. E. (2020). *State teen birth rates by race and Hispanic origin: United States, 2017–2018*. National Center for Health Statistics. https://www.cdc.gov/nchs/data/nvsr/nvsr69/NVSR69-6-508.pdf.

Haralovich, M.B. (2017). Domesticity. In L. Ouelette & J. Gray (Eds.), *Keywords for media studies* (pp. 62–65). New York University Press.

Haraway, D. J. (1991). *Simians, cyborgs, and women: The reinvention of nature*. Routledge.

Hardy, J. (2014). *Critical political economy of the media*. Routledge.

Harris, A. (2004). *Future girl: young women in the twenty-first century*. Routledge.

Hasinoff, A. A. (2015). *Sexting panic: Rethinking criminalization, privacy, and consent*. University of Illinois Press.

Haskell, R. (2018, April 9). Disney CEO Bob Iger on taking the biggest risk of his career. *Vogue*. https://www.vogue.com/article/bob-iger-disney-ceo-interview-vogue-may-2018-issue.

Hawthorne, S. (2002). *Wild politics: Feminism, globalisation, bio/diversity*. Spinifex Press.

Heller, C. (2018, April 30). *Daytime Emmy awards 2018 winners: The complete list*. E! Online. https://www.eonline.com/news/930765/daytime-emmy-awards-2018-winners-the-complete-list.

Herreria Russo, C. (2016). *Disney pulled that offensive "Moana" costume: Here's why it matters*. HuffPost. https://www.huffpost.com/entry/disney-maui-costume-brownface_n_57e0c4cde4b08cb14097b892.

Higonnet, A. (1998). *Pictures of innocence: The history and crisis of ideal childhood* (1st ed.). Thames & Hudson.

Hine, C. (2015). *Ethnography of the internet: Embedded, embodies and everyday*. Bloomsbury.

Hispanic population and origin in select U.S. metropolitan areas, 2014. (2016, September 6). Pew Research Center. https://www.pewresearch.org/hispanic/interactives/hispanic-popu lation-in-select-u-s-metropolitan-areas/.

Hough, J. (2021, April 17). *With Disneyland reopening, Disney stock can continue to climb.* Barron's. https://www.barrons.com/amp/articles/as-disneyland-reopens-bullish-investors -are-counting-on-a-disney-triple-play-parks-tv-and-streaming-51618619489?tesla=y.

Jackson, K. M. (1993). *Walt Disney, a bio-bibliography.* Greenwood Press.

Jarvey, N. (2021, March 9). Disney+ passes 100 million paid subscribers. *Hollywood Reporter.* https://www.hollywoodreporter.com/news/disney-passes-100-million-paid-subscribers ?utm_source=morning_brew.

Jimenez, T. R (2009). *Replenished ethnicity: Mexican Americans, immigration, and iden- tity.* University of California Press.

Johnson, D. (2017). Production. In L. Ouelette & J. Gray (Eds.), *Keywords for Media Studies* (pp. 149–153). New York University Press.

Jones, J. M. (2019, November 12). *Ideology: Three deep south states are the most conservative.* Gallup. https://news.gallup.com/poll/125480/ideology-three-deep-south-states-conservative .aspx.

Jorgensen, M., & Phillips, L. (2002). *Discourse analysis as theory and method.* SAGE.

Joseph, R. (2018). *Post-racial resistance: Black women, media, and the uses of strategic ambiguity.* New York University Press.

Kaplan, A. (2018, November 16). *Thanks to Sarah Silverman, we finally have a Jewish Dis- ney princess.* Kveller. Retrieved April 6, 2022, from https://www.kveller.com/thanks-to -sarah-silverman-we-finally-have-a-jewish-disney-princess/.

Kapurch, K., & Smith, J. M. (2018). Something old, something new, something borrowed, and something blue: The make-do girl of *Cinderella* (2015). In M. G. Blue & M. C. Kearney (Eds.), *Mediated girlhoods: New explorations of girls' media culture* (pp. 67–83). Peter Lang.

Kearney, M. C. (2006). *Girls make media.* Routledge.

Kearney, M. C. (2011). *Mediated girlhoods: New explorations of girls' media culture.* Peter Lang.

Keller, J., & Ringrose, J. (2015). "But then feminism goes out the window!" Exploring teen- age girls' critical response to celebrity feminism. *Celebrity Studies, 6*(1), 132–135. https:// doi.org/10.1080/19392397.2015.1005402.

Keller, J., Blue, M., Kearney, M. C., Pike, K., & Projansky, S. (2015). Mapping new method- ological approaches to girls' media studies: reflections from the field. *Journal of Children and Media, 9*(4), 528–535. https://doi.org/10.1080/17482798.2015.1091103.

Kellner, D. (1995). Cultural studies, multiculturalism, and media culture. In G. Dines & J. M. Humez (Eds.), *Gender, race, and class in media: A text reader.* SAGE.

Kennedy, M. (2014). Hannah Montana and Miley Cyrus: 'Becoming' a woman, 'becoming' a Star. *Celebrity Studies, 5*(3), 225–241. https://doi.org/10.1080/19392397.2013.839349.

Kennedy, M. (2018) "Come on, [. . .] let's go find your inner princess": (Post-)feminist gen- erationalism in tween fairy tales. *Feminist Media Studies, 18*(3), 424–439. https://doi.org /10.1080/14680777.2017.1367704.

Keys, J. (2016): Doc McStuffins and Dora the Explorer: representations of gender, race, and class in US animation. *Journal of Children and Media, 10*(3), 355–368. https://doi.org/10 .1080/17482798.2015.1127835.

Kids' audience behavior across platforms. (n.d.). Retrieved August 16, 2017, from https:// www.nielsen.com/insights/2015/kids-audience-behavior-across-platforms/.

King, M. J., & O'Boyle, J. G. (2010). The theme park: The art of time and space. In K. M. Jackson & M. I. West (Eds.), *Disneyland and culture: Essays on the parks and their influence* (pp. 5–18). McFarland.

Klein, H., & Shiffman, K. S. (2009). Underrepresentation and symbolic annihilation of socially disenfranchised groups ("Out groups") in animated cartoons. *Howard Journal of Communications; 20*(1), 55–72. https://dx.doi.org/10.1080%2F1064617080266 5208.

Koblin, J. (2017, November 2). New Netflix ratings confirm "Stranger Things" is a hit. *New York Times.* https://www.nytimes.com/2017/11/02/business/media/stranger-things-nielsen -ratings.html.

Kopan, T. (2017, August 29). *Trump's DACA decision looms.* CNN. http://www.cnn.com /2017/08/29/politics/trump-daca-immigration-decision/index.html.

Kozinets, R. V. (2001). Utopian enterprise: Articulating the meanings of Star Trek's culture of consumption. *Journal of Consumer Research, 28*(1), 67–88. https://psycnet.apa.org /doi/10.1086/321948.

Kozinets, R.V. (2010). Netnography: Doing ethnographic research online. SAGE.

Krogstad, J. M. (2016, July 28). *5 facts about Latinos and education.* Pew Research Center. http://www.pewresearch.org/fact-tank/2016/07/28/5-facts-about-latinos-and-education/.

Krogstad, J. M., & Noe-Bustamante, L. (2020). *Key facts about US Latinos for National Hispanic Heritage Month.* Pew Research Center. https://www.pewresearch.org/fact -tank/2021/09/09/key-facts-about-u-s-latinos-for-national-hispanic-heritage-month/.

Lacroix, C. (2004). Images of animated others: The orientalization of Disney's cartoon heroines from *The Little Mermaid* to *The Hunchback of Notre Dame. Popular Communication, 2*(4), 213–229. https://doi.org/10.1207/s15405710pco0204_2.

Lacy, M. G., & Ono, K. A. (2011). Introduction. In M. Lacy & K. Ono (Eds.), *Critical rhetorics of race* (pp. 1–17). New York University Press.

Latour, B. (1987). *Science in action: How to follow scientists and engineers through society.* Harvard University Press.

Le, V. (2015). The world's largest media companies of 2015. *Forbes.* https://www.forbes.com /sites/vannale/2015/05/22/the-worlds-largest-media-companies-of-2015/.

Lemish, D. (2007). Launching a new journal: Setting new research agendas. *Journal of Children and Media, 1*(1), 1–4. https://doi.org/10.1080/17482790601004994

Lemish, D. (2010). *Screening gender on children's television: The views of producers around the world* (1st ed.). Routledge.

Lemish, D. (2013). Feminist theory approaches to the study of children and media. In D. Lemish (Ed.), *The Routledge international handbook of children, adolescents and media.* Routledge Handbooks Online. https://doi.org/10.4324/9780203366981.ch8.

Lemish, D., and Russo Johnson, C. (2019). *The landscape of children's television in the U.S. and Canada.* Center for Scholars and Storytellers. https://static1.squarespace.com /static/5c0da585da02bc56793a0b31/t/5cb8ce1b15fcc0e19f3e16b9/1555615269351/The+Lands cape+of+Children%27s+TV.pdf.

LeoCamacho (2017, January 16). *Speaking Spanish with Elena of Avalor* [Video]. YouTube. https://www.youtube.com/watch?v=lCKmGb6hnII.

Leon-Boys, D. (2021a). Disney's specific and ambiguous princess: A discursive analysis of *Elena of Avalor. Girlhood Studies, 14*(2), 29–45. https://doi.org/10.3167/ghs.2021 .140204.

Leon-Boys, D. (2021b). No Spanish in Cinderella's kingdom: A situated ethnography of Disney World's engagement with *Elena of Avalor. Departures in Critical Qualitative Research, 10*(2). 50–58. https://doi.org/10.1525/dcqr.2021.10.2.50.

Leon-Boys, D., & Chávez, C. (2021). Star Wars: Galaxy's Edge as postcolonial fantasy: Disney, labor, and the renegotiation of border discourses. *International Journal of Communication, 15*(0), 2378–2396.

Leon-Boys, D., and Valdivia, A. N. (2021). The location of U.S. Latinidad: *Stuck in the Middle*, Disney, and the in-between ethnicity. *Journal of Children and Media, 15*(2), 218–232. https://doi.org/10.1080/17482798.2020.1753790.

Lerner, D. (1958). *The passing of traditional society: Modernizing the Middle East.* Free Press.

Lindlof, T. R., & Taylor, B. C. (2011). *Qualitative communication research methods* (3rd ed.). SAGE.

Livingston, G. (2009, December 11). *VIII: Family, fertility, sexual behaviors and attitudes.* Pew. Research Center. http://www.pewhispanic.org/2009/12/11/viii-family-fertility-sexual -behaviors-and-attitudes/.

Livingston, G., & Thomas, D. (2019). *Why is the teen birth rate falling?* Pew Research Center. https://www.pewresearch.org/fact-tank/2019/08/02/why-is-the-teen-birth-rate -falling/.

Livingstone, S., & Drotner, K. (2011). Children's media cultures in comparative perspective. In V. Nightingale (Ed.), *The handbook of media audiences* (pp. 405–424). Wiley-Blackwell.

Llamas, J. (2020). *Luis Miguel: La serie,* class-based collective memory and streaming television in Mexico. *JCMS: Journal of Cinema and Media Studies, 59*(3), 137–143. https://doi .org/10.1353/cj.2020.0035.

Llona, C. M. (2015, January 29). *After controversy, Disney introduces its first Latina princess: Elena of Avalor.* Fox News. https://www.foxnews.com/entertainment/after-controversy -disney-introduces-its-first-latina-princess-elena-of-avalor.

Lone, R. H. de (1979). *Small futures: Children, inequality, and the limits of liberal reform.* Harcourt Brace Jovanovich.

López Oro, P. J. (2016). "Ni de aquí, ni de allá": Garífuna subjectivities and the politics of diasporic belonging. In P. R. Rivera-Rideau, J. A. Jones, & T. Paschel (Eds.), *Afro-Latin@s in movement: Critical approaches to Blackness and transnationalism in the Americas* (pp. 61–83). Palgrave Macmillan.

Lustyik, K. (2013). Disney's *High School Musical*: Music makes the world go 'round." *Interactions: International Studies in Communication and Culture, 4*(3), 239–253. https://doi .org/10.1386/iscc.4.3.239_1.

Manning, S. (2001). *Girl net: A girl's guide to the Internet and more!* Chicken House.

Martin, H. (2018, February 9). "They're Disneyland superfans. Why a lawsuit is alleging gangster-like tactics against one social club? *Los Angeles Times.* http://www.latimes .com/business/la-fi-disneyland-social-clubs-20180209-story.html.

Martin, M. H. (1998). "Hey, who's the kid with the green umbrella?" Re-evaluating the black-a-Moor and little black sambo. *The Lion and the Unicorn, 22*(2), 147–162. https:// doi.org/10.1353/uni.1998.0027.

Martín-Rodriguez, M. M. (2019). The best Mexican is a (Day of the) Dead Mexican. In F. L. Aldama (Ed.), *Latinx ciné in the twenty-first century* (pp. 355–381). University of Arizona Press.

Mastro, D. E. (2003). A social identity approach to understanding the impact of television messages. *Communication Monographs, 70*(2), 98–113. https://doi.org/10.1080/0363775032000 133764.

Mauney, M. (2016, August 11). Disney World welcomes Elena of Avalor, first Latina princess. *Orlando Sentinel.* https://www.orlandosentinel.com/travel/attractions/the-daily -disney/os-elena-avalor-magic-kingdom-20160811-story.html.

Mayer, V. (2003). *Producing dreams, consuming youth: Mexican Americans and mass media.* Rutgers University Press.

Mayer, V., Banks, M. J., & Caldwell, J. T. (2009). *Production studies: Cultural studies of media industries.* Routledge.

Mazzarella, S. R. (2005). *Girl wide web: Girls, the internet, and the negotiation of identity.* Peter Lang.

Mazzarella, S. R. (2020). *Girls, moral panic, and news media: Troublesome bodies.* Routledge, Taylor & Francis Group.

McAllister, M. P., & Giglio, J. M. (2005). The commodity flow of U.S. children's television. *Critical Studies in Media Communication,* 22(1), 26–44. https://doi.org/10.1080 /0739318042000331835.

McDermott, M. (2016, July 12). Exclusive: How Disney brought Elena of Avalor's Latin heritage to life. *USA Today.* https://www.usatoday.com/story/life/entertainthis/2016/07 /12/meet-disney-channel-first-latina-princess-elena-of-avalor/86982644/.

McDonough, P. (2009, December 10). *Television and beyond a kid's eye view.* Nielsen Company. https://www.nielsen.com/insights/2009/television-and-beyond-a-kids-eye-view/.

McGhee, E. (2020, February). *California's political geography 2020.* Retrieved December 17, 2020, from https://www.ppic.org/publication/californias-political-geography/.

McGladrey, M. L. (2014). Becoming tween bodies: what preadolescent girls in the U.S. say about beauty, the "just-right ideal," and the "Disney girls." *Journal of Children and Media,* 8(4), 353–370. https://doi.org/10.1080/17482798.2013.805305.

McLaughlin, L., & Carter, C. (2001). Editors' introduction. *Feminist Media Studies,* 1(1), 5–10. https://doi.org/10.1080/14680770120042765.

McNary, D. (2018, January 12). Disney CEO Bob Iger's pay dropped 17% to $36.3 million last year. *Variety.* https://variety.com/2018/film/news/disney-paid-robert-iger-last-year-1202663477/.

McRobbie, A. (1982). The politics of feminist research: Between talk, text, and action. *Feminist Review,* 12(1), 46–57. https://doi.org/10.1057%2Ffr.1982.29.

McRobbie, A. (1991). *Feminism and youth culture: From "Jackie" to "Just Seventeen."* Unwin Hyman.

McRobbie, A. (2009). *The aftermath of feminism: Gender, culture and social change.* SAGE.

McRobbie, A., & Garber, J. (1993). Girls and subcultures. In S. Hall & T. Jefferson (Eds.), *Resistance through rituals: Youth subcultures in post-war Britain* (2nd ed., pp. 177–188). Routledge.

Mead, M. (1978). *Culture and commitment: The new relationships between the generations in the 1970s.* Columbia University Press.

Medina, J. (2020, October 14). The macho appeal of Donald Trump. *New York Times.* https://www.nytimes.com/2020/10/14/us/politics/trump-macho-appeal.html.

Meehan, E. R. (2005). Transindustrialism and synergy: Structural supports for decreasing diversity in commercial culture. *International Journal of Media and Cultural Politics,* 1(1). 123–126. https://doi.org/10.1386/macp.1.1.123/3.

Melanoski, B. (1961). *A scientific theory of culture and other essays.* Oxford University Press.

Mendelson, S. (2020, April 8). Box office: Expect more Disney films to skip theaters in favor of Disney+. *Forbes.* https://www.forbes.com/sites/scottmendelson/2020/04/08 /avengers-marvel-star-wars-avatar-frozen-disney-pixar-artemis-fowl-disney-plus-box -office/?sh=60baa3d95c06.

Mendible, M. (Ed.). (2007) *From bananas to buttocks: The Latina body in popular film and culture.* University of Texas Press.

Miami-Dade County, FL. (2020). Data USA. Retrieved December 17, 2020, from https:// datausa.io/profile/geo/miami-dade-county-fl.

Micheletti, M., & Stolle, D. (2012). Sustainable citizenship and the new politics of consumption. *Annals of the American Academy of Political and Social Science,* 644(1), 88–120. https://doi.org/10.1177%2F0002716212454836.

Milligan, M. (2016, July 28). "Elena of Avalor" premiere rules ratings. *Animation Magazine.* http://www.animationmagazine.net/tv/elena-of-avalor-premiere-rules-ratings/.

Mills, S. F. (1990). Disney and the promotion of synthetic worlds. *American Studies International, 28*(2), 66–79.

Milord, J. (2013, July 2). *The world's 10 largest media conglomerates.* Elite Daily. https://www.elitedaily.com/money/the-worlds-10-largest-media-conglomerates.

Mitchell, C., Reid-Walsh, J., & Kirk, J. (2008). Welcome to this inaugural issue of Girlhood Studies: An interdisciplinary journal (GHS). *Girlhood Studies: An Interdisciplinary Journal, 1*(1), vii–xv. https://doi.org/10.3167/ghs.2008.010101.

Mittermeier, S. (2021). *A cultural history of the Disneyland theme parks: Middle class kingdoms.* University of Chicago Press.

Miyashiro, A. (n.d.). *The Moana syllabus.* The Moana Syllabus. Retrieved December 1, 2016, from https://moanasyllabus.wordpress.com/.

Molina-Guzmán, I. (2005). Gendering Latinidad through the Elián news discourse about Cuban women. *Latino Studies, 3*(2), 179–204. https://doi.org/10.1057/palgrave.lst.8600141.

Molina-Guzmán, I. (2007). Salma Hayek's *Frida.* In M. Mendible (Ed.), *From bananas to buttocks: The Latina body in popular film and culture* (pp. 117–128). University of Texas Press.

Molina-Guzmán, I. (2010). *Dangerous curves: Latina bodies in the media.* New York University Press.

Molina-Guzmán, I. (2013). Commodifying Black Latinidad in US film and television. *Popular Communication: The International Journal of Media and Culture, 11*(3), 211–226. https://doi.org/10.1080/15405702.2013.810071.

Molina-Guzmán, (2018). *Latinas and Latinos on TV: Colorblind comedy in the post-racial network era.* University of Arizona Press.

Molina-Guzmán, I. & Valdivia, A.N. (2004). Brain, brow, and booty: Latina iconicity in U.S. popular culture. *The Communication Review, 7*(2), 205–221.

Morales, O. (2020). Horror and death: Rethinking *Coco's* border politics. *Film Quarterly, 73*(4), 41–49.

Moran, K. C. (2011). *Listening to Latina/o youth: Television consumption within families.* Peter Lang.

Moran, K.C. & Chung, L. (2008). Global or local identity? A theoretical analysis of the role of Viacom on identity formation among children in an international context. *Global Media Journal, 7*(12), 1–29.

Morley, D. (1993). Active audience theory: Pendulums and pitfalls. *Journal of Communication, 43*(4), 13–19. https://doi.org/10.1111/j.1460-2466.1993.tb01299.x.

Mosco, V. (1996). *The political economy of communication: Rethinking and renewal.* SAGE.

Motion Picture Association. (2020). *Theme report 2019.* https://www.motionpictures.org/wp-content/uploads/2020/03/MPA-THEME-2019.pdf.

Muir Packman, H., & Casmir, F. L. (1999). Learning from the EuroDisney experience: A case study in international/intercultural communication. *International Communication Gazette, 61*(6). 473–489. https://doi.org/10.1177%2F0016549299061006002.

Murphey, D., Guzman, L., & Torres, A. (2014). *America's Hispanic children: Gaining ground, looking forward.* Child Trends. https://www.childtrends.org/wp-content/uploads/2014/09/2014-38AmericaHispanicChildren.pdf.

Nakamura, L. (2002). *Cybertypes: Race, ethnicity, and identity on the Internet.* Routledge.

Nakamura, L. (2008). *Digitizing race: Visual cultures of the internet.* University of Minnesota Press.

National Academy of Science. (1993). *Understanding and preventing violence: Volume 1.* National Academy Press.

Navarrette, R. Jr. (2020, November 4). Why did so many Latinos vote for Donald Trump? *USA Today*. https://www.usatoday.com/story/opinion/2020/11/04/latino-vote-understanding -what-issues-important-column/6148066002/.

NCLR (2011). *Toward a more vibrant and youthful nation: Latino children in the 2010 census*. https://www.unidosus.org/publications/658-toward-a-more-vibrant-and-youthful -nation-latino-children-in-the-2010-census/.

Negra, D., & Tasker, Y. (2014). Introduction: Gender and recessionary culture. In D. Negra and Y. Tasker (Eds.), *Gendering the recession: Media and culture in the age of austerity* (pp. 1–30). Duke University Press.

Negrón-Muntaner, F., & Abbas, C. (2016). *The Latino disconnect: Latinos in the age of media mergers*. Center for the Study of Race and Ethnicity, Columbia University. http:// media.wix.com/ugd/73fa65_76876cf755864193a610131c0954daa1.pdf.

Nelson, S. (2020, November 4). Joe Biden sweeps west coast, locking in democratic electors. *New York Post*. https://nypost.com/2020/11/03/west-coast-states-go-to-joe-biden-locking -in-electors/.

Neuman, R. (2008). Disneyland's Main Street, USA, and its sources in Hollywood, USA. *Journal of American Culture, 31*(1), 83–97. https://doi.org/10.1111/j.1542-734X.2008.00665.x.

The Nielsen Company. (2019). *Descubrimiento digital: The online lives of Latinx consumers*. https://www.nielsen.com/wp-content/uploads/sites/3/2019/04/the-online-lives-latinx -consumers.pdf.

Nightingale, V. (2011). Introduction. In V. Nightingale (Ed.), *The handbook of media audiences* (pp. 1–15). Wiley-Blackwell.

Noble, S. (2013). Google Search: Hyper-visibility as a means of rendering Black women and girls invisible. *Invisible Culture: An Electronic Journal for Visual Culture*, (19). https://ivc .lib.rochester.edu/google-search-hyper-visibility-as-a-means-of-rendering-black -women-and-girls-invisible/.

Noe-Bustamante, L., Flores, A., & Shah, S. (2019, September 16). *Facts on Hispanics of Mexican origin in the United States, 2017*. Pew Research Center. https://www.pewresearch .org/hispanic/fact-sheet/u-s-hispanics-facts-on-mexican-origin-latinos/#:~:text =Mexicans%20are%20the%20largest%20population,36.6%20million%20over%20the%20 period.

Noe-Bustamante, L., Lopez, M., & Krogstad, J. M. (2020, July 7). *U.S. Hispanic population surpassed 60 million in 2019, but growth has slowed*. Pew Research Center. https://www .pewresearch.org/fact-tank/2020/07/07/u-s-hispanic-population-surpassed-60-million -in-2019-but-growth-has-slowed/.

O'Connell, E. M. (2014, September 18). *16 secret rules for Disney employees*. Guff. https://web .archive.org/web/20201113142744/http://guff.com/16-secret-rules-for-disney-employees.

Office of Adolescent Health. (2016, June 2). *Trends in teen pregnancy and childbearing*. Retrieved September 1, 2017, from https://web.archive.org/web/20170901072807/https://www.hhs.gov /ash/oah/adolescent-development/reproductive-health-and-teen-pregnancy/teen -pregnancy-and-childbearing/trends/index.html.

Ong, A. (1999). *Flexible citizenship: The cultural logics of transnationality*. Duke University Press.

O'Reilly, L. (2016, May 31). *The 30 biggest media companies in the world*. Business Insider. http://www.businessinsider.com/the-30-biggest-media-owners-in-the-world-2016-5.

Ortega, J. [@jennaortega] (2016, June 9). *The first ever Latina Princess #ElenaofAvalor is making her debut on 7/22 @7pm on @disneychannel this is such huge news* [Photograph]. Instagram. https://www.instagram.com/jennaortega/?hl=en.

Ouellette, L. (2012). Citizen brand: ABC and the do good turn in U.S. television: Cultural resistance in neoliberal times. In S. Banet-Weiser & R. Mukherjee (Eds.), *Commodity activism: Cultural resistance in neoliberal times* (pp. 57–85). New York University Press.

Ouellette, L. (2017). Citizenship. In L. Ouellette & J. Gray (Eds.), *Keywords for Media Studies* (pp. 34–38). New York University Press.

Peña Ovalle, P. (2011). *Dance and the Hollywood Latina: Race, sex, and stardom.* Rutgers University Press.

Petski, D. (2017, February 13). *"Elena of Avalor" renewed for season 3 by Disney Channel.* Deadline. http://deadline.com/2017/02/elena-of-avalor-renewed-season-3-disney-channel-1201910153/.

Pike, K. (2015). Princess culture in Qatar: Exploring princess media narratives in the lives of Arab female youth. In M. Forman-Brunell & R. C. Hains (Eds.), *Princess cultures: Mediating girls' imaginations and identities* (pp. 139–160). Peter Lang.

Pink, S., Horst, H., Postill, J., Hjorth, L., Lewis, T., & Tacchi, J. (2016). *Digital ethnography: Principles and practice.* SAGE.

Pixar animation studios—'Coco'. (n.d.). Pixar Animation Studios. Retrieved May 20, 2021, from https://www.pixar.com/feature-films/coco

Prensky, M. (2001). Digital natives, digital immigrants. *On the Horizon, 9*(5), 1–6.

Projansky, S. (2007). Mass magazine cover girls: Some reflections on postfeminist girls and postfeminism's daughters. In Y. Tasker & D. Negra (Eds.), *Interrogating postfeminism: Gender and the politics of popular culture* (pp. 40–72). Duke University Press.

Projansky, S. (2014). *Spectacular girls: Media fascination and celebrity culture.* New York University Press.

The Project on Disney (1995). *Inside the mouse: Work and play at Disneyworld.* Duke University Press.

Qvortrup, J., Corsaro, W. A., & Honig, M. (2009). Why social studies of childhood? An introduction to the handbook. In J. Qvortrup, W. A, Corsaro, & M. S. Honig (Eds.), *The Palgrave handbook of childhood studies* (pp. 1–18). Palgrave Macmillan.

Ramírez-Berg, C. (2002). *Latino images in film: Stereotypes, subversion, and resistance.* University of Texas Press.

Real, M. R. (1977). *Mass-mediated culture.* Prentice Hall.

Reuters, L. N. (2015, September 16). *Transcript: Second-tier CNN Republican Debate 2015.* CBS News. http://www.cbsnews.com/news/transcript-second-tier-republican-debate -2015-reagan-library/.

Rideout, V., & Robb, M. B. (2019). *The Common Sense census: Media use by tweens and teens, 2019.* Common Sense Media. https://www.commonsensemedia.org/sites/default /files/research/report/2019-census-8-to-18-full-report-updated.pdf.

Rideout, V., & Robb, M. B. (2020). *The Common Sense census: Media use by kids age zero to eight, 2020.* Common Sense Media. https://www.commonsensemedia.org/sites/default /files/research/report/2020_zero_to_eight_census_final_web.pdf.

Rinderle, S. (2005). The Mexican diaspora: A critical examination of signifiers. *Journal of Communication Inquiry, 29*(4), 294–316. https://doi.org/10.1177/0196859905278495.

Rios, D. I. (2003). U.S. Latino audiences of "telenovelas." *Journal of Latinos and Education, 2*(1), 59–65. https://doi.org/10.1207/S1532771XJLE0201_8.

Rivadeneyra, R., & Ward, L. M. (2005). From *Ally McBeal* to *Sábado Gigante*: Contributions of television viewing to the gender role attitudes of Latino adolescents. *Journal of Adolescent Research, 20*(4), 453–475. https://doi.org/10.1177/0743558405274871.

Roberts, E. M. (2004). Through the eyes of a child: Representations of Blackness in children's television programming. *Race, Gender & Class, 11*(2), 130–139. http://www.jstor.org/stable /41675128.

Rodriguez, C. (2013, September 9). *Disney producer misspoke: "First Latina princess" isn't Latina*. CNN. http://www.cnn.com/2012/10/25/showbiz/disney-sofia-not-latina/.

Rodriguez, G. [@hereisgina] (2016, June 6). *#MovementMondays Elena of Avalor, the first Latina Disney Princess. I have so many incredible friends who have been a part* [Photograph]. Instagram. https://www.instagram.com/p/BGUdNb6HLkp/?utm_source=ig _web_copy_link.

Rosa, J. (2019). *Looking like a language, sounding like a race*. Oxford University Press.

Rose, G. (2016). *Visual methodologies: An introduction to researching with visual materials* (4th ed). SAGE.

Rottenberg, C. (2014). The rise of neoliberal feminism. *Cultural Studies, 28*(3), 418–437. https://doi.org/10.1080/09502386.2013.857361.

Roy, I. (2019, June 19). Why Disney World bans adults wearing costumes. *Reader's Digest*. https://www.rd.com/article/why-disney-bans-adults-in-costumes/.

Salzman, M. (1996). *Going to the net: A girl's guide to cyberspace*. Avon Books.

Sammond, N. (2005). *Babes in Tomorrowland: Walt Disney and the making of the American child, 1930–1960*. Duke University Press.

Sandberg, S. (2015). *Lean in: Women, work, and the will to lead*. W. H. Allen.

Sarasohn, D. (2018, September 26). The rise of west coast democrats. *New Republic*. https:// newrepublic.com/article/151146/rise-west-coast-democrats.

Sarkar, S. (2018, February 7). *What Disney's streaming service means for Netflix subscribers*. Polygon. https://www.polygon.com/2018/2/7/16982030/disney-leaving-netflix-marvel-lucas film-pixar-streaming-rights.

Scott, R. (2019, January 22). *Lin-Manuel Miranda to create first Latina Disney princess for Moana 2?* Movieweb. https://movieweb.com/moana-2-disney-princess-latina-lin-manuel -miranda/.

Scribner, H. (2020, November 14). Here's how much money Disney lost because of the pandemic. *Deseret News*. https://www.deseret.com/entertainment/2020/11/12/21563070/disney -world-disneyland-closed-losses.

Seth, S. (2020, October 7). *The world's top media companies*. Investopedia. https://www .investopedia.com/stock-analysis/021815/worlds-top-ten-media-companies-dis-cmcsa -fox.aspx.

Sheppard, R. (2016). Mexico goes to Disney World: Recognizing and representing Mexico at EPCOT center's Mexico pavilion. *Latin American Research Review, 51*(3), 64–84. https://doi.org/10.1353/lar.2016.0034.

Shohat, E., & Stam, R. (1994). *Unthinking Eurocentrism: Multiculturalism and the Media*. Psychology Press.

Shuggart, H. A. (2007). Crossing over: Hybridity and hegemony in the popular media. *Communication and Critical/Cultural Studies, 4*(2): 115–141. https://doi.org/10.1080/14791420 701296505.

Sieczkowski, C. (2012, October 23). *Princess Sofia is not Latina, says Disney*. HuffPost. https://www.huffpost.com/entry/disney-princess-sofia-not-latina_n_2005288.

Silver, P. (2013). Latinization, race, and cultural identification in Puerto Rican Orlando. *Southern Cultures, 19*(4), 55–75. https://doi.org/10.1353/scu.2013.0032.

Silverman, H. (2002). Groovin' to ancient Peru: A critical analysis of Disney's *The Emperor's New Groove*. *Journal of Social Archaeology, 2*(3), 298–322. https://doi.org/10.1177 /146960530200200302.

Sinclair, C. (1995). *Net Chick: A smart-girl guide to the wired world*. Holtzbrinck.

Smith, T. (2018, June 26). *Play Disney parks app debuts at Disneyland Resort and Walt Disney World Resort on June 30*. Disney Parks Blog. https://disneyparks.disney.go.com/blog

/2018/06/play-disney-parks-app-debuts-at-disneyland-resort-and-walt-disney-world
-resort-on-june-30/.

Smoodin, E. (1994). *Disney discourse: Producing the Magic Kingdom*. Routledge.

Sparks, G. G., Sparks, C. W., & Sparks, E. A. (2009). Media violence. In J. Bryant & M. B. Oliver (Eds.), *Media effects: Advances in theory and research* (3rd ed., pp. 269–286). Routledge.

Sposato, S., Yep, K., & Barton, R. (2020, May 27). *Disney CEO Bob Chapek discusses why Disney World is reopening in July*. Inside the Magic. https://insidethemagic.net/2020/05/bob-chapek-discusses-reopening-sp1/.

Staiger, J. (2005). *Media reception studies*. New York University Press.

Stein, L. E. (2015). *Millennial fandom: Television audiences in the transmedia age*. University of Iowa Press.

Stern, S. R. (2002). Virtually speaking: Girls' self-disclosure on the WWW. *Women's Studies in Communication, 25*(2), 223–253. https://doi.org/10.1080/07491409.2002.10162447.

Stevenson, A. (2019, December 18). *Disney finally gave us a Jewish princess—but they got a few too many things wrong*. Femestella. http://www.femestella.com/disney-jewish-princess-elena-avalor-princess-rebekah/.

Stump, S. (2019, September 19). *Disney introducing 1st Jewish princess, actress Jamie-Lynn Sigler confirms*. TODAY.com. Retrieved April 6, 2022, from https://www.today.com/popculture/disney-s-1st-jewish-princess-will-be-voiced-jamie-lynn-t162903.

Suchar, C. S. (1997). Grounding visual sociology research in shooting scripts. *Qualitative Sociology, 20*(1), 33–55. https://doi.org/10.1023/A:1024712230783.

Suddath, C. (2015, December 17). *The $500 million battle over Disney's princesses*. Bloomberg. https://www.bloomberg.com/features/2015-disney-princess-hasbro/.

Swan, K., Meskill, C., & DeMaio, S. (1998). *Social learning from broadcast television*. Hampton Press.

Swineburn, B., & Chapek, B. (2021). *Morgan Stanley Technology, Media and Telecom Conference* [Presentation Transcript]. The Walt Disney Company. https://thewaltdisneycompany.com/app/uploads/2021/02/bc-ms-transcript-030121.pdf.

Taft, J. K. (2010). *Rebel girls: Youth activism and social change across the Americas*. New York University Press.

Tally, P. (2005). Re-imagining girlhood: Hollywood and the tween girl film market. In C. Mitchell & J. Reid-Walsh (Eds.), *Seven going on seventeen: Tween studies in the culture of girlhood* (pp. 311–329). Peter Lang.

Tampa Bay Buccaneers [@Buccaneers]. (2021, February 8). *The most magical place on Earth* [Image attached] [Tweet]. Twitter. https://twitter.com/Buccaneers/status/1358976690702217217.

Tapia, R. C. (2005). Impregnating images: Visions of race, sex, and citizenship in California's teen pregnancy prevention campaigns. *Feminist Media Studies, 5*(1), 7–22. https://doi.org/10.1080/14680770500058132.

Tartar, A., Lin, J. C. F., Dmitrieva, K., Capurro, M. E., Saraiva, C., & Pogkas, D. (2020, November 24). *Trump's new Latino voters are sending democrats a message*. Bloomberg. https://www.bloomberg.com/graphics/2020-us-election-hispanic-latino-voters/.

Tasker, Y., & Negra, D. (2007). Introduction: Feminist politics and postfeminist culture. In Y. Tasker & D. Negra (Eds.), *Interrogating post-feminism: Gender and the politics of popular culture* (pp. 1–26). Duke University Press.

Tasker, Y. (2007). Enchanted (2007) by post-feminism: Gender, irony, and the new romantic comedy. In H. Radner & R. Stringer (Eds.), Feminism at the movies: Understanding gender in contemporary popular cinema (pp. 67–89). Routledge.

Taylor, P. (2013). *Between two worlds: How young Latinos come of age in America*. Pew Research Center. http://www.pewhispanic.org/2009/12/11/between-two-worlds-how-young-latinos -come-of-age-in-america/.

Theme Index and Museum Index. (2017). *Global attractions attendance report*. http://www .inparkmagazine.com/wp-content/uploads/2018/05/2017-Theme-Museum-Index.pdf.

Torregrosa, L. L. (2020, September 17). *Trump has Latino voter support that's as strong as ever: Why haven't his insults cost him?* NBC News. https://www.nbcnews.com/think /opinion/trump-has-latino-voter-support-s-strong-ever-why-haven-ncna1240168.

The Toy Association. (2019). *Annual U.S. sales 2018 data*. Retrieved April 15, 2019, from https://www.toyassociation.org/ta/research/data/u-s-sales-data/toys/research-and-data /data/us-sales-data.aspx.

Tracy, J. F. (1999). Whistle while you work: The Disney Company and the global division of labor. *Journal of Communication Inquiry, 23*(4), 374–389. https://doi.org/10.1177/019685 9999023004005.

T.V. News Desk (2016, November 28). *Disney's* Elena and the Secret of Avalor *simulcast is 2016's No. 1 cable tv show in key demo*. Retrieved November 29, 2016, from https://www .broadwayworld.com/bwwtv/article/Disneys-ELENA-AND-THE-SECRET-OF -AVALOR-Simulcast-is-2016s-No-1-Cable-TV-Show-in-Key-Demo-20161128.

Umstead, R. T. (2016, July 28). *Disney's "Elena of Avalor" delivers royal ratings*. Multichannel News. http://www.multichannel.com/news/content/disney-s-elena-avalor-delivers -royal-ratings/406725.

Unkrich, L. [@leeunkrich]. (2017, December 14). *It takes place in 2017. #AskAboutPixar-Coco* [Tweet]. Twitter. https://twitter.com/leeunkrich/status/941382162355453952?s=20.

Urciuoli, B. (1996). *Exposing prejudice: Puerto Rican experiences of language, race, and class*. Westview Press.

U.S. Census Bureau. (n.d.). *ACS demographic and housing estimates*. U.S. Census Bureau. Retrieved May 20, 2020, from https://data.census.gov/cedsci/table?g=0500000US06037&d =ACS%205-Year%20Estimates%20Data%20Profiles&tid=ACSDP5Y2019.DP05&hidePreview =true.

U.S. Census Bureau. (2020). *Quickfacts: Los Angeles County, California*. https://www .census.gov/quickfacts/fact/table/losangelescountycalifornia/RHI725218.

Valdivia, A. N. (2000). *A Latina in the land of Hollywood and other essays in media Culture*. University of Arizona Press.

Valdivia, A. N. (2005). "Geographies of Latinidad: Constructing identity in the face of radical hybridity." In W. Critchlow, G. Dimitriadis, N. Dolby, and C. McCarthy (Eds.) *Race, identity, and representation in education* (pp. 307–320). Routledge.

Valdivia, A. N. (2007). Is Penelope to J. Lo as culture is to nature? Eurocentric approaches to "Latin" beauties. In M. Mendible (Ed.), *From bananas to buttocks: The Latina body in popular film culture* (pp. 129–148). University of Texas Press.

Valdivia, A. N. (2008a). Is my butt your island? The myths of discovery and contemporary Latina/o communication studies. In A. N. Valdivia (Ed.), *Latina/o communication studies today* (pp. 3–26). Peter Lang.

Valdivia, A. N. (2008b). "Latina Girls and Communication Studies." *Journal of Children and Media, 2*(1), 86–87.

Valdivia, A. N. (2008c). Mixed race on the Disney Channel: From *Johnnie Tsunami* through *Lizzie McGuire* and ending with *The Cheetah Girls*. In M. Beltrán & C. Forjas (Eds.), *Mixed race Hollywood* (pp. 269–289). New York University Press.

Valdivia, A. N. (2010). *Latina/os and the media*. Polity Press.

Valdivia, A. N. (2011). This tween bridge over my Latina girl back: The U.S. mainstream negotiates ethnicity. In M. C. Kearney (Ed.), *Mediated girlhoods: New explorations of girl's media culture* (pp. 93–109). Peter Lang.

Valdivia, A. N. (2017). Othering. In L. Ouelette & J. Gray (Eds.), *Keywords for media studies* (pp. 133–134). New York University Press.

Valdivia, A. N. (2018). Holding up half the sky: Global narratives of girls at risk and celebrity philanthropy. *Girlhood Studies: An Interdisciplinary Journal, 11*(3), 84–100. https://doi.org/10.3167/ghs.2018.110308.

Valdivia, A. N. (2018). Latina media studies. *Feminist Media Histories, 4*(2), 101–106. https://doi.org/10.1525/fmh.2018.4.2.101.

Valdivia, A. N. (2020). *The gender of Latinidad: Uses and abuses of hybridity.* Wiley.

Valdivia, A. N. (2021). Feminist media studies: We need to take intersectionality seriously. In S. Eckert & I. Bachmann (Eds.), *Reflection on feminist communication and media scholarship* (pp, 133–147). Routledge.

Van Zoonen, L. (1994). *Feminist media studies.* SAGE.

Vargas, L. (2009). *Latina teens, migration, and popular culture.* Peter Lang.

Velez, M. (2016, June 7). *Sorry, Disney: I'm not excited about your Latina princess yet.* Revelist. https://www.revelist.com/real-talk/disney-latina-princess-essay/2831.

Wagmeister, E. (2016, August 11). *"Elena of Avalor" renewed for season 2 on Disney.* TV by the Numbers. https://web.archive.org/web/20180614173705/http://tvbythenumbers.zap2it.com/more-tv-news/elena-of-avalor-renewed-for-season-2-on-disney/.

Wajda, D. M. (2016, August 23). *Girl Scouts, Disney create 'Elena of Avalor' leadership guide.* NBC News. https://www.nbcnews.com/news/latino/girl-scouts-disney-create-elena-avalor-leadership-guide-n636496.

The Walt Disney Company (2009). *2008 corporate responsibility report.* https://thewaltdisneycompany.com/app/uploads/FY08Disney_CR_Report_2008.pdf.

The Walt Disney Company (2011). *2010 citizenship report.* https://thewaltdisneycompany.com/app/uploads/FY10Disney_2010_CC_Report.pdf.

The Walt Disney Company (2017). *Lead like Elena contest.* Disney LOL. http://lol.disney.com/lead-like-elena-contest.

The Walt Disney Company (2018). *2017 corporate social responsibility update.* https://thewaltdisneycompany.com/app/uploads/2017disneycsrupdate.pdf.

The Walt Disney Company (2019, November 7). *The Walt Disney company reports fourth quarter and full year earnings for fiscal 2019.* https://www.thewaltdisneycompany.com/wp-content/uploads/2019/11/q4-fy19-earnings.pdf.

The Walt Disney Company (2020). *Disney investor day 2020* [Presentation transcript]. https://thewaltdisneycompany.com/app/uploads/2020/12/Disney_Investor_Day_2020_transcript.pdf.

The Walt Disney Company (2021). *2020 corporate social responsibility report.* https://thewaltdisneycompany.com/app/uploads/2021/02/2020-CSR-Report.pdf.

The Walt Disney Company (2022). *2021 corporate social responsibility report,* https://impact.disney.com/app/uploads/2022/02/2021-CSR-Report.pdf.

Warner, K. J. (2017). Plastic representation. *Film Quarterly, 71*(2). https://filmquarterly.org/2017/12/04/in-the-time-of-plastic-representation/.

Wasko, J. (2001a). *Understanding Disney: The manufacture of fantasy.* Polity.

Wasko, J. (2001b). Is it a small world, after all? In. J. Wasko, M. Phillips & E. R. Meehan (Eds.), *Dazzled by Disney? The global audiences project* (pp. 3–28). Leicester University Press.

Wasko, J., Phillips, M., & Meehan, E.R. (2001). *Dazzled by Disney? The global audiences project.* Leicester University Press.

Wasko, J. (2017). The Walt Disney Company. In B. J. Birkinbine, R. Gómez, & J. Wasko (Eds.), *Global media giants* (pp. 11–25). Routledge.

Wasko, J. (2020). *Understanding Disney: The manufacture of fantasy* (2nd ed.). Polity Press.

Wasko, J., & Meehan, E. R. (2001). Dazzled by Disney? Ambiguity in ubiquity. In J. Wasko, M. Phillips & E. R. Meehan (Eds.), *Dazzled by Disney? The global audiences project* (pp. 329–343). Leicester University Press.

Watts, S. (1997). *The Magic Kingdom: Walt Disney and the American way of life*. Houghton Mifflin.

Whelan, B. (2012). Power to the princess: Disney and the creation of the 20th century princess narrative. *Interdisciplinary Humanities, 29*(1), 21–34.

Whitten, S. (2016, October 17). *Disney princess dolls push Hasbro's revenue above Wall Street estimates*. CNBC. https://www.cnbc.com/2016/10/17/disney-princess-dolls-push-hasbros-revenue-above-wall-street-estimates.html.

Whitten, S. (2021, February 11). *Disney said Covid-related costs shaved $2.6 billion from parks' operating income in latest quarter*. CNBC. https://www.cnbc.com/2021/02/11/coronavirus-hurt-theme-parks-costing-disney-2point6-billion.html.

Whyte, A. (2018, July 26). *Disney Junior producing Elena of Avalor TV movie*. Kidscreen. http://kidscreen.com/2018/07/26/disney-junior-producing-elena-of-avalor-tv-movie/.

Williams, R. (2020). *Disney theme parks and fandom*. Amsterdam University Press.

Wills, J. (2017). *Quick takes: Disney culture*. Rutgers University Press.

Wiltz, T. (2015, March 3). *Racial and ethnic disparities persist in teen pregnancy rates*. Pew Charitable Trusts. https://www.pewtrusts.org/en/research-and-analysis/blogs/stateline/2015/3/03/racial-and-ethnic-disparities-persist-in-teen-pregnancy-rates.

Winch, A. (2013). *Girlfriends and postfeminist sisterhood*. Palgrave Macmillan.

Zacks Equity Research. (2020, April 6). *Disney (DIS) alters movie release dates, boosts Disney+ suite*. Yahoo! Finance. https://finance.yahoo.com/news/disney-dis-alters-movie-release-112511704.html?guccounter=1.

Zaslow, E. (2009). *Feminism Inc.: Coming of age in girl power media culture*. Palgrave Macmillan.

Zaslow, E. (2017). *Playing with America's Doll: A cultural analysis of the American Girl collection*. Palgrave Macmillan.

Zelizer, V. A. R. (1985). *Pricing the priceless child: The changing social value of children*. Princeton University Press.

Zorn, E., & Underberg, N. M. (2013). *Digital ethnography: Anthropology, narrative, and new media*. University of Texas Press.

Index

Note: *Italicized* page numbers indicate illustrative material.

About the Author

Diana Leon-Boys is an assistant professor in the Department of Communication and affiliate faculty in the Department of Women's and Gender Studies and the Institute for the Study of Latin America and the Caribbean at the University of South Florida. She holds a PhD in communications and media studies from the Institute of Communications Research at the University of Illinois, Urbana-Champaign.

Available titles in the Latinidad: Transnational Cultures in the United States series